THE PAINTINGS OF
ZURBARAN

PHAIDON

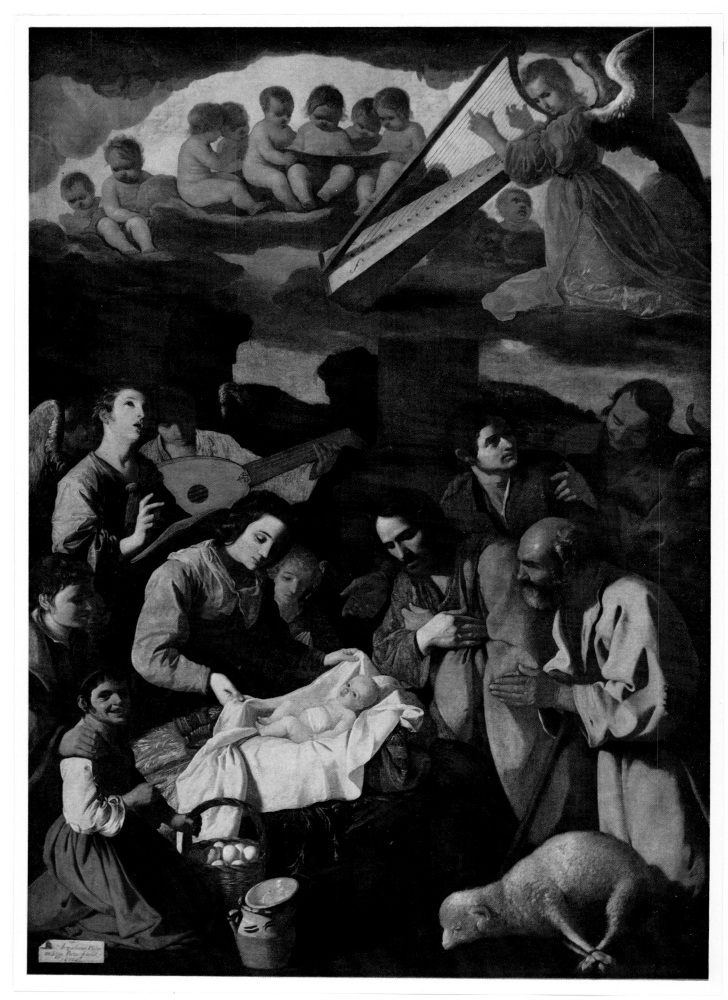

THE ADORATION OF THE SHEPHERDS. 1638. Grenoble, Museum (Cat. No. 138)

THE PAINTINGS OF
ZURBARAN

COMPLETE EDITION

by

MARTIN S. SORIA

LONDON 1955

PHAIDON PRESS

ALL RIGHTS RESERVED BY PHAIDON PRESS LTD
5 CROMWELL PLACE · LONDON · SW7
1953
SECOND, REVISED EDITION: 1955
PRINTED IN GREAT BRITAIN
TEXT AND MONOCHROME PLATES BY TONBRIDGE PRINTERS LTD · TONBRIDGE · KENT
COLOUR PLATES BY HUNT BARNARD & CO. LTD. · AYLESBURY · BUCKS.

To

MY WIFE

CONTENTS

PREFACE

IMPORTANT studies of Zurbarán's art have been made in the past and are being carried out at present. Eighteenth-century sources—Palomino, Ponz, and Ceán—describe the pictures in their original locale. More recently, since the great Zurbarán Exhibition of 1905 at Madrid, notable books and studies on the artist have been published by Elías Tormo, José Cascales, Hugo Kehrer, and August L. Mayer. The Sevillan scholar Celestino López Martínez found numerous documents, mostly signed by the artist. Valuable source material was also uncovered in the Documentos para la historia del arte en Andalucía, brought out by Prof. José Hernández Díaz at the University of Seville. In 1931 a brilliant essay on the artist's style was written by Paul Guinard, who in 1947-1949 discussed in three basic articles the original and subsequent location of Zurbarán's works. Sra. María Luisa Caturla was remarkably successful in discovering new documents on the artist's activities.

The generally accepted œuvre of Zurbarán contains many questionable attributions, including pictures belonging to the Italian school and a great many others actually done by his pupils. This study contains only those works which the author believes to be by Zurbarán himself, incorporating about forty paintings for the first time into the catalogue of the master's works. Through a new study of his stylistic development, a chronological sequence of his pictures is established and several major changes in the hitherto accepted dates of his paintings are suggested. Many datings are necessarily tentative, to be confirmed or revised as unknown works or documents are coming to light. This is believed to be the first catalogue raisonné ever compiled, based on twelve years of research during which time nearly all paintings, except those East of the Rhine, were examined first hand.

Prof. Chandler R. Post was the first to open the author's eyes to the greatness of Zurbarán. Prof. Kehrer made available his collection of photographs. M. Guinard and Sra. Caturla shared information. Don C. López Martínez *communicated many unpublished documents found by him. Don Alonso Grosso, Director of the Seville Museum, procured photographs. Don José Gudiol disclosed unknown paintings and permitted the fullest use of his great research centre at Barcelona. Don Arturo Gasull of Llerena gave useful information and kind hospitality. Don José Hernández Díaz, Don Enrique Marco Dorta, and Don Antonio Gómez Castillo, all of Seville, contributed helpful discussion and advice. Many museum directors and private collectors willingly showed their treasures. Mrs. Elizabeth Wilder Weismann read the manuscript and made valuable suggestions. To each one I wish to express my most sincere gratitude.*

M. S. S.

PREFACE TO THE SECOND EDITION

The success of the first edition has shown that the time was ripe for bringing Zubarán again before the eyes of the public. An ever wider audience is appreciating Zurbarán along with Velázquez, Rubens, Hals, Rembrandt, Poussin, Lorrain and de la Tour among the greatest painters of the seventeenth century. In the second edition it was possible to add a long lost masterpiece of great importance and thirteen other works recently found.

To the Author's regret a few paintings in the Plandiura collection at Barcelona could not be included because the owner refused access as well as photographs. It was thus impossible to clarify which works in this collection, if any, are authentic.

1954   *M.S.S.*

Numbers in *italics* refer to the Catalogue on pp. 131ff.
Small raised numbers refer to the Bibliography on pp. 193ff.

INTRODUCTION

I. SOURCES OF ZURBARÁN'S ART

THE Spanish master Francisco de Zurbarán (1598–1664) has always been highly respected in Spain and in Spanish America. His discovery beyond the Pyrenees began during the Napoleonic wars, when the French admired his paintings so much that they carried them off by the dozen from the churches of Seville. Those spoils, together with the paintings which Louis Philippe was able to acquire during the secularization of Spanish monasteries in 1835, made it possible for the French King to open his famous Spanish Gallery ([57]) at the Louvre in 1838, a sensation for the artistic world of the time. One fifth of over four hundred paintings exhibited there were attributed to Zurbarán and brought him general European acclaim. Théophile Gautier's famous verses ([31]) show how the Romanticists understood Zurbarán's art:

Moines de Zurbarán, blancs chartreux qui, dans l'ombre,	Zurbarán's monks, white Carthusians, in the darkness,
Glissez silencieux sur les dalles des morts,	Silently glide by flagstones over dead corpses,
Murmurant des *Pater* et des *Ave* sans nombre,	Murmuring *Paters* and *Aves* numberless,
Quel crime expiez-vous par de si grands remords?	What crime to atone through such keen remorses?
(From 'A Zurbarán,' 1844.)	
. . . Comme dans les tableaux où le vieux Zurbarán,	. . . As in the paintings where old Zurbarán,
Sous le nom d'une Sainte, en habit sévillan,	Under the guise of a Saint, dressed as Sevillan,
Représente une dame avec des pendeloques,	Represents a lady with glinting pendeloque,
Des plumes, du clinquant et des modes baroques.	Feathers and tinsel in fashions Baroque.
(From 'En passant à Vergara,' 1841.)	

For almost a century thereafter, the artist was esteemed as a painter of fierce, repentant monks and of saints dressed as mundane ladies. More recently the public has begun to appreciate his monumentality and his realism penetrating to the essence of objects and giving them a life of their own. We admire the disciplined design of his compositions and the bold application of deep, rich colours, placed side by side at full intensity and with surprising contrast. Both design and colour are akin to contemporary art. The modern artist, like Zurbarán, emphasizes two-dimensional relationships by the use of flat areas of colour and by avoiding a unified or a fixed vanishing-point perspective, to stress design.

Zurbarán is one of the outstanding representatives of the Baroque, that is, the style of the seventeenth century. His sources spring not only from the Middle Ages and the Renaissance, but particularly from Mannerism, as the style from about 1525 to 1600, between Renaissance and Baroque, is called. During the Mannerist period Spanish art received overpowering stimuli from Italy, as exemplified by El Greco at Toledo, Morales in Extremadura, and the Italian artists active at the Escorial. Northern influence arrived by way of the portraitists Anthony More and his Spanish pupil Sánchez Coello, as well as by Flemish and German prints, eagerly copied by Spanish artists. Flemish paintings and prints had such a profound effect that, next to Italian art, they were the primary source of Spanish painting during the Mannerist and Baroque periods. ([44])

In Andalusia, Luis de Vargas and Pablo de Céspedes were as Italianate as any of their Spanish contemporaries, or more so. Yet Seville, in a larger measure than any other Spanish town, was also influenced by Flemish artists: Pedro de Campaña (Pieter Kempeneer), Hernando (Ferdinand) Sturm, and 'Frans Frutet'. Campaña's (at Seville 1537–1562) *Presentation in the Temple* (fig. I), at Seville Cathedral, combines Italian perspective and contraposto—Raphael and Michelangelo—with Flemish sensuousness and breadth. The light background, seen through dark columns, furnished Zurbarán with one of his favourite pictorial devices. The art of Sturm (documented at Seville from 1537 to 1557) relates him to his great compatriots Heemskerck and Marten de Vos. Sturm's *Saints Catherine and Barbara* (fig. III), of 1555, reflects Flemish Mannerism in the idealized faces of oval shape, large eyes, and small mouths, the great elegance and rich jewelled dresses. It anticipates the *Virgin Martyrs* by Zurbarán, who as a Spanish and Baroque painter was to strengthen their spiritual quality. Of the Flemish trio, 'Frans Frutet' exerted the greatest influence on Zurbarán. 'Frutet' is the name given by Ponz ([3]) in 1780 for the author of an otherwise unidentified Flemish altarpiece of 1548, now in the Museum of Seville (see fig. II); this is the earliest mention of the name, however, and it has appeared in no document. A true forerunner of the Baroque, it is for its time surprisingly calm and static in composition. Zurbarán derived major elements of his art from this painting which is conceived in large, ample forms. Frutet modelled hands and faces with the ample softness and the round fleshiness they possess in Zurbarán's paintings at Santa Magdalena (*4–5*). The artist may also have taken from Frutet the notion of applying intense luminous colours to broad areas. Zurbarán borrowed specifically the Flemish idea of introducing into a picture of the Virgin and Child a low table and on it a pewter plate with luscious fruits, and he repeatedly (*25, 67*) copied the curtain above the Virgin.

Seville, during the sixteenth century one of several major artistic centres in Spain, rose to unique importance when its painters began to follow the Baroque credo. The city was predisposed for such a role by the necessary cultural and economic conditions. The trade monopoly with the Indies made her one of the wealthiest towns in the world. Here was the jumping-off place for crossing over to the Spanish Americas, and here twice a year the Indies fleet unloaded fabulous treasures. Foreign trade brought a freer exchange of ideas than elsewhere in Spain. To Seville flocked the most intelligent, most enterprising and most affluent men, Spaniards and foreigners alike. Spiritually and economically, Seville was Spain's capital. Pacheco's (1564–1654) painting academy was one of the cultural centres of the city. He stressed the importance of plastic form and lifelike illusion, as compared to mere beauty and delicacy.([58]) Thus he clearly turned away from Mannerism and embraced Baroque principles. He contrasted the materialist concept of the imitation of nature as an end in itself with a thoroughly spiritual, not to say mystical, view: painting shall lead man away from vices and to the true veneration of God. This idea is not only very Spanish but it is the most important tenet of the whole Baroque. Naturalism was merely a tool in the service of the impassioned spirituality which pervaded the entire epoch. Pacheco, as the Inquisition's watchdog to insure 'decent and proper' pictorial representations, wrote on iconography, i.e. on how to paint the sacred subjects.([58]) Zurbarán followed his instructions in painting the Crucified—with four nails— and the Immaculate Conception. 'An imperial crown which should not hide the stars should adorn her head. Under her feet is the moon . . . with the points downward.' Pacheco continues: 'In my painting I forgot the dragon, the common enemy, whose head the Virgin broke when she triumphed over original sin . . . I shall omit him whenever I can, in order not to embarrass my painting with him.' Zurbarán, too, seldom 'embarrassed' his *Purisima* by the dragon, and often painted the crown. Pacheco's paintings (see fig. VI) influenced him greatly.

The Apotheosis of Saint Thomas Aquinas (*41*), of 1631, echoes the elder Herrera's (1576?–1656) *Triumph of Saint Hermengild* (fig. IV), at the Seville Museum. Zurbarán's still lifes recall Sánchez Cotán's (1561–after 1631) compositions, simple, strong and tender, realistic and mystic at the same time. Palomino states that Zurbarán was a follower of Roelas (1558–1625), who from Venice had brought reflections of the art of Titian and Tintoretto, and was the first to introduce the Caravaggiesque tenebroso style to Seville.

I. Pedro de Campaña: *The Presentation in the Temple.* 1555.
Seville, Cathedral.

II. 'Frutet': *Virgin and Child.* 1548.
Seville, Museum.

III. Hernando Sturm: *Saints Catherine and Barbara.* 1555. Seville, Cathedral.

IV. Francisco Herrera the Elder: *The Triumph of Saint Hermengild*. About 1624. Seville, Museum.

V. Juan de Roelas: *The Virgin of Mercy*. About 1611. Seville, Cathedral.

VI. Francisco Pacheco: *The Embarkation of Saint Peter Nolasco*. About 1600. Seville, Museum. (After Stradanus, *Fishing in the Arno, Florence*, about 1570, engraved at Antwerp 1578.)

VII. Juan de Mesa: *Our Lady of the Caves*. Seville, Museum.

VIII. Juan Martínez Montañés: *The Immaculate Conception*. (Painted by Francisco Pacheco.) About 1632. Seville, University.

His influence on Zurbarán seems limited, however, although his *Virgin of Mercy* (fig. V), in the Cathedral of Seville, calls Zurbarán to mind in the contrasted lighting, the composition, the clouds and the draperies. The landscape background in Roelas' *Saint Francis Borgia,* at the Seville Museum, possesses Zurbarán's quiet melancholy and stillness.

Antonio Mohedano (about 1560–1625) appears to have been a major influence on Zurbarán, as Angulo has shown.([52]) Mohedano's paintings anticipate Zurbarán's San Pablo series (*4–5, 14–16*) in the tenebroso, the facial types, the fleshiness and plasticity. Similar, too, are the arrangement of objects and figures in an interior, the handling of clouds, and the types of putti.

Zurbarán recalls Gothic painters in his clear, cool, luminous colours and in the angular architecture of his deeply carved draperies.

Some of the altars for which Zurbarán painted canvases also contained carved wooden images, painted and gilded in the Spanish manner. This art, called 'estofado,' was carried out at Seville even by renowned painters. Thus Zurbarán was, like his colleagues, in constant touch with sculpture. During the first sixty-five years of the seventeenth century, the Sevillan school of Baroque sculpture was at its height. Zurbarán, Velázquez and Cano may owe the plastic power of their folds and figures to the image carvers, particularly to Montañés. Zurbarán preserved the statuesque quality of his figures longer than the other two painters, who, at Madrid, began to strive for a more airy fusion with the surrounding atmosphere. His style seems calmer and in a more classical temper than that of Montañés (1568–1649), who had grown up as a Mannerist. Being more nearly contemporary, the sculptors Juan de Mesa (1586–1627) and Pedro de Mena (1628–1688) are closer in mood to Zurbarán (see figs. VII, VIII).

Prints were another important influence on the artist, who, throughout his life, relied on Flemish and German engravings for many of his works ([44-45]). Like Velázquez, he usually closely followed a composition taken as model. When a design had caught his fancy, he was apt to borrow it, even if it concerned a different story requiring considerable, and sometimes bizarre, mutations. He often copied heads and gestures of one or several figures, and part of the architecture, but painted the rest according to his own invention, in a wholly imaginative way.

He studied prints by Callot (*78, 144–145*), Ribera (*86–87*), S. à Bolswert (*68, 133*), Th. Galle (*24, 26, 70, 155*), R. Sadeler (*59*), others after Abraham Bloemaert (*69*), G. Seghers (*221*), and by or after Mannerists of Flanders: F. Floris (*93, 98*), Heemskerck (*89, 159*), Marten de Vos (*26, 33, 52, 86, 89*), Jer. Wierix (*67*); France: G. Salmon (*102*); and Italy: B. Passeri (*69*). In turning to German Renaissance artists, like the Master E.S. (*27*), Dürer (*10, 176, 207–208, 223*), H. S. Beham (*100, 102*), Schongauer's *Apostles* (*47, 78*) and perhaps his *Wise and Foolish Virgins* (*46, 116, 119, 179–181*), Zurbarán deliberately strengthened the archaic aspect of his imagery.

The influence of Caravaggio, founder of Baroque painting in Italy, may have been exaggerated. As Lafuente Ferrari ([55]) explained : ' At the same time as Caravaggio in Italy, painters elsewhere veered to naturalistic painting, proving again a truth now universally recognized : changes of artistic taste are not due alone to the action of a single master, but are produced with historic logic by a general spiritual reorientation.' Everywhere, in the second decade of the seventeenth century, the time was ripe for the new Baroque techniques of naturalism and tenebroso to represent religion in a novel and dramatic way. Similar tendencies, in art and in other branches of human endeavour, often appear at many places simultaneously when the time is ripe. Painters in Spain could have developed the Baroque style from Flemish painting, from Venetian and Spanish mannerism, from the Bolognese school, from Caravaggio, or from all four. Baroque naturalism had a long ancestry : Van Eyck, Dürer, Holbein, Savoldo, Moroni. In Spain, one finds naturalism, among many others, in Juan Correa de Vivar, active about

SAINT JEROME WITH SAINTS PAULA AND EUSTOCHIUM. About 1638–40. New York, Samuel H. Kress Foundation (Cat. No. 198)

1550 at Toledo, whose *Death of the Virgin* (Prado 671) anticipates Zurbarán in the classic construction, the vivid colours, the realism of the setting, and the Flemish pewter dish with fruit on a low table. Any semblance of a relationship between the art of Correa de Vivar and that of Zurbarán may, however, be accidental, and should be taken as a further indication of the archaic spirit in the art of Zurbarán.

Three contemporary Spanish artists influenced Zurbarán particularly : Velázquez, Ribera, and Murillo.

Velázquez's impact on Zurbarán, cemented by an early and continued friendship, was strong and repeated, although Zurbarán's earliest pictures (*1–3*) do not show traits derived from his friend. Velázquez's spell was felt for the first time in 1626 or 1627 in a group of paintings including those for San Pablo (*Dominican Miracles* and the three *Doctors of the Church*, see *4–5, 14–16*), two *Saints* (*6–7*), at Cadiz, a *Marriage of Saint Catherine* (*9*), the *Holy Family* (*12*), the *Christ Child Blessing* (*13*), and *Fray Diego Deza* (*19*). These paintings have a loose, glossy technique, distinguishing the modelling of faces and folds and inspired by Velázquez : two instances of many are the hands and sleeves of *St. Jerome* (*16*), and the face of *Diego Deza*. Plate 2 and Fig. 14 reproduce two works by Zurbarán, painted only three or four years apart, one before and the other after Velázquez influenced him. The head of Deza (fig. 14) is related to such heads by Velázquez as the *Portrait of a Man with a Ruff* (Prado 1209) of 1619. The same deeply marked lights run from eye to cheek and from nose to jaw. The eyes are shadowed in both portraits, more intensely by Zurbarán, the temples and cheek highlighted and the ears modelled with great vigour. An energy unusual for Zurbarán is seen in the bold strokes of the collar, which find their more convincing counterpart in Velázquez's rendering.

The *Male Portrait* (*35*), here ascribed to Zurbarán, which in the Museum of Seville is attributed to Velázquez, could not be by the former unless he had direct knowledge of the portraits done by Velázquez at Madrid in 1625 and immediately thereafter. If one accepts the *Male Portrait* as by Zurbarán, and I see no other choice, one is almost forced to the conclusion that Zurbarán shortly after 1625 visited Velázquez at Madrid. Pose, treatment of shadow, and background are based on Velázquez's *Olivares*, dated 1625, in the Hispanic Society of America at New York. The motif of the right glove hanging down came from Velázquez's *Infante Carlos* of about 1626, at the Prado. In the *Male Portrait*, the technique in which the glove is painted, while possessing some elements of Velázquez's style, is precisely the same as that of Zurbarán's *Doctors of the Church* (*14–16*). This glove is one of the reasons for assuming that the picture, although based on Velázquez, was not painted by him.

From June 1626 until August 1628 there are no documents mentioning Zurbarán. For the stylistic reasons just discussed, one may wonder whether he journeyed from Llerena to Madrid to visit Velázquez and to obtain a court position. Since stylistic comparison makes it certain that Zurbarán executed important commissions at Seville between 1626 and 1628, his stay at Madrid, if it took place at all, cannot have exceeded six to nine months.

Subsequently, Velázquez influenced Zurbarán twice anew, on the occasion of the latter's trips to Madrid in 1634 and from 1658 onward. Thus the *Relief of Cadiz* (*103*), 1634, contains motifs of Velázquez's *Surrender of Breda*, of the same year and done for the same palace hall, while the *Doctor of Law* (*214*), painted during Zurbarán's final stay at Madrid, resembles Velázquez's style in the spontaneous brushwork of the collar and the elegant, soft execution of the hands.

The Valencian painter Ribera was from 1616 active in far away Naples. His influence on Zurbarán is first felt in 1633 or 1634, although as early as 1620 the Spanish viceroy of Naples is said to have brought paintings by him to Osuna, fifty miles from Seville. While Zurbarán could have studied Ribera's pictures there or at Madrid (if he went there in 1627 or 1628 as here tentatively suggested), he does not seem to have been interested in Ribera as yet, for not a single picture painted prior to 1633 shows any traces of that artist, either in subject matter, mood or brushwork. Zurbarán's Lisbon *Apostolate* (*78*), dated in 1633, presents the earliest paintings in which Ribera's influence may possibly be detected. The types as well as the sketchy handling of the brush, *alla prima,* may have been derived from him. Zurbarán's *Altar of Saint Peter* (*86–90*) in the Cathedral of Seville offers the earliest certain example of Ribera's influence. Dated heretofore in 1625 because of an erroneous interpretation of the documents, this altar does not fit into Zurbarán's early style.([46]) It was painted in 1633 or later, in my opinion. Kehrer([24]) has pointed out that the artist used Ribera's etching of Saint Peter for the two flanking figures (*86–87*) of that Saint. Zurbarán also employed Ribera's peculiar wet-in-wet oil technique, for instance in the scene showing *Saint Peter Healing the Lame* (*89*). This proves that by now Zurbarán had studied actual paintings of Ribera whose influence, confined essentially to the 1630's, is most evident in the *Hercules* series (*93–102*), 1634, and the works for Jerez (*124–143*) and Guadalupe (*151–162*), 1637–1639.

During the last fifteen years of his life Zurbarán fell under the spell of Murillo, who had ever since 1645 increasingly eclipsed him in popularity. The artist's economic situation became worse and worse. Murillo's influence, favoured by the *Zeitgeist* of the incipient Late Baroque, changed Zurbarán's art from virile strength to a soft, tenderly glowing quality. This was, however, due as much to circumstances in Zurbarán's own life and the general stylistic tendencies of the time as to Murillo, who had in turn in his own early period been strongly under the influence of Zurbarán.

With so many influences active on the artist, it may seem to the reader that he was a weak personality without a strong and characteristic style of his own. Nothing could be farther from the truth. The artist's greatness is supported by his ability to combine in his work traditional and progressive elements. His models and, in many ways, his spiritual affinities went back to earlier periods which lived on in his art. On the other hand, the painter incessantly searched for new solutions of problems of form, colour, chiaroscuro and space. He was truly great because he was at the same time a *retardataire* and a pioneer, one reaching into the past and into the future. He succeeded always in endowing his pictures with a deeply religious feeling, which was often lacking in his models. The many influences which Zurbarán successfully absorbed never made him waver in his direction predetermined by his very roots. He had the simplicity, individuality, and sturdy faith of the farmers in his native Extremadura.

Those who have travelled through that lonely region along Spain's western border, will better understand Zurbarán's paintings. Fertile fields and low rolling hills stretch in all directions, but everywhere vistas are held in check by distant mountains. Strong colours abound: greens and greys and the far-away luminous whites. The eye develops a keen grasp of space. Villages are few and far between. The soil rewards those who work hard, and the people are strong and virile. Serene and silent like the earth, they are a provincial and proud, highly individualistic race, which bred soldiers and leaders in the conquest of Spanish America, men like Cortés, Pizarro, and Orellana.

II. THE STYLES OF ZURBARÁN

DURING fifty years of artistic activity, Zurbarán's style changed as he grew older, because his spiritual and pictorial aims developed and altered. Several periods can thus be distinguished and a stylistic analysis is necessary in order to establish a logical sequence of his works. His earliest known picture, the *Immaculate Conception* (*1*) of 1616, is amazingly accomplished. Already his style is unmistakable and the foremost qualities of his art are obvious: radiant luminosity, striking colour contrasts, realistic treatment, and withal a mystic feeling. In spite of these virtues, the figures are modelled in high relief rather than fully in the round, and the space behind them lacks realization.

1. The early style until 1629

From 1617 to 1628, Zurbarán lived at Llerena,([6]) the capital of the priorate of San Marcos de León and of the military order of Santiago for the entire region of Extremadura, with jurisdiction over thirty-eight towns and villages, and also the seat of a tribunal of the Holy Inquisition. The war against nearby Portugal led, after 1640, to a decline of the city, but in Zurbarán's time there were many convents, now in ruins or entirely gone: San Francisco, Santo Domingo, Santa Ana, the Concepción, and the Unshod Carmelites of San Sebastián. Only the church remains of the convent of the Franciscan nuns. While the Clares still live in Santa Clara, their other establishment, Santa Isabel, was secularized in 1835. I visited the three remaining churches (Santa Clara and the two parish churches, La Granada and Santiago) but discovered paintings by Zurbarán (*112–114*) only in the main church dedicated to Our Lady of the Pomegranate, La Granada. In the surroundings of Llerena were many hermitages, but none survives. All those churches and chapels, and those of other towns in the region, undoubtedly provided the young master with much work. Not a single painting, however, has so far been rediscovered.([47])

Many citizens of Llerena emigrated to the Colonies. The brothers of Zurbarán's second wife lived at Cartagena (Colombia) and Lima. As Sra. Caturla([6]) explained: 'In Llerena, surely, began Zurbarán's connection with the New World which was to bring to America later such an important portion of his works.'

A study of the early style is based on twenty-seven paintings which can be attributed to the years from 1626 to 1629. Among them are paintings for the Sevillan churches of San Pablo (*4–5, 14–16*), the Trinitarians (*10–13*), and San Buenaventura (*24–27*), all dated or documented. In these works Zurbarán established himself as a master of sculpturesque form. Like all progressive artists of that time he applied himself to the problem of tenebroso in order to make his pictures by dramatic shadows as convincing as possible. In comparison to the following decade, however, the tenebroso contrast of his faces was still subdued and not yet sharply focused. Zurbarán, from the beginning, chose the language of realism. In his early style, this aspect of his art was, however, less pronounced than in his second, realistic period. In early paintings (*2–7, 9*) the heads were still more idealized than realistic. The modelling is somewhat hard and clumsy, and the drawing is still hesitant. The folds of the draperies are often angular and arranged in an excited zig-zag rhythm, as in the skirt of Saint Lucy (*2*), the mantle of Saint Michael (*3*), the robes of Christ (*9*), or those of the *Christ Child Contemplating the Crown of Thorns* (*20*). Stylistically the *Saint Lucy* and the *Saint Michael* (*2–3*) are slightly earlier than the rest of the group. The head of Saint Lucy (plate 2) is painted flat, dry, and in only two tones of light and dark, a uniform light area being set against a medium dark area in the shadows. The head of Fray Diego Deza (fig. 14) is plastic, glossy in modelling, and dramatic through many shades of light and dark. As suggested on p. 7, the style of this picture was derived from Velázquez, who influenced Zurbarán some time between 1626 and 1628.

The paintings for the Trinitarians (*10–13*) progress towards greater realism, a simplification of drapery folds, and greater airiness and subtlety in painting light and shade. Vermilion is used effectfully as a local colour. The space-building tenebroso deepens in the *Holy Family with Saints Anne, Joachim, and John* (*12*). The delicacy of the Virgin's face, her thin transparent scarf, and the precious flowers disclose the artist's increasing maturity. However, Zurbarán's treatment of space still falls short of the achievements to be reached by him in the 1630's.

The early style shows soft folds and broad, flat expanses of velvet-like draperies, as in the *Saint Bonaventure* series *(24–27)* ([33-34]). The draperies, however wavy, never reach out into space, but are conceived almost in a single plane. In the faces and hands brown shadows and white high-lights are used, as is the case throughout the artist's career. Backgrounds are usually dark, although the *Saint Bonaventure* series presents vistas opening on light-gray architecture. Spatial clarity is still lacking; the figures are not clearly separated from one another. Crowded together without room to move about, they produce a sense of tight atmosphere, of drama, and of pathos. These traits are usually associated with the European Early Baroque (1590–1620), but sometimes even more developed in the High Baroque (1620–1640).

The magnificent *Saint Bonaventure's Mediation at the Council of Lyon (26)*, painted in 1629, exemplifies all these qualities. It also contains incisive individual portraits. This is not surprising, because Zurbarán's intense style is very effective in single-figure studies. Indeed, his single figures of saints and monks constitute one of his chief claims to fame. His narrative scenes, too, exhibit a hidden boldness of composition, all the more inventive for being so unorthodox. A skilful camouflage of the perspective extension lines, and alternating areas of light and dark, of voids and masses, force the eye of the spectator to engage actively in the scene represented. There is no point of rest, but a perpetual moving back and forth in space.

In the *Saint Bonaventure Refers Saint Thomas Aquinas to the Saviour (25)* at Berlin, the artist set out to solve exciting problems of spatial relationships. The monks, tightly massed at the left, are balanced by the small figure of Christ at the right. A curve, accentuated by the expressive hands of the friars, leads up to the Crucified. The lights are distributed in such a way that they, too, point to the agonizing Christ. Horizontals and verticals offer an abstract mathematical construction in space, stimulating to the modern eye and akin to aspirations of contemporary art. Caravaggio and the Italian Baroque painters emphasized complicated movement into the depth of the picture and seemingly even in front of the picture surface. Zurbarán, on the other hand, like later on Cézanne, constructed a relatively flat box, in which most of the action takes place parallel to the picture plane. For this reason, both the doorway at the left and the side of the chair at the right are less foreshortened than perspective would require. Movement forward and backward is arrested by the background plane, and large, block-like forms, as in Cézanne, are provided by the figures. Zurbarán was aware of the fact that unless counterbalanced, deep space will hinder the sensation of emotional tension forces associated with the surface plane. His shallow space encourages the experience of strong emotional plane relationships, related to the four borders of the canvas.([56])

The archaic, medieval composition of the *Saint Bonaventure on his Bier (27)* is probably derived from the *Ars Moriendi* prints (about 1460) by the German Master E.S. The monumental yet quiet mood, the colours, as well as the position of the heads and the relationships of the figures call to mind Piero della Francesca. Such associations bespeak the timelessness of Zurbarán's art.

At the transition to Zurbarán's second period, the realistic style, stand four *Scenes from the Life of Saint Peter Nolasco (30–33)*, founder of the Mercedarian order for the redemption of Christians from Moorish captivity. They were painted in 1629 and 1630. The artist has deepened his spiritual message and made advances toward greater clarity and depth of the spatial arrangement. Here, for the first time, Zurbarán disclosed his gifts as a great landscape painter. The quietness, freshness, and orderly arrangement of his lakes and glades anticipate work by the best landscape painters of the nineteenth century.

A wonderful transparency and luminosity distinguish not only the paintings as a whole but especially the faces which now have the diaphanous quality of a silverpoint drawing. Indeed the only certain drawing (*34*) known today from Zurbarán's hand appears to be precisely from this period. An increased precision of draftsmanship makes the features more realistic than before. Particularly moving is the head of the inversely crucified Saint Peter, anticipating the *Blessed Alonso Rodríguez* (*39*) of 1630. As for the draperies, the large planes are now broken up, and the folds are smaller and firmer, with many subtle half-tones.

From 1626 to 1639 Zurbarán was active, almost exclusively, in the service of various religious Orders: the Capuchins, the Mercedarians, the Carthusians, and the Jeronymites, all of whom wear white habits. Thus Zurbarán developed that masterful variety in the rendering of white materials for which he is known. No one else was so skilled in painting whites, crisp as frozen snow, soft as cotton, heavy as cream. In a choice essay on the master, Paul Guinard([22]) onced called the *Saint Hugh of Grenoble Visiting the Refectory* (*69*) 'une symphonie en blanc majeur'. Unlike other Spanish artists of fame, Zurbarán specialized in serial productions for conventual halls and cloisters, as well as the main altars of churches. In this respect, too, he emulated medieval artists. For a single commission he might paint twenty, or as many as thirty-four pictures. These large orders were, perforce, partly filled by assistants working under the master's direction.

2. *The realistic style of the early 1630's*

Zurbarán's second style is exemplified by the *Vision of the Blessed Alonso Rodríguez* (*39*), 1630; the *Apotheosis of Saint Thomas Aquinas* (*41*), 1631; the three *Carthusian Scenes* at the Museum of Seville (*68–70*), about 1633; and the ten *Labours of Hercules* (*93–102*), 1634. In these works Zurbarán's art reached a realism he never surpassed. He now excelled in the most painstakingly sharp and precise draftsmanship, along with which he was also developing a more luminous colour scale, lightening his colours and simultaneously deepening his shadows. The greater tenebroso contrast made his pictures more dramatic. This development is in line with the aspirations of other outstanding painters of his age. Zurbarán now stressed, to the utmost, the plastic solidity of his figures; see, for example, the head of the Blessed Alonso Rodríguez (plate 24). In the painting of this title, the relation of the picture's width to the perspective viewing distance is about $1:\frac{1}{2}$. 'This very close viewpoint means that the lines running into depth are given the greatest possible extension.'([63]) Consequently these orthogonal lines seemingly creating depth have a maximum value as a surface pattern. The artist also guides us across the picture plane by the row of windows not drawn in perspective. The orthogonals of the floor and of both sides converge at three different vanishing points. The spatial relationships, although more three-dimensional than in the artist's previous works, are not yet clarified as much as they were to be in his later paintings. The music-making angels seem nearer the foreground than the Virgin, but the clouds indicate that they are in one and the same plane. This moving forward and backward in space by planes shifting in depth, rather than due to any ineptness, seems to be a conscious device to engage the spectator. In combination with Zurbarán's geometric pattern it gives to his paintings a surprisingly modern aspect and explains his prominence today as a precursor of contemporary masters.

In 1626, in the *Dominican Miracles* (*4–5*), Zurbarán had not made the slightest distinction in depicting saints and mortals, and the differentiation is still slight in the early 1630's. Unlike El Greco's explosive eruptions that fling the spectator skyward and so startle him that the strangest miracle seems more real and believable than an experience from daily life, Zurbarán's ecstasies are held rigidly to the ground by his sense of realism. At this time he painted heavenly figures almost as soberly as earthly ones, an approach which he was to change progressively during the second half of the 1630's, his mystic period. However, in the early 1630's he merely placed his heavenly personages on a second storey, a balcony or clouds. These differences in Greco's and Zurbarán's representations of visions are explained by the dissimilar spiritual affinities of the two artists and by a change in the prevalent characteristics of Spanish mysticism.

In the *Apotheosis of Saint Thomas Aquinas (41)*, as in so many of his other canvases, it is the Mannerist, funnel-like composition, with luminous distances framed by darks, which draws our eyes into the picture. The dark column in the middle-ground breaks into the light area of the background. It thus pulls the spectator toward the front plane again and provides increased tenebroso contrast. This is Zurbarán's most ambitious picture, rich in colour but not entirely unified in brush work or design.

Another high-point in the painter's career was reached in his three paintings for the refectory of the Carthusian monastery at Seville (68–70). *The Virgin as Protectress of the Carthusians (68)* was adapted from a print (fig. 43). Zurbarán's pristine imagination, his intensity, his simplicity, and his plastic organization give the painting an ethos towering far above that of his sources. Four colours ring forth in purest harmony: the pink of the Virgin's gown, the light and dark blues of the mantle against the warm orange of the background, and the cool whites of the monks. Chaste flowers, so tender that one is afraid of breaking them, so fresh that one can smell their fragrance, lie at the Virgin's feet. The highly imaginative shape of her gown has extraordinary power. Rising from a broad base, with folds ascending like organ pipes, the movement expands through the protectively raised arm, rests briefly in the finely modelled head of the Virgin, and swings victoriously upward along the winglike edges of her huge mantle. The metallic amplitude of the form reminds one of sculptures by Jacopo della Quercia, the plastic bulk calls to mind Michelangelo. Kneeling figures, in many shades of white, project from the background, a musical rhythm winging along the clear-cut folds of their robes. Each monk is clearly separated from his brethren, so that space, in relatively flat three-dimensional depth, is most successfully organized. This picture is a masterpiece. It shows how much Zurbarán had learned since he painted the sequence of Saint Bonaventure. One may recall the tight grouping of figures in *Saint Bonaventure's Mediation at the Council of Lyon (26)*, 1630, and the small degree of spatial clarity in the *Apotheosis of Saint Thomas Aquinas (41)*, 1631. In view of the progress in draftsmanship and brushwork made in the pictures for the Charterhouse of Seville, these cannot be dated before 1633. More symmetrical in comparison to the master's earlier paintings, the design is accompanied by an even greater precision in the rendering of detail, thus following what seems to be an unchanging principle of Spanish art from the Primitives onward, as stated by Chandler R. Post[59]: 'The union of the highest possible realism of detail with the utmost schematization of the general design.'

Symmetry, strict order, and most careful detail also distinguish the *Saint Hugh of Grenoble Visiting the Refectory (69)*. Outstanding qualities of the picture are the veracity and earnestness of the faces, the stimulating, plastic presentation of solid bodies in space, and the unity achieved by immaculate colours: gray, white, lavender, and blue. Never before had whites and grays been used with such chaste purity, such bracing precision, such visionary clarity, such strength and tenderness. This picture bridges the span from early Renaissance art to the aspirations of present-day painting. Each body is self-contained, drawn with a clean, sharp exactness reminding one of both Uccello and Picasso. All lines are related to each other. Overlapping contours and solids are keenly separated by contrasts of light and shade. Kehrer has pointed to the archaic—and one might add, modern—character of the planes, neatly parallel to the picture surface. They were Zurbarán's favourite vehicle in building a painting. A particularly spacious recession, is, however, provided by the picture on the wall, a masterpiece of integration with the total design and of imaginative landscape painting as well.   The colours are fresh, light, and airy in effect. The oblong frame acts in unison with the table cloth; between both areas a subtle tension is established. The hands and faces of the seated monks are loosely painted and sketchy, as in many other paintings by Zurbarán throughout the 1630's. Flesh colours are ruddy with whites, pinks and browns, and the darks in the shadows are still unrelieved.

In the *Urban II with his Confessor Saint Bruno* (70) the observer concentrating his attention on the individual figures will feel the supernatural life within them. The difference between the mortal Pope and the holy Saint is mystically suggested. A saintly numen emanates from Saint Bruno, a halo of sanctity which communicates itself to the spectator. Each one of Zurbarán's personages becomes a complete universe and everything that happens in his pictures happens in the inner world of the individual. Meditating quietly, only living for his spiritual vision, the Saint seems to be touched by divine grace.

Important in the construction of this painting are the two S-curves created by the two main figures, the one formed by Saint Bruno paralleled by the person behind him. The two centre figures are bound to each other by the bow-shaped design of the rug at their feet, by the straight plane of the table, and by the rectangular areas below the windows. Balancing the three horizontals are three verticals in the background. Completing this design are two arcs. One, beginning in the foreground corner of the canopy above the Pope, runs along the curtain, through the Pope's head, then along his back to the edge of the curtain at the lower left. The other circle segment begins in the curtain hiding the column at top centre, then runs along the back of Saint Bruno and ends where the rug meets the lower ledge of the garment worn by the priest at the right. The stone fruits carved in low relief at the left of the right-hand window parallel the outline of the curtain, while the fruits at the right, instead of being symmetrical, parallel Saint Bruno's back. It is clear that here, as in other pictures, the artist stressed the repetition of lines.

The oblique rectangulars in the door jamb at the right are parallel, running in the same general direction as the upper back and the arm rests of Pope Urban's chair instead of following laws of perspective which would cause them to level off as they approach the horizontal line just above the head of the Saint. In spite of his interest in realistic detail, Zurbarán was willing to sacrifice realistic vanishing-point perspective, for the sake of diagonal movements and of tensions between planes parallel to the surface of the picture. Such tensions he provided chiefly by the use of values of light and dark. Ever since the *Apotheosis of Saint Thomas Aquinas* (41) of 1631, Zurbarán would concentrate the strongest light on the figures in the foreground, set them off plastically by a dark middleground, and achieve a semblance of depth—a relative escape—by a light or medium-bright background. One may call this arrangement Zurbarán's light-dark-medium triad. Probably taken over from Flemish sixteenth-century paintings, it was used by the master throughout the 1630's and 1640's.

The composition and many details are derived from an engraving by Theodor Galle, *Saint Norbert and Saint Bernard before Emperor Lothar* (fig. 44) contained in a *Life of Saint Norbert*, of 1605, a book often consulted by the artist for source material.([44]) The arrangement of two seated figures in the foreground and a heavy solid between them in the middleground pleased Zurbarán, but since the Emperor does not enter into the life of Saint Bruno, the painter omitted him and replaced him by a stout column.

A spiritual feeling, so characteristic of the Baroque, is evident in the signed *Still Life with Oranges* (71), 1633. Fruits and flowers are brought out fully in three dimensions, but contrasting with their sharp, precise outlines are the blurred shadows on the table and among the leaves. An air of mystery is thus introduced, aided by the contrasts of textures, light and shade, and cool tones against warm ones. In their strict order, the objects are painted like gifts on the altar of God. Some writers have rightly stressed the painter's sensitivity for the humble. Paraphrasing Saint Teresa, it has been said that, in the artist's still lifes, 'God walks among the fruits and vessels'. This spiritual attitude has been contrasted with the carnal appetite rampant in Dutch and Flemish still lifes.([26])

In the coeval *Mercedarians* (*55, 58, 79–85a*) the approximate chronological order of their production is established by the extent to which the figures are made three-dimensional. In contrast to the sharp outlines and shadows and the compact, block-like forms still prevailing in the earliest examples (*55, 58*) of the series, Zurbarán in the *Mercedarians* of about 1633 created space by effects of pose and lighting which lead the eye around the figure. In these later examples (*79–83*) he used subtle half shadows to give more depth and a progressively more sketchy technique fusing the heads with the surrounding air. Wavy instead of straight draperies contribute to the three-dimensional effect. By a comparison with the *Apostles* (*78*), at Lisbon, the five 'named' *Mercedarians* may be dated about 1633. The tenebroso contrast, most intense in the early 1630's, was again decreasing. In the two *Mercedarian Saints* (*84–85*), perhaps of 1634, at Seville, an advance in enveloping airiness proves that technically Zurbarán's art was always progressive and in step with general tendencies of Baroque painting.

At the end of Zurbarán's realistic style, stand, fittingly enough, mythological subjects and battle scenes: the *Hercules* series and the *Relief of Cadiz* (*93–103*), all of 1634. Praised by Palomino and Ponz, the artistic merit of the Hercules group has since been slighted. This writer's view([27]) that Zurbarán's brush painted the entire series has been confirmed by Sra. Caturla's discovery of Zurbarán's signed receipt.([5]) Convincing evidence for the master's authorship are the modelling and the outline of the bodies, and such details as the stances, the landscapes, and the painting of the Hydra. Occasional slight deviations from Zurbarán's usual style in the facial types, and also in details of the hands and the drapery folds, may be explained by the treatment imposed by the subject matter, as well as by very minor participation of assistants.

The Mantegnesque *Hercules* series discloses a sensuality thoroughly Baroque but surprising in the painter of monks. This sensuality enhances the muscular male body, modelled by an expressive play of light and shade. Careful observation of powerful human anatomy (see plates 55-58) here reaches a climax, appropriately closing the artist's realistic period. Painted for the Hall of Realms of the Palace at Madrid, the *Labours of Hercules* hung there between Battle Scenes, further stressing the heroic character of the ensemble. With 'historic necessity' this exuberant decorative scheme was created in 1634, that is at the peak of the High Baroque. Contrasting with this vigour are some of the landscapes in the background (particularly plate 59) belonging to the most Arcadian scenes ever created. They are worthy of Poussin and Corot. Their idyllic mood anticipates the classic phase of the Baroque, usually dated from about 1640 to 1660. This combination of epic virility and lyric melancholy exemplifies the transition from High to Classical Baroque.

The bold three-dimensional thrust of the dying Hercules' right foot (*102*) may be explained by contact with the work of Caravaggio and his followers, among them Ribera. This contact probably took place during Zurbarán's stay at the Royal Palace at Madrid. However, only few paintings by Ribera, including the *Tityus* and *Ixion*, show such bold thrusts toward the spectator. Both pictures, of 1632 and at the Prado, resemble the *Hercules* paintings in subject matter and handling. The brushwork of the faces in the *Hercules* series is, in the author's opinion, one of the earliest certain instances of an adaptation by Zurbarán of Ribera's style. The monumental, virile mood and the plastic modelling of the bodies through most sensitive tenebroso lighting are characteristic of both Zurbarán and Ribera.

The portrait of *Alonso de Verdugo de Albornoz* (*104*) was painted in 1635, after the master's return to Seville, and forms a proper transition between the two styles of the 1630's: the realistic and the mystic. Realistic in subject matter, the softly melting airy treatment of the flesh indicates not only the renewed

STILL LIFE WITH ORANGES. 1633. Florence, Count Contini-Bonacossi (Cat. No. 71)

influence of Velázquez that had occurred in 1634, but also a more mystic approach, which can be felt in the earnest, soulful eyes.

3. The mystic style of the late 1630's

Zurbarán's mystic style comprises the second half of the 1630's. Main works of these years are the pictures for the Barefooted Mercedarians of San José (117–122, 163); the paintings for the Carthusians of Jerez (124–143) and for the Jeronymites of Guadalupe (151–162); the *Blessed Henry Suso* and *Saint Louis Bertram* (149–150), both for Santo Domingo Portacoeli.

In this third period the master turned from the transparent silverpoint technique and the detailed execution of the very early 1630's, as well as from the rough and sketchy handling of 1633–1634, to a more painterly, fluid, fusing and opaque application of oil impasto. The shadows are always kept very thin. He may have learned this technique from Ribera, and, undoubtedly, also through his renewed contact with Velázquez, in 1634. Following the precedent set in the two early landscapes of 1630 (33, 49) and somewhat later in the *Hercules* series and in the *Relief of Cadiz* (93–103), Zurbarán, from now on, most frequently placed his figures outdoors in a landscape. Thus he was forced to give more attention to air and atmosphere. By using a more even illumination he further diminished harsh contrasts of light and shade. As the light became softer, its diffusion mitigated the realism of the faces. This change is visible in many of the master's holy figures, beginning with the *Saint Lawrence* (117) and the *Saint Apollonia* (119), both once at the Barefooted Mercedarians. In these pictures an increasing breadth and mildness are noticeable in the features and draperies. In *Christ Crowning Saint Joseph* (120), which is probably from the same church and also of about 1636–1637, Zurbarán now differentiated between divinity on the one hand and Saints or mere mortals on the other. Both heads are airily plastic, but that of Christ is bland and visionary, while Saint Joseph's head appears firmer. Both faces show the most gentle transitions from light to shade. A mystic trend is evident in both, as well as in the grandly enveloping folds of their monumental draperies. In fact, faces and folds, while preserving the reality of outward appearance, transcend it to express spiritual qualities.

The mystic experience thus created is nowhere expressed more strongly than in the seven effigies of *Carthusian Saints* (124–130) at Cadiz. Their former location between the altar and the sanctuary of the Carthusian monastery at Jerez helps to explain their saintly mood enjoining reverent quiet. Even more important for an understanding of these panels are the rules of the Carthusian community. Living in almost perpetual silence, the monks were allowed to walk and discourse together but once a week. Eight months out of twelve they fasted, and meat was forbidden at all times. They were required to labour assiduously with their hands. Mrs. Jameson[54] remarks that their spare diet, rigorous seclusion and practice of manual labour seem to have bestowed the emaciated look, and the pale quietude felt with overwhelming intensity in these seven *Carthusian Saints*. In eloquent silence, they are wholly withdrawn from this world. 'Blessed are the eyes which are closed to the outward, but are intent on the inward' (Thomas à Kempis). Their profiles are thinly painted with the most delicate strength, sensitivity and faith. Zurbarán entered fully into the spirit of the Carthusians, with whom he is said to have lived for a few months. His brush must have been guided by prayer and mortification, such as Carducho[53] demanded from a painter of religious subjects. This would help to explain the depth of feeling, the great refinement of modelling by tenuous touches and surest outlines. Several profiles, kept in half-shadow, are set against dark backgrounds. Such use of dark against darks forces the eye to enter into the panel, to search and, like the faithful, to believe, when mysteries—no longer seen—are but felt. The dark backgrounds seem to isolate the figures from active life. Light falling on the habits and carnations reinforces, by contrast, the airy, transparent *tenebrae* of the sombre settings. Soft and enveloping folds contribute greatly to the feeling of all-embracing tenderness. The heavy wool material is more supple and less sharply delineated than in the Carthusian scenes (*68–70*) of 1633 at Seville. The broad expanses of the draperies give firm structure to the master's pictures and are the vehicle for his exciting colour contrasts, but they are not arranged solely for their monumental strength and their value in the total design. Zurbarán's folds, beneath their mere outward appearance, seem to take on an emphatic inner life, which is able to stimulate powerful moods in the spectator. Guinard(²²) rightly said: 'His fabrics have their own architecture and an independent life apart from the body they are intended to clothe. They live with singular greatness through the force of their individuality,' and one may add, through their religious piety. Zurbarán's paintings for Guadalupe and for Jerez are the most inspired works created by Spanish mysticism in the seventeenth century.

With the modifications demanded by their former location, the paintings from the main retable (*133–140*), now dispersed, conform in style to the seven *Carthusians*. These large canvases were to be seen at a distance; consequently, their execution is more sketchy and rough. The paintings are moving instances of Zurbarán's power of individual characterization. Although derived from Ribera, his types of picaresque urchins, his faces of old women and bearded old men are not easily forgotten. The four magnificent scenes of the *Birth of Christ* (*137–140*), dated in 1638 and 1639, at Grenoble, resemble each other in space construction and in lighting. The figures are spread parallel to the picture plane, thus telling the story most clearly and evidencing the artist's narrative talent. Massiveness and monumentality, recalling once more Piero della Francesca, are achieved by emphasis on the verticals, while the diagonals crossing in space provide a carefully restricted measure of dignified movement. The light is concentrated on a white object in the centre foreground: the lilies, or the Christ Child surrounded by white draperies. These pictures are the foremost examples of Zurbarán's use of the light-dark-medium triad of illumination, a design not only dramatic by its very contrasts, but also providing for a movement backward and forward in space. Essentially fantastic, though derived from Flemish and Italian buildings, is the architecture. Its planes are, primarily, parallel to the picture surface, thus once more affirming Zurbarán's concern for limiting space. In these scenes Zurbarán retained the chromatic richness of late Gothic painters. He never again equalled the many-hued variety of these colours. Such phosphorescent over-tones and intense deep blue were used by the painter only at this stage of his career. After the death of his second wife, in 1639, his colouring was to grow less varied, and, for a while, more somber.

Striking examples of the painter's power of mystic narration are the eight scenes from the life of Jeronymite brethren (*151–158*), 1638–39, at Guadalupe. These pictures show again the overwhelming strength of the spiritual element at this period in Zurbarán's development. Most of the scenes are essentially static; there is little outward drama or movement in them, but a deep desire for the introvert peace of monastic life. This compelling mood of quiescence is more important in evaluating Zurbarán's greatness than his progress in the representation of figures within space and atmosphere which took place in these years. The rushing stream of light behind the figures, for instance in *Christ Rewarding Brother Andrew of Salmerón* (*155*), divests the miracle of all earthly weight and tension. The triangular composition, of great strength and tenderness in faces and folds, is set against a magically flowing sky of yellow lines turning to mauve in the shadows. There exists a close stylistic relationship between the paintings at Guadalupe and at Jerez. Several authors have noted that the poses of the Carthusian figures were repeated in the contemporary Jeronymite series. In the backgrounds of the eight scenes of Jeronymite monks, Zurbarán used artificial perspective, designing the architecture as a receding diagonal and

IX. The Sacristy of the Jeronymite Monastery at Guadalupe, with paintings by Zurbarán (Cf. Cat. Nos. 151–8)

lessening for once the preponderance of parallel planes. This emphasis on perspective is exceptional in the artist's work (see fig. IX).

The *Flagellation* (*159*) and the *Temptation of Saint Jerome* (*160*) are painted in rich and luminous hues of yellow, green, pink, vermilion, orange, violet, and a surprisingly deep blue. The *Flagellation* shows Zurbarán's aversion to cruelty; neither angel seems to hurt or injure the kneeling Saint. In the *Temptation* the gaunt and bony Saint was painted in closest imitation of Ribera's style. Every bone, wrinkle, and hair is shown.

For their breadth and airiness the *Blessed Henry Suso* and *Saint Louis Bertram* (*149–150*) may be tentatively dated in 1638, or even a few years later. The pictures have long been admired as among the greatest creations of mystical seventeenth-century painting. Landscapes in the background extol the virtues of solitary hermitical life and the rewards of inner contemplation. Their wild and romantically Nordic character is so unmistakable, that Zurbarán must have remembered some late Mannerist Flemish print ([23]). Yet these lakes, crags, and glens seem created largely by the artist's imagination. Unreal and fantastic, they are settings for a mystic to dream in. Bands of lights and shadows alternate in hues of siennas, blue-greens, brown-grays and gray-blues. The trees are a succulent green. Their thin, wiry, and strangely live branches and the airy, tuft-like, lightly brushed-in leaves recall the best of Chinese landscapes. In their soft harmonies, these views are among the most suggestive and universal ever conceived by the artist.

4. *The solemn or classic period of the 1640's*

The death of Zurbarán's beloved second wife in the spring of 1639 left a deep impression on the painter's mind and art. Although Beatriz had borne him only one short-lived child, he must have loved her more than his first wife and a third whom he was yet to marry. The artist never recovered from this blow. His productivity fell rapidly. Between 1629 and 1639 he had painted an annual average of fifteen extant works. During the remaining twenty-five years of his life, from 1640 to 1664, the average surviving output were two paintings per year. It is symptomatic that in 1639 and the years immediately following the passing of his wife, he painted Saints reflecting on death, as well as several ideal evocations of the features of the deceased.

From this time onward one may speak of his fourth period, of the solemn or classic style of the 1640's. The artist retained, in a graver manner, the essential qualities of the preceding period, as in the various representations of *Saint Francis Kneeling* (*166–169*). These figures have become calmer, more classical, more pathetic. They seem to have been painted with a heavy heart, and their sombre mood is emphasized by dark backgrounds. It may be suggested that Saint Francis, clutching a skull to his breast, symbolizes the painter reflecting, after the cruel loss he had suffered. The signed and dated *Saint Francis Kneeling* (*167,* plate 88), of 1639, in London, is distinguished by a new largeness of conception in the design, as well as in technique. Zurbarán was no longer interested in realism of detail. He wished to create a solemn, sustained mood and a total impression. The landscape in the background, painted in dark blues and grays, is almost moon-like in its loneliness and roughness. The head and the body of the Saint are 'big' in every sense, and the folds fall with the greatest volume and amplitude. The figure is fully in the round, with a strong diagonal thrust. Both the flesh portions and the draperies are softer and more fusing than in preceding periods. The light contributes materially to a more subdued feeling. Although tenebroso contrast still sets off the figure against the dark background, light and shadow are less contrasting within the drapery and face of the figure itself. Thus the total effect is more unified than in the master's earlier works.

About contemporary may be *Pears and Flowers* (*178*), at the Art Institute of Chicago. It is a still life extraordinary in the refined colour effects of yellow, red, and white, in its luminosity, in the pure lines of the flowers and leaves, in the powerful plasticity of the fruits, and most of all in their almost magic arrangement and interrelationships. They sparkle with vitality and warmth. The white jasmine has whispering, trembling petals; nervous outlines define the twisting leaves of the yellow quince. White hedge-roses are touched with pink, and yellow marguerites grow warm-red in the shadows. Plasticity and roundness are stressed to the utmost; light and air pervade the entire space of the painting. One senses the delicacy, transparence and fragrance of the flowers, the mellow ripeness of the fruits. As with Zurbarán's other still lifes, the picture is almost religious in spirit, an image of the fullness of life and of its transitory nature—to blossom, to ripen, and to die.

The retable at Zafra (*189–197*), 1644, gives a badly needed clue for recognizing the artist's style in his forties. The nine paintings still show contrasts of light and shade, resembling somewhat the manner of various versions of *Saint Francis Standing* (*183–185*), and continuing the handling of the late 1630's and the early 1640's. There is no inkling, as yet, of the softer, more Murillesque style of the 1650's.

Probably between 1635 and 1645 Zurbarán painted, with the aid of assistants working after his designs and under his supervision, various series of life-size, standing figures. These comprise: two series of the *Twelve Apostles* (both partly by the master), one in the Franciscan Monastery in Lima ([35]) (*144*), and one at Santo Domingo of Guatemala City ([30]) (*145*); the *Founders of Monastic Orders*, at Lima (*171*, partly by the master), copied by the shop, with variations, in a series at Castellón de la Plana, and another incomplete group in Mexico; ten *Virgin Saints* (all shop work) for the Hospital de la Sangre, at Seville, now at the Museum; *Twelve Sons of Jacob* (all shop work), in the Bishop's Palace, Bishop Auckland, near Durham, England ([42]).

The transition from the solemn style to the fifth and last manner, the Murillesque style of the 1650's and 1660's, is exemplified by the *Virgin and Child Seated in Clouds* (*199*), in the Museum at Seville. This picture may be as late as 1650, since the round and flabby folds of the sleeve and the windblown draperies of the Virgin's mantle appear in many other late paintings. The flesh portions are hazy and vaporous, and lack strength of design. Closely related and contemporary is the *Immaculate Conception* (*200*), at the Town Hall of Seville. While these pictures do not yet exhibit the strong influence exerted by Murillo during Zurbarán's last years, they are less spiritual and more elegiac than Zurbarán's art had been up to this time. Comparison of these two pictures with their models, the earlier *Virgin and Child with a Dish of Fruit* (*182*) and the *Immaculate Conception Cerralbo* (*66*), indicates the direction of the path travelled by the artist; the later examples are weaker in drawing and design, but more mellow in spirit.

5. *The Murillesque mood of the 1650's and 1660's*

Zurbarán's last style may be said to begin with the *Saint Anthony of Padua* (*202*), owned by Alonso Grosso. The artist's colouring and atmospheric effects were never more silvery, lighter, and more airy. His figures possess now a new transparency and soon will be enveloped in a soft all-over glow. The master continuously progressed toward a more convincing, more gently merging representation of space. Now, in the 1650's and 1660's, he was still in step with the time's prevailing trend, which called for an impressionistic handling of atmosphere. Warm brown backgrounds characterize this period, and the paintings as a whole are often developed in grays and browns. This economy in the use of colour is typical of an artist's late style. The light-dark-medium triad of illumination, distinguishing Zurbarán's High Baroque style of the 1630's, was now abandoned, because it was too contrasting and thus counteracted pictorial unity. This change may be noticed even in figures set in a landscape background, for instance, *Christ Carrying the Cross* (204), 1653. From this time onward the master's paintings have at most two light values, not three as before. Representations of the *Virgin and Christ Child*, or of *Christ* alone, exhibit a small area of brilliant white draperies against a unified interplay of subdued grays, browns, blues, and reds. Paintings of other subjects are composed entirely in subtle, harmonizing values, chiefly of grays and browns.

In 1658, Zurbarán went again to Madrid. Removed from the simplicity and religious fervour of his monastic surroundings in Andalusia, and more than ever exposed to the artistic currents flowing toward the Late Baroque, Zurbarán's painting deteriorated in power. To the sumptuous taste of the court, his style, once so virile and unaffected, may have seemed out of date. He therefore more and more accepted influences from Murillo and from the Late Baroque, and his pictures softened considerably, both in subject matter and style. No longer did the artist paint dramatic narratives of visions and ecstasies. Except for one *Crucifixion,* his subject now was the Virgin, alone or with the Christ Child. His late pictures have an intimate, friendly, less formal spirit about them, as if the master worked for private families and small domestic chapels, rather than for ascetic monks. In the *Virgin and Child with Saint John* (206), 1658, at San Diego, the composition and details seem inspired by Murillo's version, painted about 1650, for a Sevillan convent and now in the collection of Sir John Stirling-Maxwell at Glasgow. Whereas Murillo idealized, stressing harmonious elegance, Zurbarán was down-to-earth realistic and rustic even in as late a painting as this. The illumination of the foreground is tempered in intensity, while the rest of his picture receives uniform, even lighting. Shadow contrasts are minimized. In the Christ Child one senses a relaxation of Zurbarán's former strength, and in the modelling of the Virgin's head an ever increasing tenderness. This mellow understanding, enhanced by airiness, transparency and warmth, is the outstanding quality of Zurbarán's late pictures. In this period, some of the folds appear drawn mechanically; neither they nor the pictures as a whole are always successfully organized.

In their old age, artists often return to features of their early work, and Zurbarán is no exception. The reader will easily discover parallels between the *Young Virgin Praying* (211–212), *A Doctor of Law* (214), and the *Immaculate Conception* (222), on the one hand, and, on the other, paintings done by Zurbarán forty and more years earlier. In these late pictures the artist speaks to us with very great sobriety and humility.

A great work, worthy of closing this account of Zurbarán's stylistic development, is the *Saint Luke before the Crucified* (219), of about 1635–1640. The Saviour is dead, His flesh is greenish-gray, and His face is in the shadows. His body, modelled in the round, softly fades into the *aire ambiente,* into the transparent darks of the night. The Saint looks up to Christ in a gesture of infinite pity and faith. A mystic dialogue seems to develop between them, a relationship born and borne in solitude and supported by the enveloping light of the moon.

III. ZURBARÁN'S THEMES

ZURBARÁN painted still lifes, portraits, and mythologic and historical scenes, but religious themes formed his principal subject: the life of Christ, of the Virgin, or of a Saint, single Angels, Apostles, male and female Saints. Unlike Murillo, he did not paint Old Testament subjects.

Some representations of Christ, such as the humble *Et Ponit Vestimenta Sua* (220), were chosen by few other artists. The *Christ Child Contemplating the Crown of Thorns (20)*, a theme that occupied the artist's mind repeatedly, exemplifies his unsophisticated faith. The large majority of scenes concerning Christ narrate episodes from the Passion. Four paintings depict *The Veil of Saint Veronica (63–64a, 147)*. *Christ Carrying the Cross (204)* was also painted three times, but only one example survives. Of the *Crucifixion* there exist at least fourteen authentic versions (*8, 21–23, 37–38, 50–51, 62, 114, 170, 219, 225, 227*), each one different. Zurbarán painted the Crucified alive, in the act of expiring, or dead; thrice with a Saint or a donor half length standing below the Cross, a mode of representation inherited from the sixteenth century. In more than one version did the artist succeed in suggesting the mystery of the Redemption. Only in two pictures (*38* and *219*) is there a slight indication of landscape in the distance below. The artist sought to make Christ's body appear as sculpturesque as possible, by means of a dark, empty background, and by indicating in some *Crucifixions* parallel to Christ's form a broad black shadow (*8, 37,* and *62*) and in others a thin line of light-gray (*38, 51, 170, 219*). Zurbarán took special care in painting the loin cloth as real as possible. These plastically enveloping draperies are among his greatest achievements in representing fabrics. In every example Christ is nailed to the Cross with four nails. His feet are placed side by side on a *suppedaneum*, except in the earliest and latest picture, where they are crossed and pointed downward (*8* and *219*). Before expiring, Christ looks upward; after his death his head is bent. Of the fourteen surviving *Crucifixions*, this writer dates five (*8, 21–23, 225*) in 1626–1630, four (*37–38, 50–51*) in 1631, one (*62*) in 1632–1634, one (*227*) in 1635, one (*219*) in 1635–1640, one (*114*) in 1636–1638, and one (*170*) in 1640. Dating and determining the chronological sequence are difficult and should be considered as tentative

The emphasis on Passion scenes characterizes the artist's temper. So does the absence of Murillo's favourite themes: Zurbarán did not depict the sweet *Young Christ Child,* nor *Saint Joseph Carrying the Infant Saviour,* nor the *Parables of Christ,* nor did he, like Murillo, paint numerous scenes of the *Nativity,* except for two at Grenoble (*138–139*).

Zurbarán resembles Murillo, however, in the marked preference for the *Immaculate Conception,* because this mystery enjoyed particular popularity at Seville. Among Zurbarán's scenes of the Virgin, the *Immaculate Conception* occurs ten times (*1, 59, 66, 88, 143, 200, 222, 226, 228, 236*). In the earliest version (*1*) the Virgin stands on a sun, her arms crossed on her chest. Sixteen years later, in 1632, his *Immaculate Conception with Two Children (59)* resembles a print by Sadeler (see fig. 35), omitting, however, the snake at the Virgin's feet and pointing the horns of the crescent moon downward, in accordance with Pacheco's teachings (see p. 2). As in the print, the Marian symbols are seen through rents in the clouds. His *Immaculate Conception Cerralbo (66)* parallels the print in admitting the snake and placing the horns pointing upward.

In the *Conception (88)* of the retable of Saint Peter, the draperies and arms are more three-dimensional. The mantle flares out behind the Virgin and is not taken up by her. Practically the same pose of body, arms, hands and head, and the same arrangement of the mantle can be seen in the *Immaculate Conception (143),* 1638, at Edinburgh, another reason for dating the Saint Peter altar toward the mid-thirties. The last two versions repeat, in some respects, earlier examples. The *Conception (200),* at the Townhall of Seville, thus follows the *Conception Cerralbo (66),* while the *Conception (222),* of 1661 at Budapest shows certain traits of the first one (*1*). In the *Conceptions* as in the *Crucifixions* sometimes half- or three-quarter length figures (donors, the Virgin's parents, or Angels) appear at the bottom.

The seated *Virgin with the Christ Child* is also represented frequently (*182, 199, 206–208, 218, 223*). Since Zurbarán did not paint this theme even once before 1640, it evidences a mellowing either in his own religious feelings or in those of his clients. The austere *Crucifixions* of his early, High Baroque period, gave way in the Late Baroque to friendly, melancholy *Madonnas*. Whenever the setting is an interior, a pewter platter with fruits on a table or a stool, in the Flemish sixteenth-century manner, is included in the picture. The *Holy Family* (*12, 190, 209*) occurs as an early as well as a late theme, and this is also the case with the *Young Virgin Praying* (*67, 211–212*). This subject, like that of the *Young Virgin Asleep* (*18*), has an intimate touch, informal and simple. God, Christ, and the Virgin are very near and approachable to the Spaniard, and especially to an inhabitant of Seville.

Zurbarán's narrative scenes with Saints are painted with wise economy and sobriety, concentrating the action in a few figures and taking care not to overload the composition. Since the Spanish sense of dignity does not favour the introduction of trivial detail, anecdotal subject matter is minimized. Dignity is expressed by Zurbarán's preference for large monumental masses and the avoidance of Caravaggiesque movement in space or of exaggerated poses. This sense of serenity is responsible also for the careful, unhurried execution seen even in the master's larger paintings.

Few ages have exalted martyrdoms, as well as ecstasies and visions, more than did the Baroque. At Seville and particularly in the work of Zurbarán, however, martyrdoms were exceedingly rare, as Angulo has emphasized (²⁹, ⁶⁰). Zurbarán was truly a mystic rather than an ascetic. He preferred not to show expressions of pain or cruelty. Most of his pictures concern heavenly visions, ecstasies and miracles, treated not in the imaginative, dynamic manner of El Greco, but in the most natural, human way possible. It should be stressed that Zurbarán, the mystic, painted particularly Saints famous for their ecstatic visions: Anthony of Padua, Augustine, Benedict, Bruno, Carmelo, Cyril, Diego of Alcalá, Francis of Assisi, Hugh, Jerome, John the Baptist, Nicholas of Tolentino, Peter, Peter Pasqual, Peter Thomas, and Henry Suso.

The master's most frequent subjects were devotional, single figures of Angels, Apostles or other Saints. Over eighty of them survive. Where he painted one and the same Saint more than once, he usually repeated with minor variations the same formula, just as he repeated frequently the same favourite poses. All female Saints and, until 1636, practically all standing figures of male Saints are placed indoors against a plain grey background. Beginning in 1636, all full-length standing male Saints, with the exception of *183–185,* are seen in a landscape.

There are fourteen versions of *Saint Francis* (*44, 61, 91, 108, 166–169, 172, 183–185, 215–216*), usually kneeling, against a cave and meditating over a skull. The earliest kneeling version (*61*) may derive from a painting by El Greco, who, like Zurbarán, painted this Saint more often than any other. Other themes frequently depicted by both artists are the *Veil of Saint Veronica, Christ Carrying the Cross, The Crucifixion, The Holy Family, Saint Jerome, Saint John the Baptist,* and the *Repentant Saint Peter.* A relatively rare subject in seventeenth-century painting, the *Apostolate,* was painted repeatedly by El Greco and by Zurbarán (the latter with studio assistants). One might see in these parallels the indication of a spiritual affinity between the two painters, mystics both, but it would seem wiser to interpret them as another sign for the strongly continuing Mannerist trend in Zurbarán's art.

Three times *Saint Francis* (*183–185*) is shown standing alive on top of his tomb, as he was found in 1449 by Pope Nicholas V, when he visited the crypt where the Saint had been buried two hundred years earlier. Zurbarán painted him with a bold black shadow giving the sensation of a double image. Did the artist intend to render the Saint just this side of the thin line dividing life and death and, simultaneously, in the world of shadows yonder?

While El Greco's scintillating impassioned driving for a spiritual union with God is paralleled in poems of Fray Luis de León and San Juan de la Cruz, Zurbarán's serene mysticism is related to verses by Lope de Vega and by Saint Teresa who wrote:

VIRGIN AND CHILD WITH SAINT JOHN. About 1660. New York, Paul O. Berliz (Cat. No. 218)

Nada te turbe,	Nothing disturb thee,
Nada te espante,	Nothing dismay thee,
Todo se pasa,	All things pass,
Dios no se muda . . .	God never changes . . .

From 1570 to 1582 Llerena had been the centre of the Spanish *alumbrados,* a Quietist movement preaching inner withdrawal, 'to be alone with God'. Even more active was the Sevillan group (1616–1630) during the very years of Zurbarán's artistic formation. Ten years after the painter's death, there appeared a book which in passages recalled the spirit of Zurbarán's art, yet went far beyond the aims of the artist, so far, indeed, that it led its readers by stages toward nothingness and complete nihilism. No wonder that, having enjoyed a brief vogue of extraordinary popularity, it was confiscated by the Inquisition. Its author, the Spanish priest Miguel de Molinos (1628–1696), was one of the foremost, although last, representatives of Spanish Quietism. His philosophy is contained in the book's title: 'Spiritual guide which frees the soul and leads it along the inner road to reach perfect contemplation and the rich treasure of inner peace.' Zurbarán's Carthusian paintings (*68–70, 124–130*) come to mind. In his work Molinos said: 'I have only tried to teach—humbly, simply and clearly—the naked truth', a sentence well applicable to Zurbarán's art. Or 'the soul shall leave behind it all that is of the senses and recollect itself in its pure and deepest centre where the image of God resides: there [with] loving care, silence and oblivion of all things, the will [shall be] applied with complete resignation, listening to and being with Him so alone as if in all the world none existed but the two.' 'You will know that you are very far from perfection if you do not find God in all things.' 'Your soul is the seat of God . . . you must keep it . . . pure of guilt and defects, quiet of fears, empty of affections, desires and thoughts, peaceful in trials and tribulations.' For Molinos, as for Zurbarán, 'the inner withdrawal is faith and silence in the presence of God. . . . surrendering oneself and binding oneself to God with reverence, humility and submission.' Like Molinos, Zurbarán must have believed that 'the soul gains more in a quarter hour of prayer in complete withdrawal of the senses and mental powers as well as resignation and humility, than in five days of penitent exercises, hair shirts, disciplines, fasts and sleeping on hard boards. All this only punishes the *body,* but by withdrawal the *soul* is purified.' This passage may give a hint why Zurbarán preferred to paint Saints in mystic contemplation rather than cruel martyrdoms. It is most interesting that Molinos' assertion: 'there are two ways of praying—tenderly, fondly, lovingly and full of feeling—or humbly, dryly, without comfort and darkly', seems to contrast the religious approach of Murillo and that of Zurbarán.

Among Zurbarán's most widely known works are his Virgin Saints: *Saint Agatha (46), Saint Apollonia (119), Saint Casilda (181), Saint Catherine (110), Saint Elizabeth (111, 179), Saint Euphemia (115), Saint Margaret (56), Saint Rufina (180),* and *Saint Ursula (116).* To these may be added another *Saint Margaret (57)* which is lost, and Zurbarán's earliest Virgin Martyr, *Saint Lucy (2),* apparently done about 1625–1626 ([47]). The *Saint Lucy,* differing in style from the other Virgins, was therefore doubted until now, in the belief that all Virgin Saints were painted around 1640. Actually they seem to range in date from about 1625 to approximately 1645.

These Saints have been interpreted in various ways. Romanticists saw in them a sensuous mundanity which reflected the spirit of these nineteenth-century writers rather than that of Zurbarán ([32]). Ever since, however, critics have echoed this note. Probing more deeply, Angulo remarked that these Saints appear to walk in a procession or across a stage, like the figures of a performing clock ([28]). Emilio Orozco Díaz ([41]), who has thrown much light on the essence of the Baroque in Spain, speculated that these Saints refer to the transitory quality of life, to the quickly fading glories of this world. He believed that the pictures symbolize the great capacity and subconscious disposition of the Spaniards toward the transcendental. However, many engravings made at Antwerp prove that this way of thinking was not exclusively Spanish. Orozco Díaz quoted Spanish seventeenth-century verses speaking of ladies portrayed as saints; he inferred that the *Virgin Saints* of Zurbarán were commissioned portraits and that they express the very Spanish exaltation of the ego, the longing to secure—by a saintly portrait—eternity even in this world. Many such portraits of ladies as Saints exist, however, also outside of Spain. The Prado Catalogue claims that Zurbarán's *santas* are clothed in dresses worn by noble ladies of the epoch, but such attire was not fashionable at that time in Spain (1630–1650), nor anywhere else. Such dresses, a late Gothic survival, do occur throughout western Europe in many sixteenth-century paintings and prints. Marten de Vos, Heemskerck and others showed Jewish worthies, men and women, in similar elaborate dresses of oriental splendour. Even at the beginning of the seventeenth century, Saints are still thus luxuriously attired. In many Flemish engravings, such as the *Saint Cecilia* by Peter de Baillin (fig. 126, see also fig. 127), and in Zurbarán's *Saint Casilda* (fig. 128) one finds a brocaded mantle falling back over the shoulder, borders of precious stones and pearls, and rich jewelled chains. Zurbarán thus neither freely invented nor copied from life the rich and startling garments clothing his *Virgin Saints*.

None of Zurbarán's *Virgin Martyrs* represents a lady wishing to be immortalized as a Saint. As to the alleged portrait-like quality of their faces, most of them are not sufficiently realistic, and in Zurbarán's figures this very fact is indicative of saintliness. He was a good portraitist, capable of characterizing incisively the heads of specific persons. If his Saints or his posthumous portraits seem individual portraits from life, it is only because, as has often been observed, to the Spaniard everything is a reflection of life, a portrait. Even inanimate objects have their own physiognomy. The Spaniard is not interested in the 'ideal', nor in the 'general'. He exalts the individual, because, in the last analysis, what matters is the individual's personal salvation. The *Saint Elizabeth* (*179*), *Saint Rufina* (*180*), and the *Saint Agatha* (*46*) suggest the same idealized model. *Saint Elizabeth* and *Saint Rufina* are companion pieces and, by reasons of style, datable about 1640. They may have been evocations of Zurbarán's recently deceased wife. In 1644 he married for the third time and stopped painting *Virgin Saints* altogether.

Zurbarán's *Still Lifes* (*71–74, 175* (?)*, 178*), show the artist's deep religious piety and his great humility. As Sánchez Cantón ([26]) said, 'They, too, are things worthy to be comprehended, are things of God.' In these pictures the artist did by no means invent an entirely new iconography. His themes derive from the most humble and yet spiritually portentous *Still Lifes* created by Sánchez Cotán. Zurbarán seems to have been influenced also by Van der Hamen and by an unpublished excellent *Still Life* without figures, by Velázquez, in the Contini-Bonacossi Collection.

The only surviving mythological scenes by Zurbarán are the ten paintings of *Hercules* (*93–102*), but the artist had also decorated the ship *Holy Saint Ferdinand* with secular allegories. The Hercules series shows Baroque and yet unexpected sides of the painter's art: sensuousness, strength, virile vigour, tension, violence and a study of anatomy.

Of at least three historical paintings ([5]) only two still exist, and one of these (*133*) is, strictly speaking, a religious subject. The other, *The Relief of Cadiz* (*103*), a battle-scene, seems to be an original creation, It accents a few large figures conceived as portraits, against a most spacious, somewhat topographic landscape.

The list of portraits painted by Zurbarán comprises now only fourteen, all but five probably done long after the death of the person portrayed and all but four representing clerics. Documents mention a number of other portraits, presumably lost.

Of great importance in Zurbarán's art is a theme for which, until now, the master has not been given due recognition: his landscapes. Although there exist no landscapes *per se,* many of his pictures contain landscape backgrounds, and some of these are most distinguished. All were painted between 1630 and 1639, except one (*202*) which may be as late as 1650. Particularly moving qualities in these landscapes are their tranquillity, their spacious airiness; their succulent and unusual colours in silvery greys, greens, red brown and salmon; their fresh perception, balanced order and deep recession into distance. Many landscape backgrounds contain water, an element particularly precious in Andalusia. In their depth, silence and crystal clarity, these dark bluish-green bodies of water seem symbolic of Zurbarán's art. (see plate 59)

IV. PUPILS AND FOLLOWERS OF ZURBARÁN

THERE exist hundreds of paintings by Zurbarán's assistants, but no attempt has been made, as yet, to attribute them to individual pupils. Only two of these, Antonio del Castillo Saavedra (1618–1668) and Juan del Castillo (1584–1640), are at present well-defined artistic personalities (figs. XII, XIII). Other pupils mentioned by ancient authors are Bernabé de Ayala, Francisco and Miguel Polanco, Francisco Reina, Juan Martínez de Gradilla, José Sarabia, Juan Caro Tavira, Gerónimo de Bobadilla, and Francisco Cubrián. Of most of these little more is known than their names, but I have seen in Lima a signed *Virgin of the Kings* (after the statue venerated in Seville Cathedral), dated in 1662 by Bernabé de Ayala (fig. X), and at Pollock House in Glasgow a signed *Portrait of King Philip IV* by Gradilla (fig. XI).

Zurbarán's son, the painter Juan de Zurbarán, may have signed the still life *Pottery and a Chocolate Mill* (*175*). Although this picture lacks the religious spirit found in the father's own still lifes and

X. Bernabé de Ayala: *The Virgin of the Kings.* 1662.
Lima, National Board of Historic Monuments

XI. Juan Martínez de Gradilla: *Portrait of King Philip IV.*
1666. Glasgow, Sir John Stirling Maxwell Coll.

 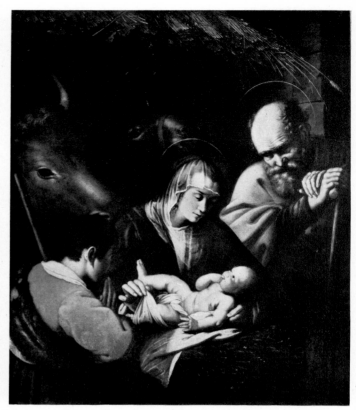

XII. Antonio del Castillo Saavedra: *Saint Peter penitent*. About 1635–40. Kansas City, William Rockhill Nelson Gallery.

XIII. Juan del Castillo: *The Nativity with a Shepherd*. About 1630–40. Mexico City, Franz Mayer Coll.

although the objects are heaped without space to breathe, there subsists a slight doubt whether or not an abbreviated 'Fran' (for Francisco) was misread as 'Juan'. If the picture were definitely established as a work by the son, it would draw with it a number of other paintings.

During the second half of the seventeenth century, Zurbarán became enormously popular throughout colonial Spanish America, where numerous painters were influenced by his style and where many pictures are still attributed to the master ([42b]). In the nineteenth century he was much admired by Courbet and by Manet. In our own time, Picasso and his friends have taken the Spanish master to their hearts as a kindred soul ([51]). Francisco de Zurbarán's art has stood the test of time.

V. ZURBARÁN AND BAROQUE PAINTING: A SUMMARY

In reaction against anti-classical Mannerism, the thirty years from 1590 to about 1620 saw the rise of the Early Baroque. Caravaggio and others presented the style in a new language of dramatic realism, in which the tenebroso becomes the principal device of pictorial expression. Zurbarán's early works attempted to embody the advances of the style in naturalism and sculpturesque form, while the dramatic tension was further heightened by the crowded front planes. Many Spanish painters had preceded Zurbarán in understanding the aims of the Early Baroque, but of all Spanish artists he may have come closest to Caravaggio, both spiritually and formally.

The High Baroque, from about 1620 to 1640, brought greater balance in composition; the shadows were lightened up, and the paintings grew more colourful and airy. Zurbarán participated in these developments; he increased not only the lucid clarity of his renditions but also the precision of his draftsmanship to reach his most realistic period between 1630 and 1635. Throughout Western Europe,

SAINT AGATHA. About 1630–2. Montpellier, Musée Fabre (Cat. No. 46)

it was the time of greatest drama, intensity and exuberance. Zurbarán reflected these tendencies. His trip to Madrid brought him into direct contact with the art of Ribera, to whom he may have felt attracted by certain basic parallels of character, but the influence was mainly restricted to brushwork and the borrowing of certain male types.

The visit to the court, instead of deflecting Zurbarán's style, strengthened his belief in the sources of his inspiration, the devout spirit of the Andalusian monasteries. Upon his return to Seville, Zurbarán became ever more mystic, mitigating the precision of his realism in his divine countenances to give them a glow of saintly tenderness and breathing spiritual meaning even into his draperies. To be sure, both elements, the realistic and the mystic, were always to some extent present in his art. But from 1635 to 1639 Zurbarán's paintings exhaled a profound spirituality, a divine grace—more moving for being so unobtrusive— which places them among the greatest creations of Spanish Baroque art. Even in his youth he had been less dramatic, less violent, (in subject matter, *not* in design) than most Early and High Baroque artists. He had been a Spanish de la Tour. Now during the 1630's, the period of his greatest artistic power—unfortunately of short duration—Zurbarán's style was completely attuned to his artistic temperament, which had always tended toward monumental sobriety. His paintings express a classical spirit also in the ordered, tectonic arrangement emphasized by horizontal and particularly by vertical accents. His art is in many ways representative of the Classical Baroque, which is exemplified by the heroic style of Poussin, based on order, reason and harmony. Spiritually the Classical Baroque, which flourished especially between 1640 and 1660, meant a turn from Rubens' *joie de vivre* to a quieter, more solemn mood. The spirit of Zurbarán's paintings was influenced not only by this general movement, but also by the death of his second wife, in 1639, which affected him profoundly and contributed to make his art heavy, grave and, gradually, more elegiac. He relinquished somewhat the former sobriety and strength of feeling. In his last period, his works became more intimately domestic and sentimental.

A certain *détente* in spiritual power as well as in competent organization and significant draftsmanship, during Zurbarán's old age at Madrid, cannot be accounted for solely by lack of contact with the pious atmosphere of the monasteries nor by the influence of a court which had become increasingly opulent. Everywhere, after the middle of the century, Baroque pathos reached a point where it was in danger of becoming outward show, unsupported by strong inner feeling. Mysticism changed to magic, faith to doubt and indifference, contemplation to affectation and egoism. Mystic poetry became prosaic and sentimental. Spanish political strength decayed ever more rapidly after the peace of Utrecht in 1659. At the same time Spanish heroic and epic poetry also declined. As Karl Vossler has stated so well: in order to exist, the poetry of inner withdrawal needed as its counterpart a joy of living, an aggressive outlook on life, and lust for temporal power and conquest. In the 1660's and especially in the 1670's a new style, the Late Baroque, began to forgo classical order and sobriety in favour of sumptuous elegance and theatricality. Neither Murillo nor Valdés Leal in Seville, and even less the painters in Madrid could or would wholly escape these qualities of the Late Baroque.

The decrease of religious values was not accompanied, however, by a corresponding decline in the formal achievements of the style. On the contrary, throughout the whole Baroque period there was a steady quest for clearer organization of space in depth, for softening of solids and fusion with the surrounding atmosphere, for unification and integration. In this respect Zurbarán was also a child of his time, and it is possible to observe his consistent progress. The early paintings with their crowded front planes have poorly organized spatial relations. Throughout the 1630's and 1640's he attended ever more to air and atmosphere and to the structural arrangement of his compositions, and finally, in the last phase, Zurbarán achieved great mellowness and pictorial unity.

In Velázquez's paintings pictorial unity was established not only through such factors as air and atmosphere, but in a large measure through a new system of colour relations. Velázquez sensitively recorded the many changes of colour, brought about by reflected light, in a harmonious system of interrelated hues, frequently emphasizing neutralized, grayish intensities. Zurbarán, on the other hand, like medieval artists, used his hues preferably at full intensity, without gradation. On first sight his colours instead of being harmonious are often surprisingly dissonant, a quality stimulating to modern eyes. This highly original use of colour during the 1630's operated, to a certain extent, against the Baroque aim of unity and integration. It was therefore increasingly modified by the artist, who, after 1650, achieved a subtle blending of hues.

Zurbarán's style not only has modern parallels but appears 'primitive' when seen against the Baroque splendour of rich cathedrals and luxurious palaces. His patrons were the austere, strictly regulated monasteries, then outnumbering the secular churches by three to one. No wonder that the artist satisfied the chastised monks with his disciplined religious paintings suggesting the ringing silence of monastic contemplation. An intimate kinship existed between Zurbarán and the monks, so that he can be considered to represent seventeenth-century conventual Spain. The court, too, remained stiff and ceremonious well into the first half of the century, and this was reflected in the few rigidly posed portraits which the artist painted during and after his visit to Madrid in 1634.

Even in his draperies one senses a fusion between the medieval and the Baroque. From folds embodying a medieval feeling of rhythm the artist distilled a Baroque expression of monumental struggle.

His works overwhelm by their virile devotion, their ascetic simplicity, by their disciplined order and their strength of construction. His outstanding contribution as a Baroque artist is the extraordinary, haunting power with which he expressed mysticism and realism. These qualities dominated the art of many Baroque masters, and particularly the whole Sevillan school of the seventeenth century. In Zurbarán's art, however, mysticism reached an intensity equalled in Spain only by El Greco, and the precision of his realism was surpassed only by Velázquez.

Zurbarán's foremost artistic qualities may, perhaps, be enunciated as a sober solemnity, strong and tender, born of a firm and settled faith; a rustic and archaic dignity, veracity, purity and simplicity; an essential stillness and static quality in the literal action; the avoidance of unnecessary detail; a sensitive draftsmanship, bringing out the inner life of objects; a design stimulating and dramatic by its imaginative unaffectedness; a limited movement back and forth in depth, balancing the tense and vigorous structure in the picture plane; and finally, the integration, in a geometric pattern, of forceful outlines, broad areas, and sculpturesque forms.

An estimate of the artist's style may be gathered from poignant evaluations made in three different epochs.

Ceán Bermúdez, the great Spanish art historian and friend of Goya, said in an unpublished *History of the Art of Painting,* written about 1800: '. . . he composed with precision and economy, eschewing mass scenes, the confused heaping of objects, and the repetition of foreshortenings. He painted in large masses of colour, with purity, with great force, and with much chiaroscuro effect.'

In 1863, Eduardo Mier([25]) gave this excellent appreciation: 'He is one of the painters most worthy to be studied by modern artists, because of his energy, the vigour of his brushwork, the spontaneity and purity of his artistic conception, his magnificent colouring, correct drawing, and the simplicity and good taste with which he composed. For his sobriety, restricting his scenes nearly always to few figures in natural and dignified poses, he is a classical painter, in the best sense of the word.'

The significance of Zurbarán for artists of the twentieth century has never been more excellently summarized than by Christian Zervos([51]) who, in 1927, said: 'Zurbarán is close to us modern painters by his feeling of vitality, by his dryness and precision through which a soul, a human soul, seems ready to break; he is close to us by the absence of pathos or anecdote, by the search for means of expression of most sober refinement, by the use of large areas of pure dominant colours, by his constant attention to ordered structure, and by the hidden audacity and the inventive spirit in which he composes.'

XIV. *Head of Francisco de Zurbarán.* Red chalk drawing, 1650–60.
Paris, Louvre. Attributed to the artist (Cat. No. 224).

VI. THE LIFE OF ZURBARÁN

1598

November 7.[20] Baptized in the parish church, Fuente de Cantos, Extremadura, Western Spain, son of Isabel Márquez and of Luis de Zurbarán, a well-to-do shopkeeper[17] of Basque descent. Childhood at Fuente de Cantos until

1614

January 15.[20] Apprenticed at Seville to the painter Pedro Díaz de Villanueva, none of whose works are known. He was a 'pintor de ymagenería', that is a painter of religious figures on panel or on canvas, not primarily of polychromed, gilded wood sculptures.

1616

Dated and signed an Immaculate Conception (1).

1617

Moved to Llerena,[6] two days from Seville and fifteen miles from his birth place. Resided at Llerena, then the most important town of lower Extremadura, until 1628, except for brief journeys.

1617

Married, at nineteen, to María Paez, nine years older and the daughter of a gelder, then a despised profession.[6]

1618

February 2. María, first child, baptized at Llerena.[6]

1618

Made a drawing for a fountain in Llerena's main square.[6] Built by Sevillan craftsmen, it survived until the Civil War (1936).

1619

Received payment for a painting placed inside Llerena's city gate.[6]

1620

July 19.[6] Juan de Zurbarán, son and future painter, baptized at Llerena.

1622

February and August. As 'resident of Llerena' signed two contracts at Fuente de Cantos, one for a processional bier, the other for fifteen scenes of the mysteries of the Rosary to be painted for an altar of that devotion in the parish church.[17]

1623

July 13. Isabel Paula, another daughter, baptized at Llerena.[6]

1623 or 1624

María Paez, his first wife, died.

1625

Married Beatriz de Morales, a widow, probably ten years older and daughter of a wealthy patrician of Llerena.[18]

1626

January 17.[11] Signed first contract for work at Seville with the prior of the Dominican convent of San Pablo el Real, to paint within eight months twenty-one pictures, fourteen of the life of St. Dominic and the other seven of the four *Doctors of the Church, St. Bonaventure, St. Thomas* and *St. Dominic*. Five of these pictures survive (4–5, 14–16).

1626–1628

Some time between June 1626 and August 1628 a conjectured visit, perhaps of several months' duration, to his friend Velázquez at Madrid.[47]

1626–1628

Worked on Sevillan commissions: for the Upper College of Magister Rodrigo (17), for San Pablo (including a lost *Crucifixion*, said by Ponz[3] to have been dated 1627), and for the Trinitarians an altar of St. Joseph with eight scenes from the life of the Saint and of the Virgin, as well as the ciborium door (10–13).[23] In September 1629, the altar is recorded as 'having been painted'.[12]

1627

Painted a *Crucifixion* for the Capuchins at Seville.[3]

1628

August 29.[15] As resident of Llerena visiting Seville, Zurbarán contracted with Fray Juan de Herrera, prefect of the Mercedarian convent, for the painting of twenty-two canvases, 184 × 230 cm. each, telling the story of St. Peter Nolasco, who had been canonized earlier in the same year. Zurbarán was to come to Seville in September with his helpers and was at this time, at the latest, head of a shop. Four paintings by Zurbarán (30–33) remain, finished in 1630.

1629

June.[20] The town of Seville officially asked Zurbarán to move there from Llerena. '. . . Seville would be honoured . . . and favour him . . . considering that the art of painting is one of the major embellishments of the State. . . .' Zurbarán accepted the offer and lived at Seville until 1658.

1629

Resided at no. 27 Alcazar Street, in the shadow of the royal castle, with his wife Beatriz de Morales; the three children of his first marriage; a relative, Isabel de Zurbarán, and eight servants.[18]

1629

Four paintings (24–27) for San Buenaventura, Franciscan church at Seville.

1630's or 1640's

Painted for San Pablo and for the Mercedarians at Cordova.[3] No pictures survive. Those attributed to Zurbarán in the Cordova Museum seem to me shop work.

1630

Altar (39) for the sacristy of Jesuit church at Seville.

1630

May 23.[20] Alonso Cano and other painters asked that as a recent arrival Zurbarán be examined by the painters' guild. The city council upheld the artist's protest against this demand, and to honour him further, ordered, on June 8,[23] an *Immaculate Conception* for the Town Hall.

1631

January 21.[11] Signed contract with Fray Alonso Ortiz Sembrano, Rector of the Dominican college of St. Thomas Aquinas, to paint the Apotheosis of the Saint (41). For the carved frame Jerónimo Velázquez received over six times as much as Zurbarán did for the picture.

1630–1632

One or two altars for the Carmelite Church of San Alberto (42–49).[23]

1631–1634

Standing effigies of Mercedarians for the Mercedarian Monastery (55, 58, 79–85a).

1633

Twelve *Apostles* (78), largely by the shop, for São Vicente de Fora, Lisbon.[40]

1633?

Three scenes (68–70) for the sacristy of the Carthusian convent of Our Lady of the Caves, near Seville.

1633–1635

Five paintings (86–90) for the Altar of St. Peter, in the Cathedral. Three others there are by the shop, and the central *Enthroned St. Peter* by an earlier hand (about 1620).[46]

1634

April to November.[5] Painted at Madrid for the Hall of Realms of the royal Buen Retiro Palace, ten *Labours of Hercules* (93–102) and two *Battle Scenes* (103 extant, the other lost). Received payment in November. Given title of court painter to Philip IV, which he used in a document of January 16, 1638.

1635

Back at Seville, painted a portrait (104).

1636

Many paintings for the church of St. Joseph[23] of the Barefooted Mercedarians (*117–122*, others lost), including thirty-eight small martyrdoms of Mercedarian friars (*163*, executed by his assistants).

1636

August 8.[23] Living at Seville, contracted to paint the main altar of the chief parish church of Llerena (*112–114*, the remainder lost).

1637

May 26.[15] Obligated himself to paint an altar for the convent of the Annunciation at Arcos de la Frontera, near Jerez. It consisted of the two *St. Johns*, *St. Francis*, *St. Clare*, the *Annunciation* in the centre, and the *Crucifixion* above. Final payment was received August 27, 1638. None of these pictures survive.

1637–1639

Painted the main altar (*133–141*) and other paintings for the Carthusian Monastery of St. Mary of Protection at Jerez (*124–132, 142*).[13]

1638

January 16.[16] Gave his daughter María, in view of her marriage to Joseph Gasso, a dowry of 2000 ducats.

1638–1640

Repeatedly took steps to collect debts owed him in Lima, Peru, where he may have sent paintings since about 1637.[16]

1638

Painted, together with Alonso de Deza, the interior decorations, including pictures of classical allegories, for the ceremonial ship *El Santo Rey Don Fernando*, transported overland to the small lake of the Retiro Palace at Madrid, as a gift of the people of Seville to King Philip IV.[43]

1638–1639

Painted eleven large and ten small paintings (*151–162*) for the Sacristy of the church of the Jeronymite Monastery of Guadalupe, Cáceres Province, in Extremadura, Spain.

1638?

Painted two side altars for Santo Domingo Portacoeli, of Seville (*149–150*).

1638?

Painted, together with his assistants, two series of the twelve *Apostles*, one in (and for?) the sacristy of San Francisco, Lima, the other for (?) the sacristy of Santo Domingo, Antigua, Guatemala, now in Guatemala City (*144–145*) [30, 35]

1638

Painted the main altar of San Román (*148*).

1639

Painted a *St. Francis* (*167*) and a *Christ at Emmaus* (*176*).

1639–1642

Lived on Rosario Street in the Sevillan parish of the Magdalena.[16]

1639

May 28.[10] His second wife, Beatriz de Morales, was buried.

1639–1655

Many documents testify to the artist's continuing residence at Seville.[16]

1639–1645

Painted three sequences of *Founders of Monastic Orders*, one series partly by the shop (*171*), and of the others, only three paintings of one series (*186–188*) and two of another (*164–165*) still in existence. Shop copies abound.

1640

Dated a *Crucifixion with a Donor* (*170*), his last dated picture for a period of thirteen years.

1643 or 1644

Painted nine pictures for an altar in the parish church at Zafra near Llerena (*189–197*).[7a]

1644

February 7.[18] Married Leonor de Tordera, his third wife. She was the daughter of Jerónimo and sister of Juan and Miguel, goldsmiths all, from whom she received a tidy dowry.[16] Her first husband, Diego de Sotomayor had died in Puebla, Mexico.

1644

April 13.[16] Contracted with Jacinto de Santaella, of Carmona, to paint two pictures (307 × 215 cm., both now lost), the *Miracle of St. Reginald of Orleans* and the *Miracle of Our Lady of the Rosary*, the latter a rather gory martyrdom.

1645

Murillo established his reputation by paintings for the Franciscan monastery at Seville. Zurbarán's popularity was increasingly eclipsed.

1645–1655

Six children were borne him by Leonor de Tordera, all of them baptized in the cathedral. All, or at least five of them, probably died very young.[20]

1645

Since March lived in a house belonging to the royal Alcazar and, according to a document of 1647, spent over a thousand ducats in new rooms, doors, windows with iron grilles, floors, ceilings and other improvements.[18]

1647

May 22.[15] Obligated himself to paint thirty-four pictures, now lost, for the Nuns of Our Lady of the Incarnation, the oldest convent in Lima. Ten were of the Life of the Virgin, 414 × 223 cm. each: *The Tree of Jesse, the Angel Appearing to Joachim and the Meeting at the Golden Gate, the Birth of the Virgin, the Presentation in the Temple, Marriage, Annunciation, Birth of Christ, Ascension of Christ with Virgin and Apostles Enthroned in Heaven, the Death and the Assumption of the Virgin*, and the *Coronation*. Furthermore twenty-four *Virgin Saints*, all life size. To be ready by Easter 1648. Payment on account was received in September and November of 1647.

1647

May.[15] Received 1000 pesos from Lima, the proceeds of paintings sold there.

1647

September 23.[15] Signed power of attorney to collect the money due for twelve canvases of *Roman Emperors on Horseback*, each 253 cm. high, sent to Lima to be sold on consignment. These pictures are lost.

1647 and 1648

Appointed agents to collect debts, possibly due for paintings, at Montemolín, a town near Fuente de Cantos.[15–16]

1648

December.[16] Gave a receipt of payment for paintings delivered to the Count of La Puebla de Maestre.

1649

February 28.[7] Receipt signed at Buenos Aires by Felipe de Atienza Ibáñez and Alvaro Gómez de Santa María for fifteen *Virgin Martyrs*, fifteen *Kings and Famous Men*, twenty-four *Saints and Patriarchs*, all full-length and some damaged, plus nine Flemish landscapes, six pounds of colour and various brushes, for sale on Zurbarán's account. The whereabouts of these pictures, presumably mostly shop work, are unknown, unless *171* and a poorly painted series, by assistants, of the *Twelve Sons of Jacob*, at the Third Order of St. Francis at Lima, belonged to this shipment.

1650

March.[16] Was paid for portraits of the sons of the Marquis of Villanueva del Río.

1653

Signed a *Christ Carrying the Cross* (*204*).

1658

Lived on Abbades Street, opposite the archbishop's palace, probably in a house to which the Cathedral Chapter had granted life-time rights to one of his daughters on December 14, 1657.[20] His household was shared by his wife, one of her relatives and three servants. No children are listed, and in 1659 his wife lived there alone, with a Manuela Zurbarán, probably a daughter, and two servants.[18] Zurbarán was no longer in Seville.

1658
May.[9] Moved to Madrid in search of commissions to repair his sinking fortunes and repay his debts.

1658
December 23.[9] Testified at Madrid in behalf of his friend Velázquez in proceedings admitting the latter to the Noble Order of Santiago.

1658
Painted an *Annunciation* (*210*), a *Virgin with the Christ Child and St. John* (*206*), and a *Virgin Nursing the Christ Child* (*207*).

1658?
Painted a *St. James of the Marches* (*213*) for the chapel of San Diego, at Alcalá de Henares.

1659
Dated four pictures (*208–209, 216–217*).

1660
September 28.[7] Signed a document, repeated in 1662, as 'resident of Madrid, formerly of Seville'.

1661
Worked at San José,[4] church of the Barefooted Carmelites at Madrid, and dated at least two pictures (*220, 222*).

1662
January 2.[4] In a letter to the Bishop of Badajoz stated that he worked much for the King, an assertion corroborated by Palomino[2] who mentioned early in the eighteenth century the existence of many paintings by Zurbarán in the Casa del Campo—the Royal Hunting Lodge—and other royal palaces, but none appear in the official inventories until 1814 and even then only two (*181* and perhaps *61*, both painted before 1645).

1662
Painted for Santo Domingo de Atocha, at Madrid.[4]

1662
Dated a *Virgin and Child with St. John* (*223*), his last known picture.

1662
Is mentioned as living in Madrid by Lázaro Díaz del Valle.[19]

1664
February 28.[20] Appraised the estate of a deceased colleague.

1664
August 27.[8] Died in Madrid.

A comparative table of Zurbarán's earnings shows that per picture he received only about $20 as a young man at Llerena, $50 as a beginning master at Seville, $300–350 at the height of his fame, and after 1650 probably less than $100. According to the present gold value of the coin the '*real de vellon*' may be set at $0.30, the ducat (11 *reales*) at $3.30, and the *peso* at $4.
The table is more indicative of comparative amounts than of actual dollar values.

Year of contract		$ per picture
1618	Drawing for fountain at Llerena, 6 reales	1.80
1619	Gate, Llerena, painting of the Virgin, 77 reales	23.00
1626	San Pablo, Seville, twenty-one pictures for 4000 reales ($1320)	63.00
1627–9	Trinitarians, Seville, eight pictures for 1430 reales ($429)	53.00
1628	Mercedarians, Seville, twenty-two pictures for 1500 ducats ($4950)	225.00
1631	Santo Tomas, Seville, one triple-size picture for 400 ducats	1320.00
1634	Retiro, Madrid, twelve pictures for 1100 ducats ($3630)	302.00
1636	Parish church, Llerena, probably fifteen pictures for 1500 ducats ($4950)	330.00
1637	Nuns of Encarnación, Arcos, six pictures for 7000 reales ($2100)	350.00
1638	Ship San Fernando, Seville, 914 reales	275.00
1647	Nuns of Encarnación, Lima, thirty-four pictures for 2000 pesos ($8000)	235.0–
1650	Marquis of Villanueva del Río, two or three pictures for 600 reales ($180)	60.000
		90.00

THE PLATES

I. THE IMMACULATE CONCEPTION WITH THIRTEEN ANGELS. 1616. Bilbao, Felix Valdés (Cat. No. 1)

2. SAINT LUCY. About 1625–6. Washington, National Gallery of Art (Gift of Chester Dale) (Cat. No. 2)

3. THE HOLY FAMILY WITH SAINTS ANNE, JOACHIM AND JOHN. About 1628. Madrid, Marquise of Campo Real (Cat. No. 12)

4. THE BIRTH OF THE VIRGIN. About 1627. Florence, Count Contini-Bonacossi (Cat. No. 10)

5. VIRGIN AND CHILD. Detail from Plate 3

6. THE CHRIST CHILD CONTEMPLATING THE CROWN OF THORNS. About 1629–30.
Seville, Manuel Sánchez Ramos (Cat. No. 20)

7. THE CRUCIFIXION. About 1627–9. Seville, Museum (Cat. No. 21)

8. SAINT SERAPION. 1628. Hartford, Conn., Wadsworth Atheneum (Cat. No. 28)

9. SAINT BONAVENTURE PRAYING. 1629. Dresden, Gallery (Cat. No. 24)

10. SAINT BONAVENTURE'S MEDIATION AT THE COUNCIL OF LYON. 1629. Paris, Louvre (Cat. No. 26)

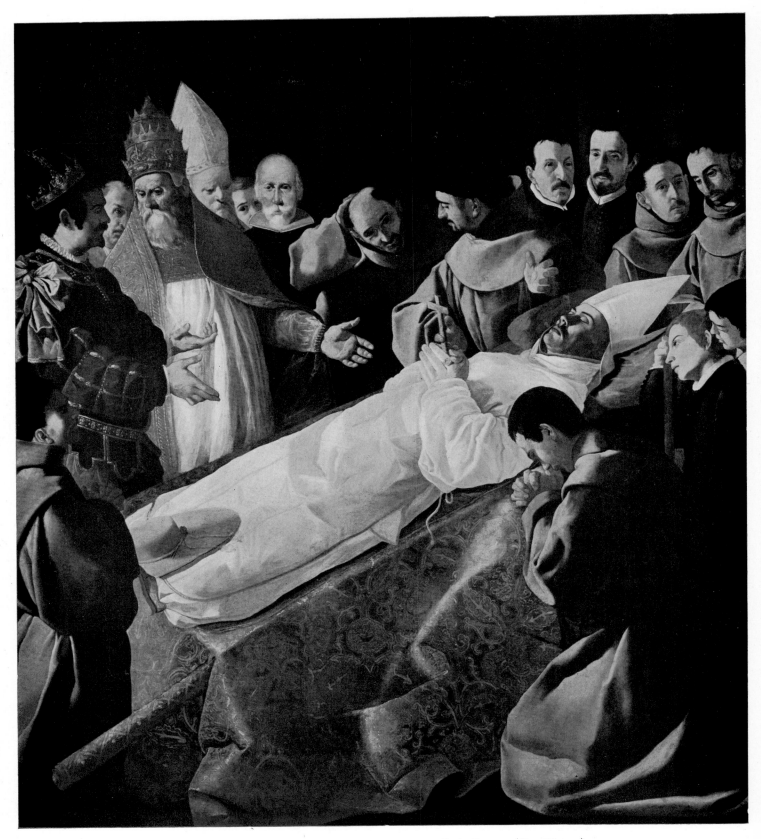

II. SAINT BONAVENTURE ON HIS BIER. 1629. Paris, Louvre (Cat. No. 27)

12. SAINT PETER NOLASCO DREAMING OF THE HEAVENLY JERUSALEM. 1629. Madrid, Prado (Cat. No. 30)

13. THE APOSTLE PETER APPEARING TO SAINT PETER NOLASCO. 1629. Madrid, Prado (Cat. No. 31)

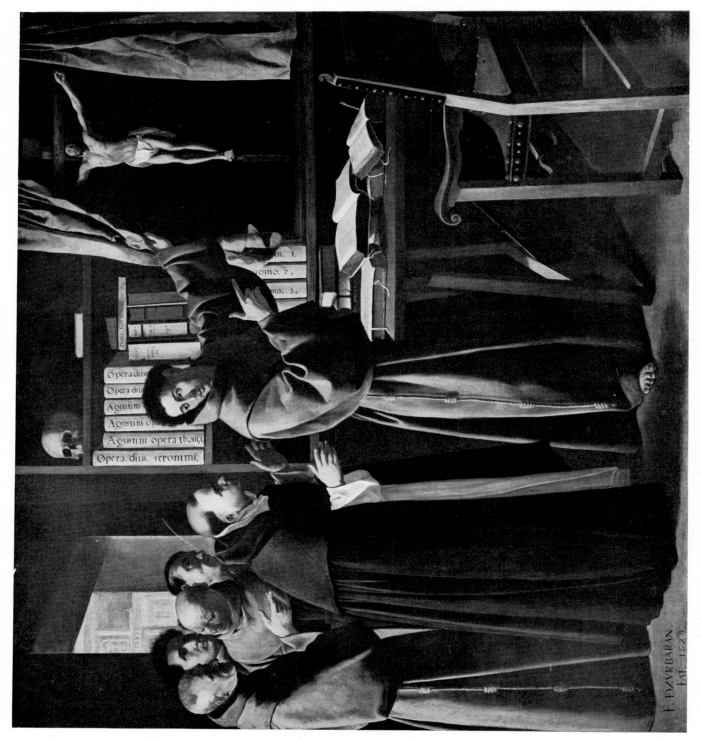

14. SAINT BONAVENTURE REFERS SAINT THOMAS AQUINAS TO THE SAVIOUR. 1629. Berlin, Kaiser Friedrich Museum (Cat. No. 25)

15. SAINT PETER NOLASCO RECOVERING THE IMAGE OF THE VIRGIN. 1630. Cincinnati, Art Museum (Cat. No. 32)

16. HEAD OF A BOY (JUAN DE ZURBARÁN?). Detail from Plate 15

17. HEAD OF A MONK. About 1629. London, British Museum (Cat. No. 34)

18. THE APPARITION OF THE VIRGIN IN SORIANO. 1626-7. Seville, Santa Magdalena (Cat. No. 5)

19. THE VIRGIN HEALING SAINT REGINALD OF ORLEANS. 1626–7. Seville, Santa Magdalena (Cat. No. 4)

20. THE DEAD CHRIST ON THE CROSS. 1627. Chicago, Art Institute (Cat. No. 225)

21. Detail from Plate 20

22. THE VISION OF THE BLESSED ALONSO RODRIGUEZ. 1630. Madrid, Academy (Cat. No. 39)

23. SAINT PETER OF ALCÁNTARA. About 1630. Seville, L. Koidl (Cat. No. 36)

24. HEAD OF SAINT PETER OF ALCÁNTARA. Detail from Plate 23

25. HEAD OF THE BLESSED ALONSO RODRÍGUEZ. Detail from Plate 22

26. THE VISION OF SAINT FRANCIS IN LA PORCIUNCULA. 1630–1. Cadiz, Museum (Cat. No. 40)

27. THE APOTHEOSIS OF SAINT THOMAS AQUINAS. 1631. Seville, Museum (Cat. No. 41)

28. SAINT AMBROSE AND SAINT GREGORY. Detail from Plate 27

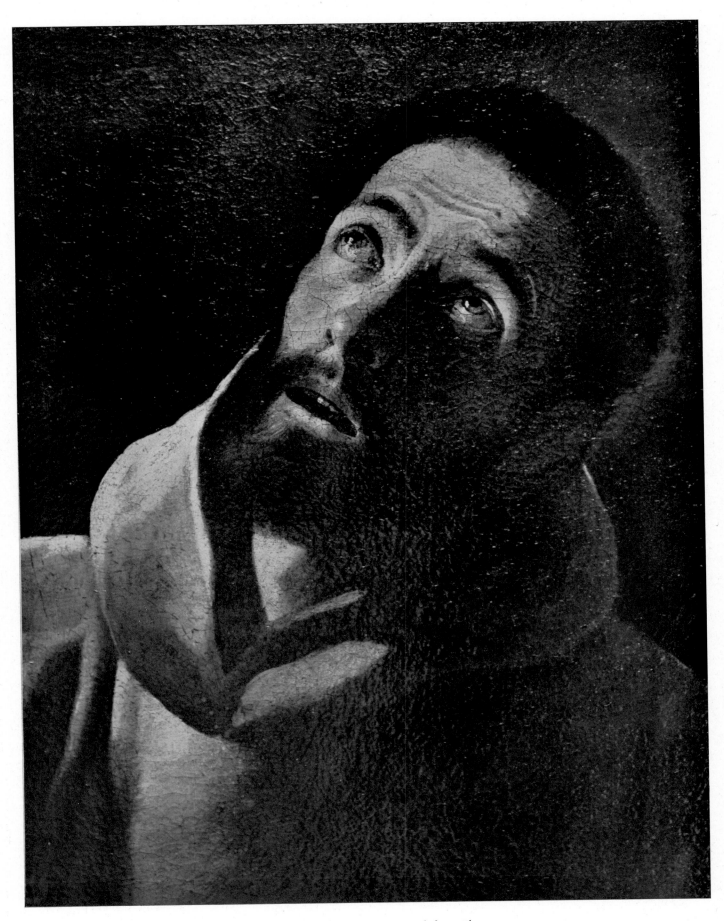

29. HEAD OF SAINT FRANCIS. Detail from Plate 26

30. SAINT PETER THOMAS.
About 1630–2. Boston, Museum of Fine Arts (Cat. No. 42)

31. SAINT FRANCIS.
About 1630–2. St. Louis, City Art Museum (Cat. No. 44)

32. UNKNOWN MERCEDARIAN. About 1631–2. Madrid, Academy (Cat. No. 55)

33. SAINT MARGARET. About 1631–2. London, National Gallery (Cat. No. 56)

34. HEAD OF SAINT MARGARET. Detail from Plate 33

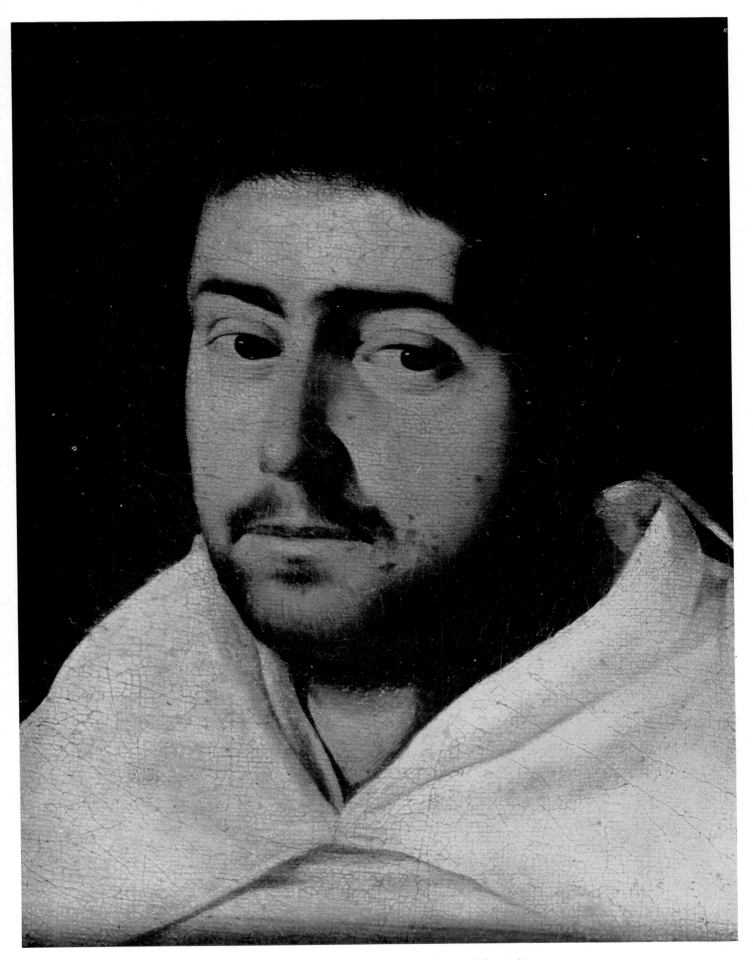

35. HEAD OF AN UNKNOWN MERCEDARIAN. Detail from Plate 32

37. 'MY SOUL DOTH MAGNIFY THE LORD'. About 1630–1. Barcelona, Felix Millet (Cat. No. 52)

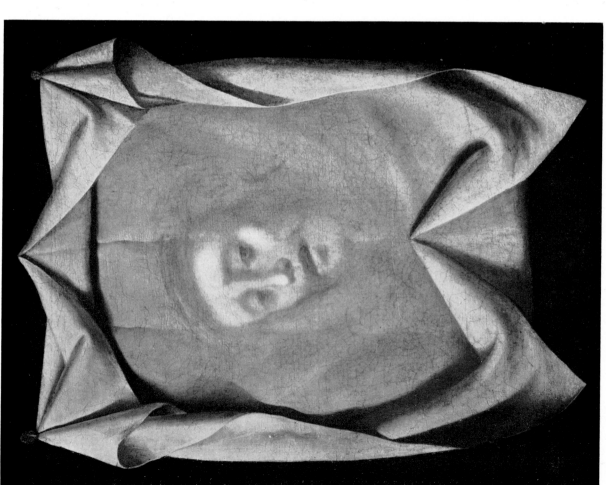

36. THE VEIL OF SAINT VERONICA. About 1631–6. Keir, William Stirling of Keir (Cat. No. 64a)

38. THE VISION OF SAINT JOHN THE BAPTIST. About 1630–2. Barcelona, José Molas Rifa (Cat. No. 49)

39. THE YOUNG VIRGIN PRAYING. About 1632. New York, Metropolitan Museum (Cat. No. 67)

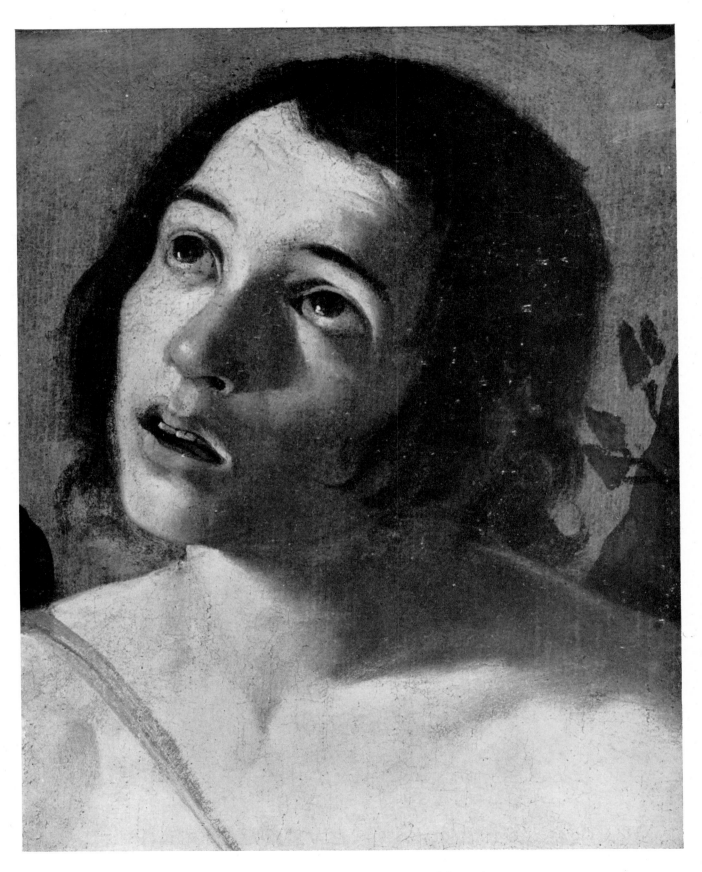

40. HEAD OF SAINT JOHN THE BAPTIST. Detail from Plate 38

41. THE VIRGIN AS PROTECTRESS OF THE CARTHUSIANS. About 1633. Seville, Museum (Cat. No. 68)

42. SAINT HUGH OF GRENOBLE VISITING THE REFECTORY. About 1633. Seville, Museum (Cat. No. 69)

43. SIX CARTHUSIANS. Detail from Plate 41

44. FOUR CARTHUSIAN MONKS. Detail from Plate 42

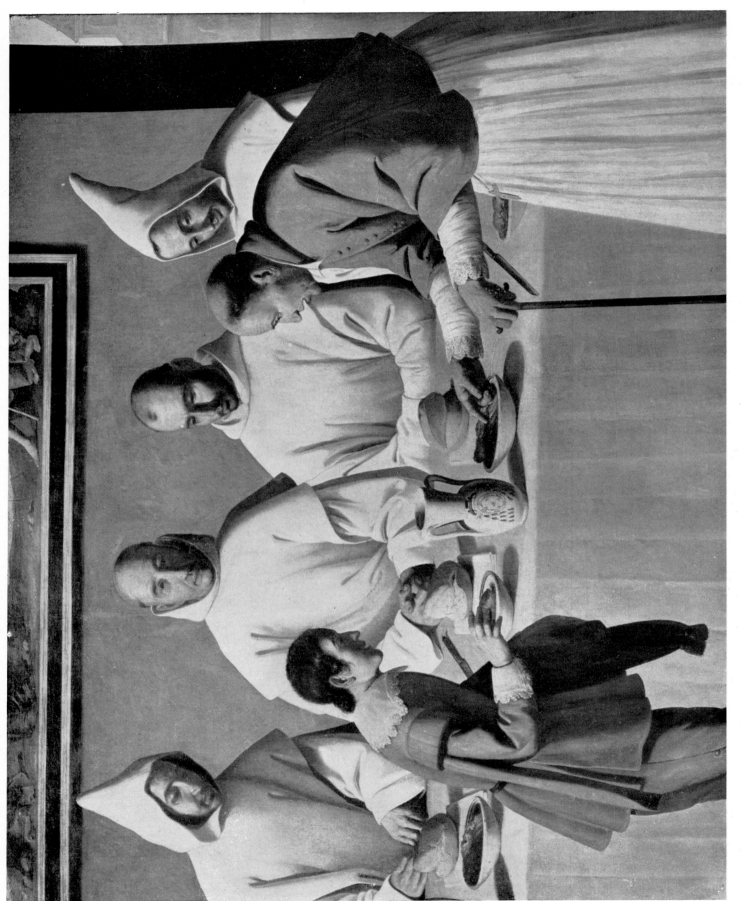

45. SAINT HUGH OF GRENOBLE AND FOUR MONKS. Detail from Plate 42

46. URBAN II WITH HIS CONFESSOR SAINT BRUNO. About 1633. Seville, Museum (Cat. No. 70)

47. STILL LIFE WITH ORANGES. 1633. Florence, Count Contini-Bonacossi (Cat. No. 71)

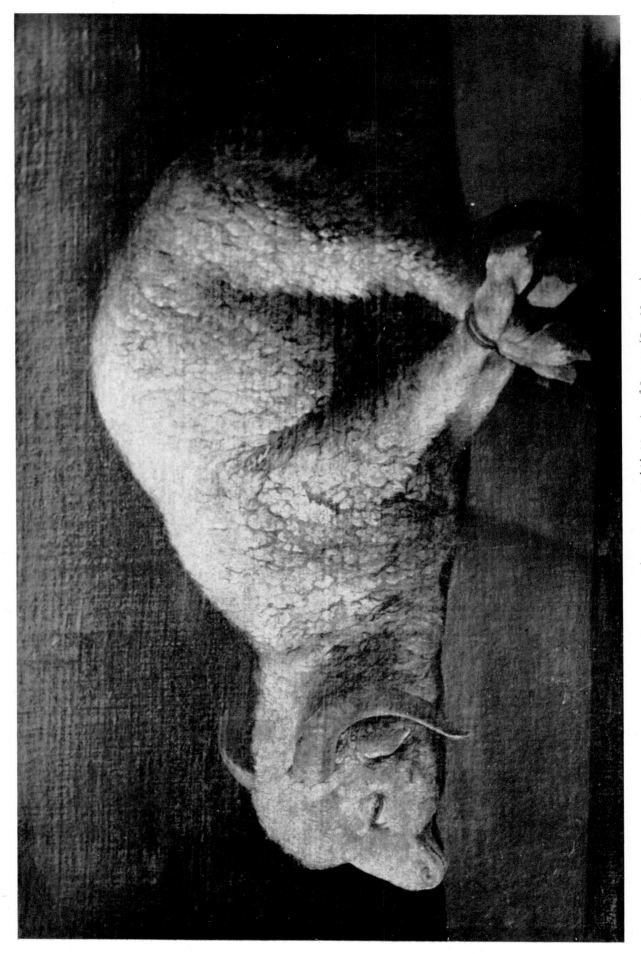

48. A LAMB. About 1635–40. Madrid, Marquise of Socorro (Cat. No. 77)

49. FRAY PEDRO MACHADO. About 1633. Madrid, Academy (Cat. No. 80)

50. HEAD OF FRAY FRANCISCO ZUMEL. About 1633. Madrid, Academy (Cat. No. 81)

51. SAINT PETER. 1633. Lisbon, Museum (Cat. No. 78a)

52. SAINT SIMON. 1633. Lisbon, Museum (Cat. No. 78c)

53. HEAD OF SAINT PETER. About 1633-5. Detail from Fig. 56. Seville, Cathedral (Cat. No. 86)

54. HEAD OF SAINT PETER. About 1633–5. Detail from Fig. 57. Seville, Cathedral (Cat. No. 87)

55. HERCULES KILLING THE HYDRA OF LERNA. 1634. Madrid, Prado (Cat. No. 94)

56. HERCULES KILLING KING ERYX. 1634. Madrid, Prado (Cat. No. 98)

57. HERCULES FIGHTING THE NEMEAN LION. 1634. Madrid, Prado (Cat. No. 93)

58. HERCULES SEARED BY THE POISONED ROBE. 1634. Madrid, Prado (Cat. No. 102)

59. LANDSCAPE. Detail from Fig. 67 (Cat. No. 97)

60. THE RELIEF OF CADIZ. 1634. Madrid, Prado (Cat. No. 103)

61. THE DUKE OF MEDINASIDONIA, SON OF THE ADMIRAL OF THE SPANISH ARMADA(?) Detail from Plate 60

62. THE BATTLE OF EL SOTILLO. 1638. New York, Metropolitan Museum (Cat. No. 133)

63. CHRIST CROWNING SAINT JOSEPH. About 1636-7. Seville, Museum (Cat. No. 120)

64. SAINT JOSEPH. Detail from Plate 63

65. THE BLESSED JOHN HOUGHTON. 1637–8. Cadiz, Museum (Cat. No. 127)

66. SAINT HUGH BISHOP OF LINCOLN. 1637–8. Cadiz, Museum (Cat. No. 129)

67. ANGEL WITH CENSER. 1637–8. Cadiz, Museum (Cat. No. 131)

S.POLO
NIA.

68. SAINT APOLLONIA. About 1636. Paris, Louvre (Cat. No. 119)

69. THE ANNUNCIATION. 1638. Grenoble, Museum (Cat. No. 137)

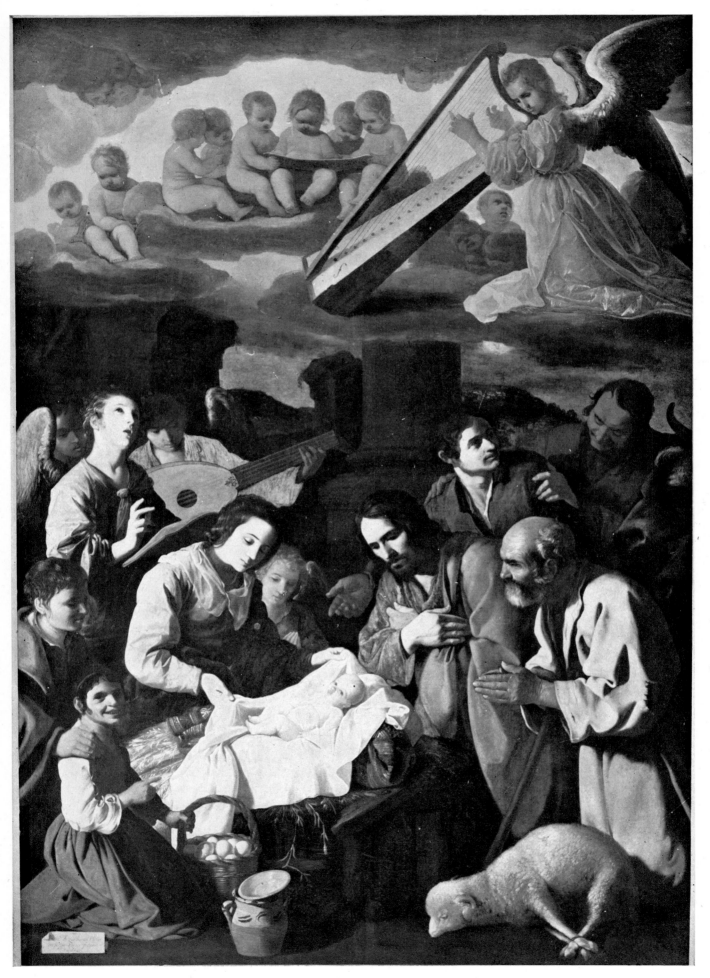

70. THE ADORATION OF THE SHEPHERDS. 1638. Grenoble, Museum (Cat. No. 138)

71. THE VIRGIN. Detail from Plate 69

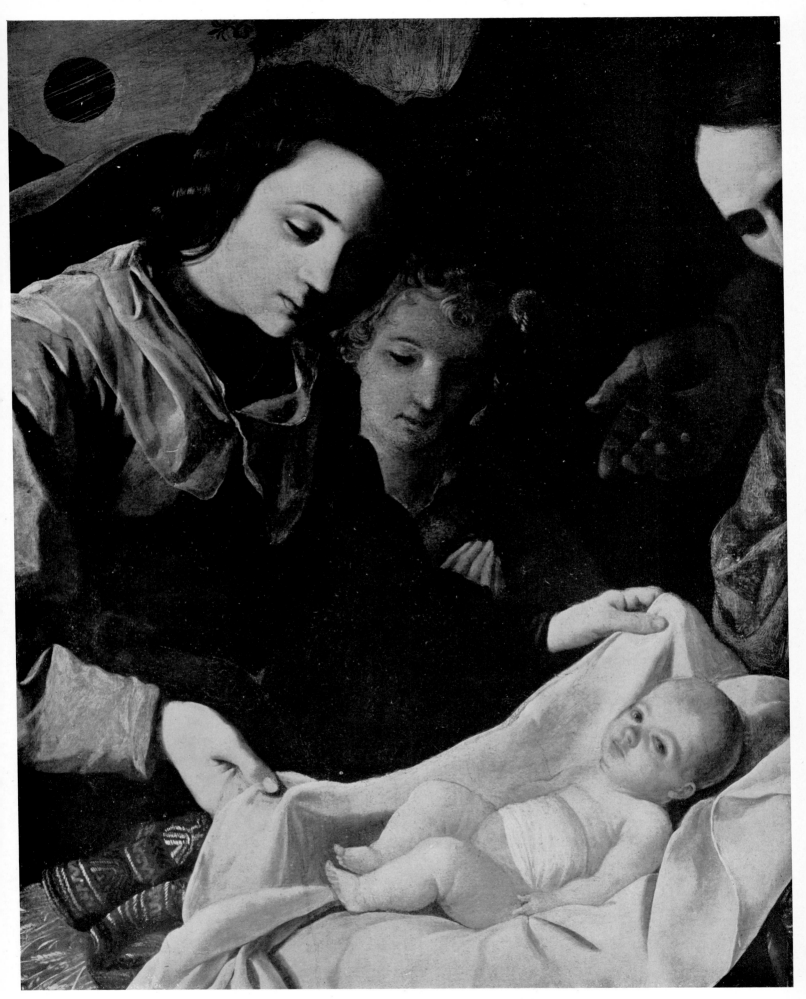

72. THE VIRGIN AND CHILD. Detail from Plate 70

73. SAINT JEROME WITH SAINTS PAULA AND EUSTOCHIUM. About 1638–40.
New York, Samuel H. Kress Foundation (Cat. No. 198)

74. CHRIST AS SAVIOUR OF THE WORLD. 1638. Barcelona, Felix Millet (Cat. No. 146)

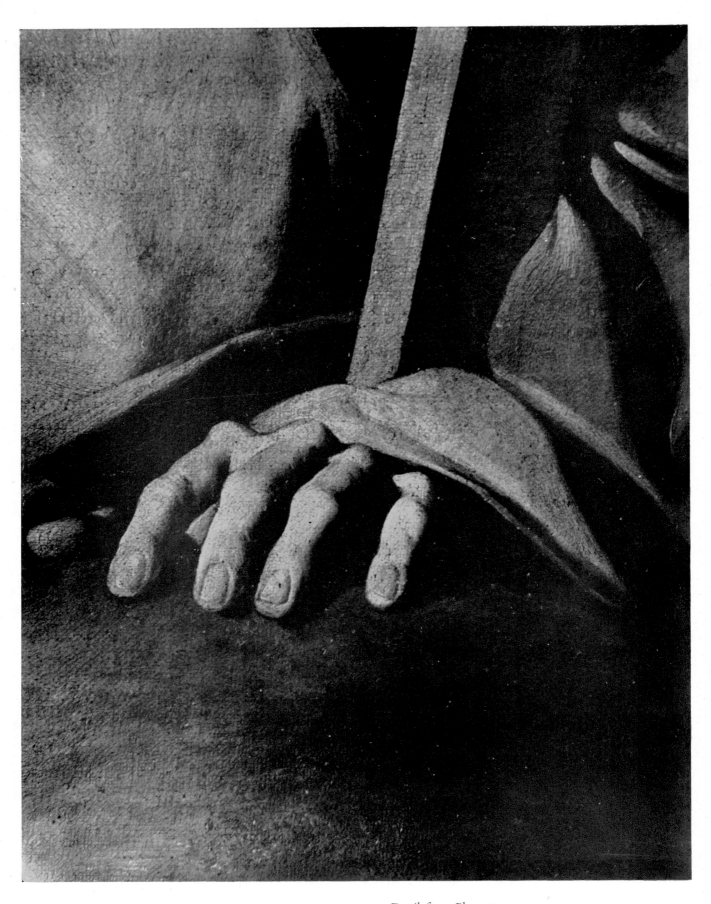

75. THE LEFT HAND OF CHRIST. Detail from Plate 74

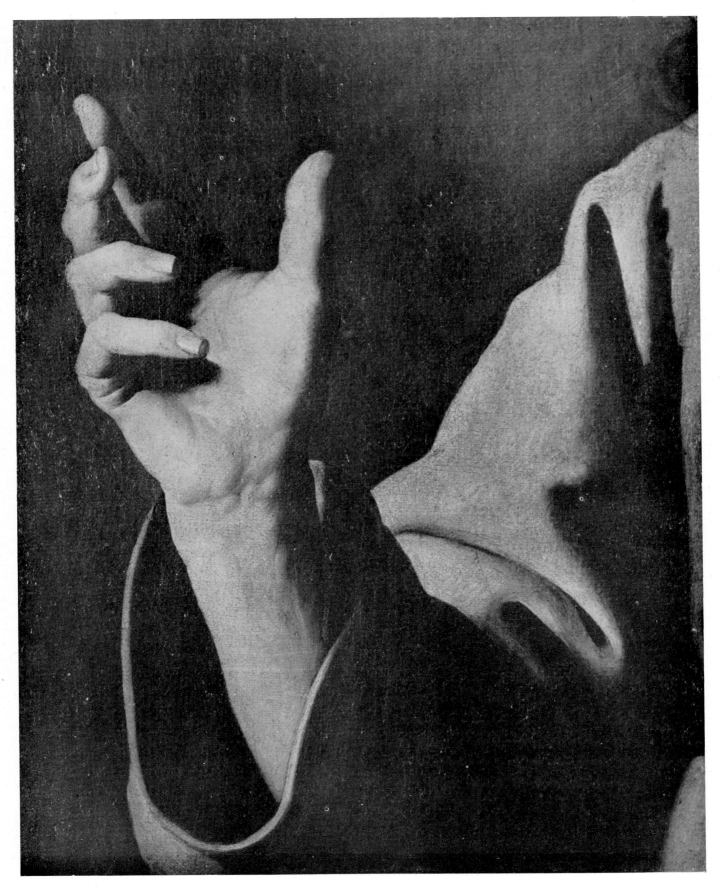

76. THE RIGHT HAND OF CHRIST. Detail from Plate 74

77. SAINT ROMANUS AND SAINT BARULAS. 1638. Chicago, Art Institute (Cat. No. 148)

78. SAINT LOUIS BERTRAM. About 1638. Seville, Museum (Cat. No. 150)

79. GONZALO DE ILLESCAS, BISHOP OF CORDOBA. 1639. Guadalupe, Monastery (Cat. No. 156)

80. THE MASS OF FATHER PETER OF CABANUELAS. 1638. Guadalupe, Monastery (Cat. No. 157)

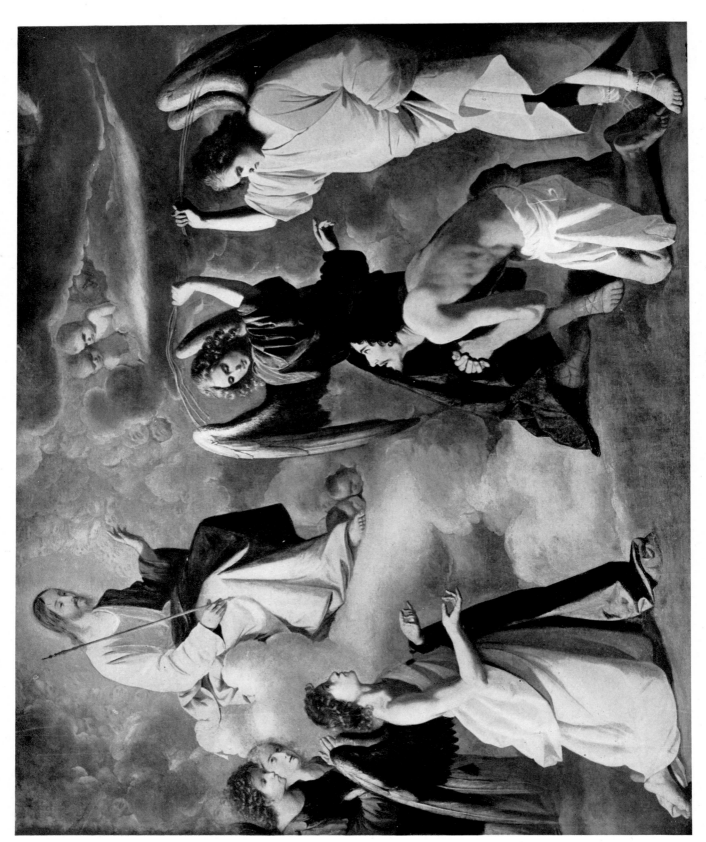

81. THE FLAGELLATION OF SAINT JEROME. 1638-9. Guadalupe, Monastery (Cat. No. 159)

82. THE TEMPTATION OF SAINT JEROME. 1638–9. Guadalupe, Monastery (Cat. No. 160)

83. HEAD OF SAINT JEROME. Detail from Plate 82

84. AN ANGEL. Detail from Plate 81

85. THE TEMPTERS. Detail from Plate 82

86. SAINT JOHN THE BAPTIST. 1638. Cadiz, Museum (Cat. No. 135)

87. SAINT FRANCIS KNEELING. About 1639. London, National Gallery (Cat. No. 166)

88. SAINT FRANCIS KNEELING. 1639. London, National Gallery (Cat. No. 167)

89. SAINT RUFINA. About 1638–42. New York, Hispanic Society of America (Cat. No. 180)

90. A DOCTOR OF LAW. About 1658–60. Boston, Isabella Stewart Gardner Museum (Cat. No. 214)

91. CHRIST CARRYING THE CROSS. 1653. Orléans, Cathedral (Cat. No. 204)

92. THE YOUNG VIRGIN PRAYING. About 1660. Leningrad, Hermitage (Cat. No. 211)

93. HEAD OF SAINT JEROME. Detail from Fig. 133. About 1640–5. San Diego, Fine Arts Gallery (Cat. No. 188)

94. SAINT FRANCIS IN MEDITATION. About 1658–60. Munich, Alte Pinakothek (Cat. No. 215)

95. THE HOLY FAMILY. 1659. Budapest, Museum (Cat. No. 209)

96. THE VIRGIN AND CHILD WITH SAINT JOHN. 1658. San Diego, Fine Arts Gallery (Cat. No. 206)

97. THE ANNUNCIATION. 1658. Philadelphia, Museum of Art (Cat. No. 210)

99. SAINT LUKE BEFORE THE CRUCIFIED. About 1660–4. Madrid, Prado (Cat. No. 219)

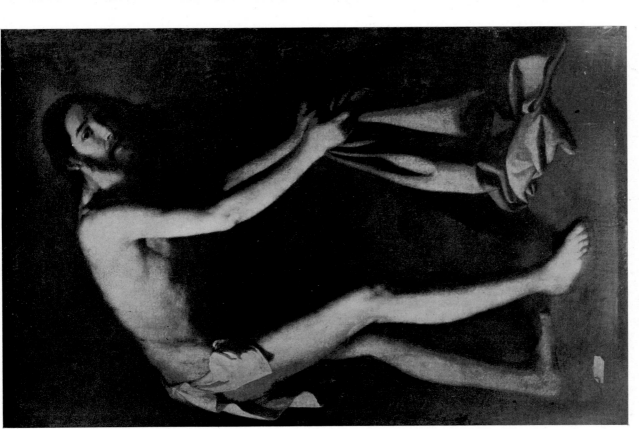

98. 'ET PONIT VESTIMENTA SUA'. 1661. Jadraque, Parish Church (Cat. No. 220)

100. THE IMMACULATE CONCEPTION. 1661. Budapest, Museum (Cat. No. 222)

CATALOGUE

CATALOGUE

1. THE IMMACULATE CONCEPTION WITH THIRTEEN ANGELS. Bilbao, Felix Valdés. 193 × 156 cm. Signed: Franco de Zurbaran fac/ 1616. Plate 1

History: Manuel López Cepero sale, Seville, May 15–30, 1860, No. 66.
Exh: Madrid, 1905, No. 31.
Lit: Tormo, *Época*, March 31, 1905; Mayer, *Sevillaner Malerschule*, pp. 147, 150–151; Cascales, pl. X; Kehrer, pp. 32–33.

Virgin in white and light grayish-blue. Golden-orange background. Recognizing the Italian derivation of the playing angels, Tormo pointed to Donatello's and della Robbia's putti friezes and to a drawing by Pordenone, while Mayer suggested Titian. Compare Titian's *Bacchanale*, Prado; Domenico Campagnola's print of *Twelve Dancing Children*, 1517; and Marco Dente of Ravenna's *Eight Dancing Amorini*, engraved after Raimondi. See pp. 7–9, 21, 30.

2. SAINT LUCY. Washington, The National Gallery of Art. 105 × 77 cm. About 1625–6. Inscribed: S. LUCIA. Plate 2

Collection: Paul Somazzi, Smyrna, Turkey; Gift by Chester Dale, 1943.
Dating: The dark background and the flatness of face, body and draperies suggest an early date, before Velázquez's influence was felt. Modelling of draperies, hands and face related to 4–5, 7.
Lit: Mayer, *ZfbK*, 1927–28, LXI, p. 291 ('1635–1640'); S. I, 166; Cook, *GdBA*, 1945, pp. 82–83; S. VII, 254, 256–260.

White sleeves. Venetian-red bodice with blue bow. Green cloak. Gold jewelry. Wreath of pink, white, red and yellow flowers. In spite of a certain clumsiness, authenticity confirmed by the transparent shadows and transitions between hair and cheek, the design of the sleeves, and the crisp, characteristic drawing of the flowers. See pp. 7, 9, 23–4, 191.

3. SAINT MICHAEL CASTING OUT LUCIFER. New York, Metropolitan Museum of Art, No. 89-15-17. 164 × 110 cm. About 1625–6. Figure 1

History: Bensusan, Cadiz; Gift by H. G. Marquand, 1888.
Dating: Mayer 'early period'; Kehrer 'about 1640'; Angulo, verbally, 'by a follower of Zurbarán, about 1660–1670'; Wehle 'unknown Andalusian painter, second half of the seventeenth century'.
Lit: Mayer, *Arts and Decoration*, 1916, IV, p. 221; Kehrer, pl. 65, pp. 106–107; Wehle, *Metropolitan Museum, Catalogue*, 1940, p. 236; S. VII, 254, 256–260.

Violent colours: pinks, vermilions, blues and greens against a pink and golden sky. For modelling of face, hands and angular drapery design, cf. 2. Similar dramatic, broad and expansive folds in 9, 11, 13 and 20. For the nude Lucifer, cf. 93–102. The same subject repeated in 192, painted in 1644, in a less crowded, more three-dimensional composition, with lighter background. See pp. 7, 9.

4. THE VIRGIN HEALING SAINT REGINALD OF ORLEANS. Seville, Santa Magdalena (formerly called San Pablo), Chapel of the Rosary. 190 × 230 cm. 1626–7. Plate 19

History: One of fourteen scenes, of which twelve unaccounted for, from the life of St. Dominic, commissioned on January 17, 1626, for San Pablo, Seville. Companion piece: 5. Of seven other pictures, including four Doctors of the Church, for the same commission, only 14–16 survive.
Dating: The head of St. Reginald should be compared to that of *Deza*, 19. Both are influenced by Velázquez, and thus later than 2, 3.
Condition: The faces do not show any repaint.
Exh: Seville, 1929–1930, Palacio de Bellas Artes, Arte Antiguo, room VI, Nos. 1 and 7.

Lit: Pal. III, 108; Ceán VI, 50; *Documentos*, II, 182; Lafuente Ferrari, *El realismo en la pintura*, 1935, p. 107; S. I, 40; G. II, 196–198.

Virgin: pink and blue. St. Reginald: white. St. Dominic: black and white. First woman: pink gown, ochre cloak slashed with green. Second woman: vermilion gown, green mantle, wine-red belt. Guinard rediscovered the subject of the picture. Influence of Montañés in the face of the Virgin, and of Sánchez Cotán in the still life on the table. See pp. 2, 6, 7, 9, 11, 30, 32 and fig. II.

5. THE APPARITION OF THE VIRGIN IN SORIANO. Seville, Santa Magdalena (formerly called San Pablo), Chapel of the Rosary. 190 × 230 cm. 1626–7. Plate 18

History, Exhibitions and Lit: See 4.
Dating: Same as other extant paintings of the Dominican series, 4, 14–16. Note the plain draperies; effects of lighting emphasized by dark backgrounds; subdued chiaroscuro contrasts.

The Virgin, in light pink and blue, points to the image of St. Dominic which, in 1530, she brought to the Italian monastery of Soriano. The crowned St. Catherine wears pink and vermilion. St. Mary Magdalene: white chemise, orange skirt, light-grey cloak with green and pink flowers. Vermilion in the tiled floor and in Dominican standard at upper left.

FIG. I   Cat. No. 3

FIG. 2   Cat. No. 6   FIG. 3   Cat. No. 7   FIG. 4   Cat. No. 8

6. SAINT NICHOLAS OF TOLENTINO. Cadiz, Emile Huart. 73 × 47 cm. About 1626.   Figure 2

History: see 7.

Dating: Angulo believed 6 and 7 contemporary with paintings for Jerez and Guadalupe, *124–143, 151–162*, painted 1637–1639. The face recalls, however, that of the kneeling monk in *5*, documented in 1626. The fleshy modelling relates the picture to the Dominican group, *4–5, 14–16*.

Lit: Angulo, *Arch. esp. de arte*, 1944, no. 61, pp. 6–7.

Born in 1249 and one of the greatest miracle workers of his time. The partridge is the Saint's symbol. During his last illness, his brethren brought him a dish of that fowl to restore his strength. Wasted as he was, he refused to eat meat, and stretched his hand over the partridges, whereupon they rose from the dish and flew away. Zurbarán repeated the expressive outline of the black Augustinian habit, years later, in the *Saint Augustine (164)*. See pp. 7, 9, 22.

7. SAINT ANTHONY OF PADUA. Cadiz, Emile Huart. 73 × 47 cm. About 1626.   Figure 3

History: Together with 6, perhaps the 'St. Anthony and another Saint', two paintings of equal size, 63 × 42 cm., 1810 in Alcazar of Seville, room 1, no. 94. There attributed to Bernabé de Ayala, as was *120*. Private collection, Seville, 1880; private collection, Jerez.

Dating: see 6. Modelling, pose and expression are related to those of the St. Mary Magdalene in *5*.

Lit: see 6.

The radiant Christ Child, nude beneath a white, finely transparent shirt, and standing on the gospel, symbolizes Saint Anthony's powers of preaching. The Saint's habit is olive-green. Slate-blue background.

8. CHRIST GIVING UP THE GHOST. Seville, Museum of Fine Arts, No. 211. 124 × 80 cm. About 1626-8.   Figure 4

Dating: Related in drapery style to the paintings for San Pablo, *4–5, 14–16*.

Condition: Found, torn and neglected, by the author in the deposits of the Seville Museum in 1948. Ably restored by Manuel López Gil, of the Museum of Fine Arts, Cadiz.

The overpoweringly realistic expression of the head, in agonized pain, is heightened by the red colour of the eyelids. In modelling,

the face resembles that of the boy in the painting at Cincinnati (pl. 16), of the *Male Portrait (35)*, and the face of Christ in pl. 22. The crossed feet, seen also in Zurbarán's last version of the *Crucified, 219*, are derived from Montañés' famous statue, the *Christ of Mercy*, at Seville Cathedral. St. Bridget in her *Revelations* (I, 10) had stated that Christ's feet were crossed and that four nails were used. See p. 21.

9. THE MARRIAGE OF SAINT CATHERINE OF SIENA. Keir, Scotland, William Stirling of Keir. 109 × 100 cm. About 1626.
                                                                        Figure 5

FIG. 5   Cat. No. 9

History: Probably Aniceto Bravo collection, Seville, about 1825; brought to England, before 1835, by Sir John M. Brackenbury, who sold it, in 1850, to Sir William Stirling-Maxwell, grandfather of the present owner.

Dating: The drapery folds correspond to the early period, cf. *2–5*. For the modelling of Christ's head and hands, see *19*; for the hands also *16*.

Condition: The Virgin's head has been overcleaned, removing her crown.

Exh: Art of the Seventeenth Century, Royal Academy, London, 1938, No. 231; Spanish Paintings, National Gallery of Scotland, Edinburgh, 1951, No. 42.

Lit: G. I, 183.

Christ: plum-coloured cloak over wine-red robe. Virgin: pink gown, light-blue cloak. St. Catherine: in black and white. In their intensity, these hues are characteristic of Zurbarán. The two female figures are less convincing in modelling than that of Christ. See pp. 7, 9.

10. THE BIRTH OF THE VIRGIN. Florence, Count Contini-Bonacossi. 141 × 109 cm. About 1627.   Plate 4

History: Until 1880, see *11*. Owned by Count Theodore von Berckheim, Paris, in 1925.

Dating: Mayer 'before 1630'. See *11*.

Exh: Galerie Charpentier, Paris, 1925, No. 118; Contini-Bonacossi Exhibition, Rome, 1930, No. 63.

Lit: Ponz IX, 5, 6; Ceán VI, 49; López Martínez, I, 6–8; Mayer, *Apollo*, 1930, XII, p. 3; idem, *Pantheon*, 1930, V, pp. 291, 296; G. II, 189, 191; S. V, 74.

Standing woman at right: yellow skirt, light-blue upper garment with barely visible vermilion undersleeves, white lace collar. Her contemporary dress and the pose indicate a portrait. Woman at the left: orange-sienna skirt, light-blue jacket. Woman tending baby: green skirt. Sparkling white linen, bright vermilion bedspread, carmine curtains. Colour scheme and modelling, harmonizing with *11–12*, prove that all three belonged to same altar. Benesch noticed that the arrangement of the whole and many details were copied from Dürer's woodcut (B. 80) of the same subject. See pp. 9, 30, 32.

FIG. 6   Cat. No. 11

FIG. 7   Cat. No. 13

11. THE VIRGIN AND HER PARENTS. Florence, Count Contini-Bonacossi. 127 × 108 cm. About 1627.   Figure 6

History: One of eight scenes from the life of the Virgin, once forming a side altar at the epistle side, Shod Trinitarians, Seville; all eight in Marquis of Salamanca collection, Paris, sold about 1880. Five unrecorded since.

Dating: By Mayer 'between 1630–1635', too late, because related by Guinard to Trinitarian altar, mentioned as 'in existence' on September 26, 1629, but done, to judge by style, about 1627. See *10*, *12–13* from same church, and same date.

Exh: Contini-Bonacossi Exhibition, Rome, 1930, No. 64.

Lit: Ponz IX, 5, 6; Ceán VI, 49; Mayer, *Burl. Mag.*, 1924, XLIV, p. 212; López Martínez, I, 6–8; S. I, 40; G. II, 189, 191.

Virgin: blue skirt ornamented in gold, white blouse with black borders, dark-blue bodice. St. Anne: yellow-ochre cape, violet skirt. St. Joachim: dark rose-vermilion. See pp. 9, 30, 32.

12. THE HOLY FAMILY WITH SAINTS ANNE, JOACHIM AND JOHN. Madrid, Marquise of Campo Real. 136 × 128 cm. About 1628.   Plates 3, 5

Collections: Alberto Berges Gastiarena, Madrid; Marquise of Perinat, mother of present owner, Madrid.

Dating: Slightly later than the other two extant paintings, *10–11*, from the altar of the Trinitarians, because stronger and surer in modelling and more varied in the draperies.

Lit: Ponz IX, 5, 6; Ceán VI, 49; López Martínez, I, 6–8; Gaya Nuño, *Zurbarán*, 1948, pl. XXIV.

FIG. 8   Cat. No. 14   FIG. 9   Cat. No. 15   FIG. 10   Cat. No. 16

Virgin: white, pink and deep blue. Christ Child: green-blue. St. John: bright vermilion. St. Anne and St. Joseph: orange browns and green umbers. St. Joachim: green-grey headkerchief striped in lilac. Pink, white, orange, vermilion and violet flowers. See pp. 7, 9, 22.

13. THE CHRIST CHILD BLESSING. Moscow, Pushkin State Museum of Fine Arts. 42 × 27 cm. About 1627. Panel.   Figure 7

History: The long lost 'gracioso niño Dios', seen by Ponz and Ceán as ciborium door in the main altar of the church of the Shod Trinitarians, Seville; Alcazar, Seville, 1810, No. 280; Countess Schuwaloff, St. Petersburg; Hermitage, Leningrad, as 'Infant St. John the Baptist' attributed to Meneses Osorio, until recognized as a Zurbarán by K. Malitzkaya.

Dating: Stylistically related to and contemporary with 10-12, from same church. Compare the facial expression and the drapery patterns.

Lit: Ponz IX, 5, 6; Ceán VI, 49; K. Malitzkaya, *Burl. Mag.*, 1930, LVII, p. 17; G. II, 191; K. Malitzkaya, *The Spanish Painting*, Moscow, 1947, pp. 109, 114; Pemán, II, 155-156.

Wearing a red garment, white at the neck. On the reverse a carved and gilded Phœnix, symbol of the suffering and resurrected Christ. See pp. 7, 9, 30.

14. SAINT GREGORY. Seville, Museum of Fine Arts, No. 191. 198 × 125 cm. 1626-8.   Figure 8

Inscribed: S GREGOVS.

History: See 4.

Dating: Compare with 4-5 and 15-16.

Lit: Pal. III, 108; Ponz IX, 3, 24; Ceán VI, 49; Matute, *Archivo Hispalense*, 1887, III, p. 337, no. 48; Kehrer, pl. 25, pp. 62-63; *Documentos*, II, 182; S. I, 40; G. II, 194-195.

Vermilion cope, embroidered in gold and silver. White surplice. Salmon-vermilion gloves and book edges. Golden tiara. Mild chiaroscuro. Influence from Velázquez. See pp. 6-7, 9, 30, 32.

15. SAINT AMBROSE. Seville, Museum of Fine Arts, No. 192. 205 × 98 cm. 1626-8.   Figure 9

History, Dating, and Lit: See 4 and 14.

Carmine and yellow ochre cope, yellow ochre mitre. Vermilion book edges. For the facial expression, compare 6 and the kneeling monk in 5. Uncertain whether originally different in size from 14 and 16, or cut later.

16. SAINT JEROME. Seville, Museum of Fine Arts, No. 193. 198 × 125 cm. 1626-8.   Figure 10

History, Dating and Lit: See 4 and 14.

Brownish complexion. Vermilion vestments of a Cardinal. A brown lion in the shadows at the left. Two later, more impressive versions, 188, 193, show the Saint pointing to the trumpet of the Last Judgement. See pp. 6, 7, 22.

17. MAGISTER RODRIGO FERNÁNDEZ DE SANTAELLA. Seville, Seminary, Rector's Hall. 208 × 158 cm. About 1626-7.   Figure 11

History: Still in its original place.

Dating: Colouring and setting, recalling fifteenth-century Flemish paintings, are in Zurbarán's early style.

Lit: Ceán VI, 50; González de León, *Noticias artísticas de Sevilla*, 1844, I, p. 145; Gestoso Pérez, *Sevilla monumental y artística*, Seville, 1888, III, p. 35; G. II, 200-201, ill.

Founder of the Upper College (later University) of Seville, begun in 1472. Clad in black and white, grey-green cloak. Kneeling on a red pillow before a statue of the *Virgin de la Antigua*, in white and gold. The Virgin holds a rose in her right hand; on her left the Christ Child, dressed in blue. Blue curtain before the image, red curtain overhead. Reddish table cloth changing to green. Interior setting with dark background. See. p. 24, 30.

17a. SAINT ANTHONY OF PADUA. São Paolo, Museu de Arte. 160 × 104 cm. 1627-9.   Figure 13

Collection: Acquired in 1950 in England from a collection in Milan, Italy.

Dating: The modelling of the folds, the lighting and the stiff, frontal pose are related to 14-16.

Lit: Recognized as an early Zurbarán by R. Longhi (letter 1933).

Life-size, kneeling and looking to the upper left where the small figure of the Christ Child blessing is disclosed in a cloudburst. At the lower left an open book and a branch of lilies. See p. 22.

FIG. 11   Cat. No. 17

18. THE YOUNG VIRGIN ASLEEP. Jerez de la Frontera, Collegiate Church. 109 × 90 cm. 1627–9.   Figure 12

Dating: Pictorial elements recall *4–5, 14–16*, but the more three-dimensional organization of space suggests the date given above.
Lit: Mayer, *Apollo*, 1928, VII, p. 181.

Rose-vermilion gown, blue cloak. On a brown table, a plate and cup of blue china holding pink roses, white lilies, and a carnation. Fairly dark background. Mayer pointed to the expressive rendering of Spanish mysticism. Thus the mood of the thirties is anticipated. See p. 22.

19. FRAY DIEGO DEZA, ARCHBISHOP OF SEVILLE. New York, M. Knoedler & Co. 174 × 143 cm. About 1629.   Figure 14

Inscribed: Do⟨mi⟩nus Didacus Deca Archiep ⟨iscopus⟩ Hisp⟨aliae⟩ elect⟨us⟩ Toletan⟨i⟩ inquisit⟨or⟩ gen⟨eralis⟩ n⟨oste⟩r illustrissimus fundator. Coat of arms of this famous founder (1444–1523) of the Dominican College of Santo Tomas Aquinas, Seville, and protector of Columbus.

History: Cell of the prior of the College; Alcazar, Seville, 1810, No. 66; Virginia Gómez Acebo de Pérez, Madrid.
Dating: Face and hands related to *13–15*. Free and ample draperies anticipate *40*.
Lit: Ponz X, I, 128; Ceán VI, 48; Matute, *Archivo Hispalense*, 1887, III; *Arch. esp. de arte*, 1929, V, p. 169; González de Léon, I, p. 131.

Dominican blacks and whites against the deep red of the table

FIG. 12   Cat. No. 18

FIG. 13   Cat. No. 17a

cloth. A copy, on loan to the Museum of Seville, has hitherto been accepted as the original (see G. II, 285). It differs in many details, particularly the space relationships. The original is far superior in modelling. The composition repeats Italian sixteenth-century ecclesiastical portraits. See pp. 7, 24.

20. THE CHRIST CHILD CONTEMPLATING THE CROWN OF THORNS. Seville, Manuel Sánchez Ramos. 128 × 85 cm. 1629–30.
Plate 6

History: By tradition once in the Carthusian Monastery of Our Lady of the Caves, Seville, and probably identical with the picture seen by Ceán in the anteroom of the prior's hall.
Dating: One of the earliest interior backgrounds not entirely dark. Related to 41.
Exh: Madrid, 1905, No. 33; Seville, 1929–1930, room I, No. 23.
Lit: Ceán VI, 49; Cascales, pl. XII; Kehrer, p. 63; C. Serra Pickman, *Discursos leídos ante la Academia de Bellas Artes de Santa Isabel de Hungría de Sevilla*, Seville, 1934, pp. 32–33; S. I, 43; G. III, 5–6.

In blue-lavender and reds, pressing a drop of blood from his finger. Transparent glass vase with pink, white and yellow flowers. Vermilion curtain disclosing a Baroque wall, oval in shape with shallow niches. The placing of each object and setting as a whole emphasize spatial depth. A painting of the same subject in the Museum of Seville is different in pose and dates probably after 1640. Therefore and because of weak design and handling, it cannot be a study. It should be attributed to Zurbarán's shop. See pp. 9, 21.

21. CRUCIFIXION. Seville, Museum of Fine Arts, No. 206. 252 × 172 cm. 1627–9.
Plate 7

History: Mentioned by Ponz and Ceán in the Capuchin Church, Seville.
Dating: Lights and shadows in the loin cloth are close in feeling to *4–5, 14–16*. As yet, no shadow is thrown by the body.
Lit: Ponz IX, 5, 9; Ceán VI, 50; Kehrer, pl. 6; G. II, 192.

FIG. 15   Cat. No. 23

The detail shows increasing mastery of realistic, form-giving modelling and ability to express spiritual values by dramatic foreshortening. See p. 21.

22. THE DEAD CHRIST ON THE CROSS. Barcelona, Juan Guitart. 167 × 108 cm. About 1628–30.

Dating: Apparently contemporary with *21, 23*.

Head downward and inclined to left. Feet half overlapping. Voluminous loin cloth. Sign overhead inscribed 'INRI'. See p. 21.

23. CRUCIFIXION. Madrid, Manuel de Longorio. 168 × 119 cm. About 1629–30.
Figure 15

Dating: The draperies are less excited and more orderly than those of *21*. Thus probably slightly later in date, and contemporary with *30–33*, dated 1629 and 1630.
Exh: Madrid, 1905, no. 34. Unrecorded since.
Christ, his arms pitifully emaciated, is very human and not idealized. The loin cloth is of a type repeated in *62* and *170*. Sebastián Llano Valdés copied the upper part in a *Crucifixion*, signed in 1666, at Seville Cathedral. See p. 21.

24. SAINT BONAVENTURE PRAYING. Dresden, Gemäldegalerie, No. 696. 239 × 222 cm. 1629.
Plate 9

History: One of four scenes from the life of St. Bonaventure, *24–27*, for the Franciscan college of that name at Seville; Alcazar, 1810,

FIG. 14   Cat. No. 19

FIG. 16   Cf. Cat. No. 24

FIG. 17   Cf. Cat. No. 26

No. 70 (as 'Saint Anthony with an Angel'); Returned to College, 1814–1835; Galerie Espagnole, Louvre, 1838, No. 348 (as 'Saint Francis Meditating'); Louis Philippe sale, 1853, No. 206, for £68 to the Dresden Gallery.
Dating: See 25.
Lit: Ponz IX, 3, 42; Ceán VI, 47–48; Justi, *JKPK*, 1882, IV, p. 152; idem, *ZfbK*, 1911, XLVII, p. 25; Cascales, pl. XVI; Kehrer, pl. 15, pp. 48–49; idem, *Spanische Kunst*, pp. 182–183; Kleinschmidt, *Archivum Historicum Franciscanum*, 1926, XIX, pp. 3–16; G. I, 266–270; S. IV, 254. For the subject, see Pietro Galesini, *Vita S. Bonaventurae*, in *Opera Omnia de San Bonaventura*, Rome, 1588, I, p. 26.

After the death of Clement IV, at Viterbo, the cardinals, unable to agree on a successor, asked St. Bonaventure to designate the next pope, even if he should propose himself. The kneeling Saint humbly prays for God's guidance. A Caravaggiesque angel points to the absent future Gregory X, elected Pope in 1271. Inspired by an engraving by Theodor Galle, *Finding of the Relics of St. Gereon at Cologne* (fig. 16), part of a *Vita S. Norberti*, by Van der Sterre, Antwerp, 1605. Zurbarán repeated the general composition, but transformed a conventional print into a scene of silent, mystic introspection. See pp. 9–10, 30.

25. SAINT BONAVENTURE REFERS SAINT THOMAS AQUINAS TO THE SAVIOUR. Berlin, Kaiser Friedrich Museum, No. 404A. 226 × 256 cm. Signed: FCO. DE (interlaced) ZURBARAN/FATA 1629.
Plate 14

History: See 24. Taken from Seville, in 1810, by Marshal Soult; bought at Soult sale, Paris, 1852, No. 23, frs. 19500. Wantonly destroyed by fire, May 5–10, 1945.
Lit: See 24. Also Cascales, pl. XV; Kehrer, pl. 14; Grautoff and Pevsner, *Barockmalerei in den Romanischen Ländern*, Potsdam, 1928,

colour plate; Ch. Norris, *Burl. Mag.*, 1952, XCIV, pp. 337–346. For the subject, see Galesini, *l.c.*, I, p. 15.
Saint Thomas Aquinas, amazed at the force and richness of Saint Bonaventure's mystic theology, visited the young teacher at the University of Paris and asked to see his library. In reply, St. Bonaventure pointed to the image of the Crucified as the sole source of his knowledge. Cool, clear colours, predominantly grey, sienna, black and blue, produce an ensemble of great force and dignity. See pp. 2, 9–10.

26. SAINT BONAVENTURE'S MEDIATION AT THE COUNCIL OF LYON. Paris, Louvre, No. 1738. 250 × 225 cm. 1629.   Plate 10

History: See 24. Alcazar, Seville, 1810, No. 69 (as 'A Council'); Soult sale, Paris, 1852, No. 22, bought in at frs. 19500 and sold to the Louvre in 1858.
Dating: See 25.
Lit: See 24. Also Cascales, pl. XVII; Kehrer, pl. 16, pp. 50–51; Matrod, *Chronique des arts*, December 31, 1922 (as 'Reception of the Ambassadors of Emperor Paleologus'); S. I, 41.

Known under various erroneous titles. Father Kleinschmidt rightly suggested that St. Bonaventure's activities at the Council of Lyon, in 1274, are represented. From an engraving showing *St. Norbert at the Council of Fritzlar* (fig. 17), in the *Vita S. Norberti* (see 24), Zurbarán borrowed the general arrangement of the main diagonal aligning the seated figures as against the standing one at the left, also the raised platform with a canopy, the opening in the background, and even the profile head at the extreme left. Zurbarán replaced the print's deep vanishing-point perspective by planes parallel to the picture surface. His architecture, modern in its pure, geometric volumes, co-operates with the monumental figures, painted in vermilion, light grey, blue-grey, black and yellow. Red curtains and coverings. Yellow ochre, blue-green and white rug. See pp. 10, 12.

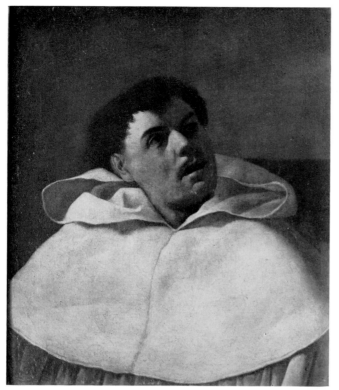

FIG. 18   Cat. No. 29

27. SAINT BONAVENTURE ON HIS BIER. Paris, Louvre, No. 1739. 250 × 225 cm. 1629.   Plate 11

History: See *24*. Soult sale, Paris, 1852, No. 24, bought in at frs. 5000, and sold to the Louvre in 1858.
Dating: See *25*.
Lit: See *24*. Also Cascales, pl. XVIII; Kehrer, pl. 18, pp. 51-52; S. V, 75; Guinard-Baticle, p. 88 ill. in colour.

The Saint's death took place on July 15, 1274. Emperor Michael VII Paleologus, Pope Gregory X, and the Archbishop of Lyon, all of whom attended the Council, stand at the Saint's feet. The Emperor in blue-green, gold and lavender. The Pope in gold, carmine and white. Franciscans in mouse-grey alternate with noblemen and priests in black. The Saint, in white edged with gold, rests on a blue-grey pillow and a deep-lilac chasuble, a vermilion hat at his feet. Gold and carmine bier, the gold ranging from raw sienna to yellow, whitish in the lights and grayish in the shadows. See p. 10, and *34*.

28. SAINT SERAPION. Hartford, Conn., The Wadsworth Atheneum. 120.5 × 103.5 cm. Signed: Franco de Zurbaran fabt. 1628. Inscribed: B⟨eatus⟩ Serapius.   Plate 8

History: Painted for the 'De Profundis' hall, in the Mercedarian Monastery, at Seville; see *30* for a commission of August 29, 1628; Alcazar, Seville, 1810, No. 227 (105 × 84 cm.); Julian Williams, Seville; bought there about 1832 by Richard Ford; his sale, Rainey's Auction Rooms, London, June 9, 1836, No. 33 to Sir Montague John Cholmeley, Easton Hall, Grantham, Lincolnshire, until 1947; David Koetser, New York.
Lit: Ponz IX, 3, 48; Matute, *Archivo Hispalense*, 1887, III, p. 377; Ceán VI, 49; G. II, 172-173; Pemán III, 207-208; *Art News*, Nov. 1951, p. 31, ill. in colour, p. 60.

A most dramatic, yet essentially tranquil presentation of the English bishop who preached the gospel to the Mohammedans and was martyred in 1240 in North Africa. Three-quarter length, wearing the white, red, and gold insignia of the Mercedarians on his chest. The

white draperies create a pattern suspended in mid-air, still in death, floating downward, yet aspiring to heaven. Eminently fit for the room where the bodies of monks were placed before burial. See p. 30.

29. BUST OF A MERCEDARIAN MONK. Madrid, María Cruzat de Rumeu de Armas. 69 × 56 cm. About 1628.   Figure 18
Collections: Marquis of Casa Argudín, Madrid, 1905.
Dating: The modelling of the head may be compared to that of *28*.
Condition: Repaint in the face and in the white habit.
Exh: Madrid, 1905, No. 30.
Lit: Gaya Nuño, *Zurbarán*, 1948, pl. XI; G. III, 37 (perhaps part of series: *55, 58, 79-82*). See also *83-85a*.

Perhaps a companion piece to *28*. Brownish-yellow face. Dark hair.

30. SAINT PETER NOLASCO DREAMING OF THE HEAVENLY JERUSALEM. Madrid, Prado, No. 1236. 179 × 223 cm. 1629.
Signed: Fco DE (interlaced) F. Z.   Plate 12

History: Together with *31-33*, one of twenty-two scenes from the life of St. Peter Nolasco, commissioned on August 29, 1628, for the Shod Mercedarians, at Seville; Dean López Cepero, Seville, before 1808; given by him to King Ferdinand VII. Another picture of this series, St. Peter Nolasco Taking the Mercedarian Habits, 112 × 225 cm., was in the Manuel López Cepero sale, Seville, May 15-30, 1860, No. 749.
Dating: See *31*.
Lit: Ponz IX, 3, 47; Ceán VI, 49; Kehrer, pl. 12, pp. 42-43; Sánchez Cantón, *La Merced*, January 24, 1922; S. I, 42; G. II, 162-171; Guinard-Baticle, p. 90 ill. in colour.

To the sleeping Saint, in white, appears an Angel in pink and light blue. Light-grey city with bluish walls and pink roofs. Dark background. A pupil, possibly Francisco Reina, painted four other pictures of the series, now at Seville Cathedral (reproduced by Kehrer, pl. 8-11). See pp. 10, 30, 32.

31. THE APOSTLE PETER APPEARS TO SAINT PETER NOLASCO. Madrid, Prado, No. 1237. 179 × 223 cm. Signed: FRANCISCUS DE (interlaced) ZURBARAN/FACIEBAT 1629.   Plate 13
History: See *30*.
Lit: See *30*. Also Kehrer, pl. 13.

The startled Saint beholds St. Peter, crucified head down on an inverted cross. The Apostle's head is among the artist's most realistic. See p. 10.

32. SAINT PETER NOLASCO RECOVERING THE IMAGE OF THE VIRGIN. Cincinnati, Cincinnati Art Museum, No. 1917-58. 164 × 208 cm. Signed: FRANCO DE (interlaced) ZURBA⟨RAN⟩ FATI./1630.
Plates 15, 16

History: See *30*. From the Mercedarians to the Galerie Espagnole, Louvre, 1838, No. 398; Louis Philippe sale, London, May 6-21, 1853, No. 416, £65, to Pearce; Pearce sale, at Phillips, London, April 23, 1872, No. 500, £79 to Myers; Charles T. D. Crews sale, Christie's, July 2, 1915, No. 294, to Sulley & Co.; gift of Miss Mary Hanna, Mr. and Mrs. Charles P. Taft and Mr. Stevenson Scott, 1917.
Exh: Toledo, Ohio, 1941, No. 69.
Lit: See *30*. Also *Acta Sanctorum*, January, III, 1866, pp. 595-605; Fray P. N. Pérez, *San Pedro Nolasco*, Barcelona, 1915, p. 94; Fray G. Vázquez, *La Merced*, August 15, 1929, p. 286; F. W. Robinson, *Bulletin, Cincinnati Art Museum*, 1936, VII, pp. 17-27.

In 1237, St. Peter Nolasco recovered the image of the Virgin of El Puig, near Valencia. The sacred tablet, hidden during the Moorish occupation, was brought to light, together with the old church bell, in the presence of James I of Aragon. The King wears blue armour, grey pantaloons gold-embroidered, and light-grey hose. Soldiers in yellow, vermilion, and greyish-green painted over pink. Blue-grey helmets, bell, and landscape. Portrait head of a boy (pl. 16), perhaps the artist's ten-year-old son Juan, painted upon completion of the picture. Cut 7.5 cm. on the sides, 15 cm. above.

FIG. 19 Cat. No. 33

33. SAINT PETER NOLASCO WITH THREE NOBLES. Dallas, Texas, Col. Harry E. Stewart. 171 × 212 cm. 1630. Figure 19

History: See *30*. From the Mercedarians to the Galerie Espagnole, Louvre, 1838, No. 397; Louis Philippe sale, No. 415, £30 to Drax; J. C. W. Sawbridge-Erle-Drax sale, Christie's, May 10, 1935, No. 153, £252, to A. Seligmann.
Dating: See *32*.
Lit: See *30* and *32*. Also Pal. III, 107; R. Ford, *Atheneum*, London, 1853.

The Saint, in tan, vermilion and yellow ochre, inquires his way from a knight of the order of Malta and two companions. Guinard identified the picture with one described by Palomino, and called attention to the deeply recessed landscape. The composition, in the main figure and in the landscape background, recalls an engraving of *Christ Meeting the Pilgrims on the Road to Emmaus*, after Marten de Vos, in Geeraard de Jode's *Thesaurus sacrarum historiarum veteris et novi Testamenti*, Antwerp, 1579–1585, p. 365. The three figures at the left are by a different, less skilful hand. Cut 11 cm. at the left, and 8 cm. along top. See pp. 10, 25.

34. HEAD OF A MONK. London, British Museum, No. 1895–9–15–873. 28 × 19.4 cm. About 1629. Black chalk drawing, light-cream paper.
 Plate 17

Collections: Madrazo, Madrid; John Malcolm of Poltabloch (*Catalogue*, by J. C. Robinson, London, 1876, No. 424).
Dating: Cf. pl. 17.
Lit: Mayer, *Sevillaner Malerschule*, p. 160; idem, *Handzeichnungen Spanischer Meister*, pl. 46; Kehrer, *Spanische Kunst*, p. 211.

Life-size drawing, apparently study of a dead monk from nature, perhaps intended as sketch for *27*. Vigorously modelled. Finely shaded. Bistre lightly added at the moustache, chin, and outline of the face at the right. Features coherently organized. Curvy parallel lines define face and hood. Contrasting chiaroscuro kept light and transparent, as in the master's portraits in oil of this period. Attributions to Zurbarán of other drawings, at Hamburg, London, and elsewhere, do not seem convincing. See p. 11.

35. MALE PORTRAIT. Seville, Museum of Fine Arts. 210 × 130 cm. About 1630. Figure 20

History: Until now attributed to Velázquez. Called Andrés Count of Ribera, on account of an inscription which disappeared in a recent cleaning.
Dating: The approximate date, and Zurbarán's authorship, are suggested by comparison with *32*, particularly the head of a boy (pl. 16), that of the helmeted soldier next to it, and of the other soldier at the left. Cf. the modelling of the eyes, nose, cheeks, and jaw. Velázquez already by 1625 painted in a more airy and three-dimensional style.
Condition: Recently restored, removing several layers of old repaint. The restorer, believing the picture to be by Velázquez, seems to have softened Zurbarán's chiaroscuro contrasts. Most of the right hand repainted, left hand and glove almost entirely restored. Hair, moustache, and Van Dyck beard reinforced by recent repaint.

Dressed in black, before a grey background. Healthy tanned face, pale-rose lips, greenish-grey facial shadows, as in *32*. Right glove, in grey with white high lights, is original. Pose of legs repeated in central figure of *103*. Pose and relationship of arms and hands similar in *104*. See p. 7.

FIG. 20 Cat. No. 35 FIG. 21 Cat. No. 37 FIG. 22 Cat. No. 38

36. SAINT PETER OF ALCÁNTARA. Seville, L. Koidl. 67 × 54 cm. About 1630.   Plates 23, 24

History: Brought to the author's attention by Alfonso Grosso.
Dating: The loose, pigmented modelling of the face and the drawing of the fleshy hands indicate a date close to 1630.

Saint Peter of Alcántara (1499-1562), a Franciscan, was the founder of the Stricter Observants of the rule of St. Francis and a counsellor of St. Teresa. Beatified in 1622, the ardent mystic was famous for his tender, human sympathy. The head anticipates that of *St. Jerome 188* in truthfulness of expression. The folds of the sleeve are characteristic of the artist.

37. THE DEAD CHRIST ON THE CROSS. Bilbao, Felix Valdés. Life size. 1630-1. Said to be signed on the cross.   Figure 21

Collections: Marquis of Villafuerte, Seville.
Dating: In the draperies close in feeling to *39*, and probably contemporary.
Lit: Cascales' reproduction, pl. XXIII, claiming to be of this picture, is actually of the similar one in Seville Museum, No. 202 (*62*).

Zurbarán's earliest and best representation of the Dead Christ. The dark background further emphasizes the brilliant whites of the loincloth, simply designed and moving. See p. 21.

38. CRUCIFIXION. Seville, Museum of Fine Arts, No. 195. 232 × 167 cm. About 1631.   Figure 22

History: Seen by Ponz and Ceán in the Capuchin Convent at Seville.
Dating: Recalls *41* in modelling. Compared to *37*, which may be a year earlier, the chiaroscuro contrast is considerably increased and the shadows darker.
Lit: Ponz IX, 5, 10; Ceán VI, 50; Kehrer, pl. 5; G. II, 192.

The body is set against a reddish-brown background. Below are ashen-gray and dark-yellow ochre hills and the towers of Jerusalem. See p. 21.

39. THE VISION OF THE BLESSED ALONSO RODRÍGUEZ. Madrid, Royal Academy of Fine Arts. 266 × 167 cm Signed: FCO DE (interaced) ZURBARAN FA (interlaced)/1630.   Plates 22, 25

History: In the eighteenth century still in the sacristy of the Jesuit church, Seville.
Lit: F. Fita, *Boletín de la Real Academia de la Historia*, 1917, LXX/LXXI; *Arch. esp. de arte*, 1929, V, p. 176; Kehrer, pl. 23, pp. 57-58; Cascales, pl. LX; S. I, 44; G. III, 6-7; Guinard-Baticle, p. 92 ill. in colour.

The pious janitor of the Jesuit college at Mallorca, in a vision, received into his own body the hearts of Christ and of the Virgin Mary. Zurbarán could have known Alonso Rodríguez's (1530-1617) features from an engraving by Anthony Wierix 'ex vivo expressus'. The Virgin is clad in white and blue, Christ in light vermilion. The angel has an orange-yellow dress and blue wings with touches of carmine. On the ground, Thomas à Kempis' book inscribed: 'Contentus mundi', Rodríguez's daily reading. One of Zurbarán's chief works. Its spiritual power causes the onlooker to experience, bodily, the burning faith of the old man. See pp. 11, 30.

40. THE VISION OF SAINT FRANCIS IN THE PORCIUNCULA. Cadiz, Museum of Fine Arts, No. 63. 248 × 167 cm. 1630-1.   Plates 26, 29

History: Seen by Ponz in the choir of the Capuchin church at Jerez; entered the Museum in 1836.
Dating: Resemblances in modelling to *39*, give an approximate date.
Condition: Recently cleaned and restored by Manuel López Gil.
Lit: Ponz XVII, 5, 70; Ceán VI, 51; *Catálogo, Museo de Pinturas*, Cadiz, 1876, No. 63 ('1631-1633'); Cascales, pl. LXI; Kehrer, pp. 74, 76; G. III, 21.

Christ, upon the intercession of the kneeling Virgin, grants to St. Francis the Jubilee of the Porciuncula. The writ in Christ's hand confirms this privilege of a year of indulgence. The Porciuncula is the plot of land where St. Francis rebuilt a church dedicated to the Virgin. Greys and browns below contrast with blue, pink, white and yellow above. See p. 22.

41. THE APOTHEOSIS OF SAINT THOMAS AQUINAS. Seville, Museum of Fine Arts, No. 199. 475 × 375 cm. Signed: Franco de Zurbaran facb 1631.   Plates 27-28

History: Commissioned on January 21, 1631 for the main altar of the Dominican College church of St. Thomas Aquinas, at Seville, to be ready on St. John's day (June 18th) of 1631. During the War of Independence taken to Paris, exhibited at the Louvre in 1813; soon afterwards restored to Spain, and after a few years in Madrid, returned to Seville, in 1819.
Lit: Ponz IX, 3, 25; Ceán VI, 45-46, 48; Lefort, *Histoire de la peinture espagnole*, Paris, 1890, p. 145; Cascales, pl. VII; Gestoso Pérez, *Catálogo, Museo Provincial de Sevilla*, 1912, pp. 83-86; Kehrer, pl. 24, pp. 58-60; *Documentos*, II, p. 183; S. I, 43; G. I, 263-265.

At the top, Christ in light blue, the Virgin in rose and blue, St. Paul in lavender-grey and yellow ochre, and St. Dominic. In the main tier, around St. Thomas: St. Ambrose, in blue-grey, red and gold; St. Gregory, in green, vermilion and gold; St. Jerome, in vermilion; St. Augustine, in gold. Below, at the left, Archbishop Deza, founder of the college, in light blue. Emperor Charles V, at the right, in dark-blue armour, violet and gold breeches, white hose and tan boots. He wears an orange-ochre cape embroidered with gold and silver and a rose bow. At either side, three kneeling ecclesiastics in dark blue, one of them sometimes, without adequate proof, considered the artist's self-portrait. Kehrer saw a continued use of Raphael's *Disputà* formula of Renaissance composition, executed in Baroque chiaroscuro style. Lefort cited the influence of Roelas' *Death of St. Isidoro* and of Herrera's *Triumph of St. Hermengild*, which has a similar composition, distribution of masses, use of light and shade, and colouring. See pp. 2, 11-3, 30, 32.

42. SAINT PETER THOMAS. Boston, Museum of Fine Arts, No. 23-554. 91 × 32 cm. About 1630-2. Inscribed: S. P⟨EDR⟩° THOMAS.   Plate 30

History: Probably from the Carmelite church of San Alberto, Seville, where a number of altars were erected between 1629 and 1633, and where Palomino, Ponz and Ceán saw an altar by Zurbarán. Alcazar, Seville, 1810, Nos. 268-271 (together with our *43-45*, companion pieces as Guinard recognized); taken by Marshal Soult; sold, 1835, to the Duke of Sutherland; his sale, Stafford House, at Christie's, July 11, 1913, no. 145, £168, to Knoedler & Co.; Gift by Mrs. Zoe Oliver Sherman, Boston, 1922.
Dating: Close to *41* in modelling, recalling the head of St. Ambrose.
Exh: British Institution, London, 1836, Nos. 2 and 5; Royal Academy, London, 1870, Nos. 65 and 31; 1876, Nos. 137 and 141; 1890, Nos. 142 and 144.
Lit: Head, *Handbook of the History of the Spanish and French Schools of Painting*, London, 1848, p. 131; Waagen, *Treasures of Art in Great Britain*, London, 1854, II, p. 67; *Studio*, New York, February 8, 1890, p. 103; Mayer, *Sevillaner Malerschule*, p. 150; Kehrer, pl. 70 and 71, p. 108; S. I, 39, 44; G. I, 270-273.

Archbishop of Crete, later Patriarch of Constantinople, a Carmelite († 1366). Clad in white and brown Carmelite habits. The pose anticipates *124* and *126*, at Cadiz. See pp. 22, 30.

43. SAINT CYRIL OF CONSTANTINOPLE. Boston, Museum of Fine Arts, No. 22-642. 91 × 32 cm. About 1630-2. Inscribed: S. CIRILLO.   Figure 23

For History, Dating, Exhibitions and Literature: See *42*.
General of the Carmelite Order († 1225) and a fervent champion of the dogma of the Immaculate Conception, so greatly venerated at Seville, particularly in Zurbarán's time. Dressed in white and brown. A somewhat similar position repeated in *130*, at Cadiz. See p. 22.

SAINT FRANCIS. 1632. Buenos Aires, Dr. Alejandro E. Shaw (Cat. No. 61)

FIG. 23   Cat. No. 43   FIG. 24   Cat. No. 46   FIG. 25   Cat. No. 47   FIG. 26   Cat. No. 48

44. SAINT FRANCIS. St. Louis, City Art Museum, No. 47-1941. 91 × 32 cm. About 1630-2.   Plate 31

History: See *42*. Soult sale, May 19-22, 1852, No. 38, frs. 690; bought 1941, from A. Seligmann, Rey & Co., New York.

Dating: See *42*.

Lit: S. I, 170; G. I, 270-273.

Franciscan cord and grey-brown habit. Guinard suggests that it is St. Francis because so identified in the Alcazar, in 1810, No. 271. In the Museum of Historic Art of Princeton University is a copy, by the shop; less precise in modelling of face, hands and feet; the draperies lacking Zurbarán's sculpturesque form. This copy was in the Galerie Espagnole, Louvre, 1838, No. 358; Louis Philippe sale, No. 265, £41, to Graves for Lord Northbrook; Lord Northbrook sale, Christie's, May 3, 1940, No. 44, £241, to David Koetser, New York, who sold it to Princeton. Another copy (56 × 33 cm.) in the Museum, Pontevedra, Spain, on deposit from the Prado, reproduced in *The Studio*, CXL, July-December 1950, p. 143. See p. 22.

45. SAINT BLAISE. Sinaia, Pelesh Castle, formerly King Michael of Roumania. 92 × 31 cm. 1630-2. Inscribed: S. BLAS.

History: See *42*. Soult sale, May 19-22, 1852, No. 37 bought by Sacchi; Barclay; Bamberg, Nice; King Charles I of Roumania.

Dating: See *42*.

Lit: L. Bachelin, *Tableaux anciens de la Galerie Charles I, roi de Roumanie*, Paris, 1898, No. 175; V. von Loga, *Malerei in Spanien*, Berlin, 1923, p. 217; G. I, 270-273.

To judge from a photograph, appears partly by the shop.

46. SAINT AGATHA. Montpellier, Musée Fabre, No. 171. 130 × 61 cm. 1630-2.   Figure 24

History: Guinard suggested that, with *47-48* and a *St. Ferdinand*, it formed an altar in the Carmelite church of San Alberto, Seville. *42-45* were in the same church. Alcazar, Seville, 1810, No. 232; Soult sale, 1852, No. 34.

Dating: Same as *42-45, 47-48*.

Exh: Musée de Montpellier, Paris, Orangerie, 1939, No. 105.

Lit: F. B. Mercey, *Étude sur les Beaux-Arts*, Paris, 1855, pp. 265-266; Mayer, *Historia de la pintura española*, 1942, p. 332 ('early'); G. I, 273; S. IV, 256.

Dark green-blue bodice, citron sleeves, plum-coloured skirt, vermilion mantle. The *St. Ferdinand*, companion piece in the Alcazar, 1810, and in the Soult sale, No. 39, is probably identical with a painting reproduced in the catalogue of the Dollfus sale, Paris, November 11-13, 1912, No. 81, measuring 125 × 63 cm., and shop work to judge by the illustration. See pp. 23-4.

47. SAINT ANDREW. Budapest, Museum of Fine Arts. 146 × 60 cm. 1630-2.   Figure 25

History: See *46*. Alcazar, Seville, 1810, No. 63; taken to Paris by Marshal Soult; sold, 1835, to Duke of Sutherland; his sale, Stafford House, at Christie's, July 11, 1913, No. 144, £273, to Knoedler & Co., London; Baron Herzog, Budapest.

Dating: As *42-45, 46, 48*. Face and draperies related to *41*.

Exh: British Institution, 1837, No. 63; Royal Academy, London, 1870, No. 137; 1890, No. 143.

Lit: Waagen, *Treasures, op. cit.*, II, p. 67; Mayer, *Sevillaner Malerschule*, p. 150; Kehrer, frontispiece, p. 110; S. I, 44; G. I, 270-273; C. Garas, *Bulletin du Musée Hongrois des Beaux-Arts*, September 1949, pp. 24-7.

The pose may have been suggested by Schongauer's engraving of *St. Andrew*. This Saint was considered a Carmelite, because, according to *John* I, 40, before joining the Apostles he was a disciple of St. John the Baptist. St. John is said to have lived following the rule of the Prophet Elias (*Matt.* XI, 14 and XVII, 12-13; *Luke* I, 17), whom the Carmelites have always claimed as their true founder.

48. SAINT GABRIEL. Montpellier, Musée Fabre, No. 170. 146 × 61 cm. 1630-2.   Figure 26

History: See *46*. Alcazar, Seville, 1810, No. 62; Soult sale, 1852, No. 29, frs. 2555.

FIG. 27   Cat. No. 50   FIG. 28   Cat. No. 51   FIG. 29   *Cf.* Cat. No. 52

Dating: Same as *42–47*.

Exh: Musée de Montpellier, Paris, Orangerie, 1939, No. 104.

Lit: F. B. Mercey, *l.c.*, pp. 264–265; S. I, 44; G. I, 273.

Not part of an Annunciation, but companion piece of *47*. Resplendent white robe, over light-rose garment turning to crimson in shadows. Grey wings, painted in white, black and yellow ochre, are outlined by a grey line against dark gray-blue sky. Tree with green and red ochre leaves. All colours are applied in thin glazes. Great luminosity, refinement of colour contrasts, most careful execution. Rich, variegated draperies. Landscape background is as yet not recessed and is still minimized in importance.

49. VISION OF SAINT JOHN THE BAPTIST. Barcelona, José Molas Rifa. 119 × 196 cm. About 1631.   Plates 38, 40

History: Standish Collection, Louvre, 1842, No. 172 (as 'school of Zurbarán'); Frank Hall Standish sale, Christie's, 1853, No. 215 (as 'school of Zurbarán'), to Drax; J. S. W. Erle Drax sale, Christie's, February 19, 1910, No. 132, £6, to Quinto.

Dating: Same as *42–48*. Close to *41*.

St. John hearing the voice of God in the wilderness (*Luke* III, 2). At the right, fresh landscape in blue-green, blue and warm red-brown. In the background, the Baptism of Christ in the river Jordan, the heavens opening, and the Spirit of God descending as a Dove and lighting upon Him (*Matt.* III, 13–17). St. John is linked in his Gospel, chap. I, to the Prophet Elias. Marco Antonio Alegre de Casanate, in his *Paradisus Carmelitici Decoris* (Lyon, 1639, p. 142), quoted that 'Ioannes Baptista verus fuit Religionis Carmeli observator et Princeps cum discipulo suo S. Andrea'. The painting therefore may have come from the Carmelite church of San Alberto, together with *42–48*. An altar, painted at San Alberto about 1630 and still in place, is topped by a painting of similar oblong shape. See pp. 15, 22, 30.

50. CRUCIFIXION. Rome, Private Collection. 214 × 144 cm. About 1631.   Figure 27

History: In 1914 belonged to Dr. M. K. Rohe, Munich.

Dating: More linear and less fusing than *51*, thus slightly earlier.

Lit: Kehrer, pl. 3–4.

Related in pose to *51*, but sharper, more precise and dry in modelling. Mayer believed it to be a shop piece. The author has not seen it, nor a similar version at Castro Urdiales (Santander) (*42a*). See pp. 21, 191.

51. CRUCIFIXION. Motrico, Guipuzcoa, Parish Church. 272 × 198 cm. About 1631.   Figure 28

Dating: Softer, less dramatic and probably slightly later than *38*.

Lit: Tormo, 'Un Zurbarán, el Cristo de Motrico', *Cultura Española*, 1906, IV, p. 1140.

The draperies of the loincloth are related, in a general manner, to *38* and *50*, but are more delicate and sensitive. See p. 21. In the sacristy of the Merced, Cusco, Peru, there attributed to Velázquez, is a shop variant, perhaps with touches by Zurbarán. A copy of that picture is in San Pedro at Cusco. See p. 191.

52. MAGNIFICAT ANIMA MEA DOMINUM. Barcelona, Felix Millet. 115 × 92 cm. About 1630-1. Signed: F. Z. Inscribed: MAGNIFICAT ANIMA MEA DOMINVM.   Plate 37

History: Discovered by Manuel Gómez-Moreno at Sanlúcar de Barrameda.

Dating: The simple, unaffected modelling of the face and of the warm, fleshy hands is in the manner of *41*.

Exh: *Siete obras maestras*, Sala Parés, Barcelona, 1949–50, pls. LXV–LXVIII (as by Velázquez).

The text follows *Luke* I, 46: 'My soul doth magnify the Lord'. The pose and the cartouche are derived from an Antwerp engraving of the subject after Marten de Vos, published by Philip Galle in Geeraard de Jode's *Thesaurus sacrarum historiarum*, 1579-1585, p. 37 (fig. 29). Light blue cloak, crimson gown, yellowish-grey scarf. Yellow sky, grey cartouche, white clouds with touches of pink and yellow. Markedly medieval in its devout, earnest emotion, and its silent contemplation. Attributed to Velázquez, but characteristic of Zurbarán also in the colours, the w-shaped folds at the left shoulder, the sharp outlines of the cloak and of the inner veil.

53. SAINT FERDINAND. New York, Frederick A. Mont. 127 × 102 cm. 1631-2.   Figure 30

History: Unnamed sale, at Sotheby's, London, July 3, 1946, No. 173 (as by Sustermans).

Dating: The conception of space, the painting of the costume, and the lighting of the hands are close to *41*.

The Liberator of Seville from the Moors was a popular subject, repeatedly painted by Zurbarán and his assistants. Black cap, white feathers, steel-grey half-armour, pink baldric, salmon pantaloons, white hose, tan boots. Zurbarán painted the hands, which are modelled with exciting play of light and shade, the ghost-like sword, the crisp pantaloons, and the animated outline of the legs. Face, armour, baldric and chair disclose the brush of an assistant.

54. SAINT DIEGO OF ALCALÁ. Madrid, Prado, No. 2442. 93 × 99 cm. 1628–33. Figure 31

Collections: José Luis de Sola, Cadiz, 1905; purchased from his son, 1932.

Dating: Mayer 'close to 1640'. However, an early date explains the lack of organic plastic structure in the heads, the crowding of figures at the left, and a certain flatness of space. For the sketchy handling of some of the faces, cf. St. Joachim in *12*. The technique of the Saint's face is closer to *55, 58, 79–83*.

Exh: Madrid, 1905, No. 80.

Lit: Mayer, *Historia de la pintura española*, 1942, p. 342; S. I, 169.

By a miracle, at the approach of a superior and two friars, the bread for alms furtively carried in his lap by Saint Diego of Alcalá is changed into violet and yellow flowers. All four friars wear grey Franciscan habits. See p. 22.

55. UNKNOWN MERCEDARIAN. Madrid, Royal Academy of Fine Arts. 204 × 122 cm. About 1631–2. Plates 32, 35

History: One of eleven full-length Mercedarians, by Zurbarán, seen by Ceán in the Library of the Mercedarians, Seville. Entered the Academy in 1813 with the confiscated collection of Prime Minister Godoy.

Dating: The earliest of the series, comprising also *58, 79–83* and *85a*, which see.

Lit: Ceán VI, 49; Mayer, *Boletín soc. esp. excursiones*, 1936, XLIV, p. 44; S. I, 46; G. II, 173–175.

In power of conception, precision, and refined draftsmanship, the most successful of the series. Pronounced portrait-like character, as if painted from life, in contrast to *79–83*. Stylistically related to *56*. Eight cm. added at either side. See pp. 14, 30, 191.

FIG. 31 Cat. No. 54

56. SAINT MARGARET. London, National Gallery, No. 1930. 194 × 112 cm. About 1631–2. Plates 33, 34

History: Possibly collection of Prince Charles (later Charles IV of Spain) in the Casa de Campo (Casita del Príncipe) at El Escorial by 1789; perhaps one of three pictures said to be from the Escorial and to have been presented by the King of Spain (c. 1855?) to the Second Baron Ashburton († 1864); Lady Ashburton collection, 1871; purchased from her son-in-law, the Marquess of Northampton, in 1903 (see MacLaren, infra).

Dating: The painting of the face recalls *55* and *67*.

Condition: Cut down to 163 × 105 cm., but enlarged after 1871 to present size.

Exh: Royal Academy, London, 1871, No. 74; Arts Council Spanish Paintings Exh. 1947, No. 41.

Lit: Kehrer, pl. 60; *Studio*, November 1937, repr. in colour; S. I, 167; G. III, 30–31; N. MacLaren, *National Gallery Catalogues, The Spanish School*, 1952, pp. 85–6 ('perhaps of the middle thirties').

Zurbarán's only Virgin Saint in contemporary dress, that of a Spanish shepherdess. Vermilion skirt edged in green, blue jacket lined with crimson, white chemise, grey sheepskin top jacket over dark-red bodice. Whitish wool saddle-bag, striped in red, blue-green and yellow. Green sandals. The pose, derived from *4*, reappears in *46, 119, 183*, and inverted, in *179*. See pp. 23–4.

57. SAINT MARGARET. Madrid, Royal Palace (formerly). 156 × 91 cm. About 1631 (?). Figure 32

History: In 1794 engraved by Bartolomé Vázquez, and then in the Royal Palace, Madrid. Unrecorded since.

Lit: Ceán VI, 50; G. III, 30–31; MacLaren, p. 86.

The dragon, attribute of St. Margaret, was thought to be vice attacking a virtuous soul walking serenely on her straight path. Ceán described the picture and identified the Saint. It differs in pose from *56*, which is also larger. Studio copies in the Seville Museum (from the Hospital de la Sangre), and the Göteborg Museum (Louis Philippe sale, No. 389, Drax and Northcliffe sales, April 20, 1923, No. 44, Anonymous sale, Christie's, May 10, 1935, No. 18; Göteborg Museum, *Arstryck*, 1942, No. 1160, ill.). MacLaren, p. 86, rightly calls pastiches the versions at Buckingham Palace (Louis Philippe sale, No. 390) and the Detroit Institute of Arts. Another later copy (190 × 116 cm.) owned by Sra. María Antonia Rius de Armenteros, Madrid. See pp. 23–4.

FIG. 30 Cat. No. 53

FIG. 32   Cat. No. 57   FIG. 33   Cat. No. 58

58. UNKNOWN MERCEDARIAN BISHOP. Pau, Museum. 190 × 115 cm. About 1631–2.   Figure 33

History: See 55. Gift of La Caze, 1872.

Dating: Less compact in the hands and more wavy in the folds, than 55, thus slightly later. See 85.

Condition: Coat of arms and face are entirely repainted.

Lit: Ceán VI, 49; Lafond, *Revue de l'art ancien et moderne*, 1899, V, p. 421; S. II, 134 (as by Francisco Reina); G. II, 174–175.

White Mercedarian robes, next to a red table on which two books, one of them inscribed: 'Biblia sacra'. See pp. 14, 30.

59. THE IMMACULATE CONCEPTION WITH TWO CHILDREN. Jerez de la Frontera, Heirs of Pedro Aladro. 252 × 168 cm. Signed: FRAN^CO DE(interlaced) ZURBARAN FACIE 1632.   Figure 34

Lit: Kehrer, p. 61 (cited the signature); Mayer, *Apollo*, 1928, VII, p. 181; S. I, 45; Pemán II, 170–172.

Raphael Sadeler's engraving (fig. 35), printed at Munich in 1605, anticipates the pose of the Virgin, and the transparent, dynamic clouds. Symbols of the Immaculate Conception are, at the left: the heavenly door (*porta coeli*) and the *stella maris;* at the right, the *scala coeli* and the *speculum sine macula;* below, the tower (*turris Davidica*), cypress (*quasi cipressus*), *templum Dei*, well (*puteus aquarum*), fountain (*fons signatus*), the *hortus conclusus*, palm tree (*quasi palma*), the olive, and the cedar. Omitted are the *vellus Gideonis*, *porta clausa*, *civitas Dei*, and *flos campi*. The inscriptions 'Quae est ista' and 'Aurora consurgens' are from the *Song of Songs*, VI, 10: 'Who is she that looketh forth as the morning, fair as the moon, clear as the sun, and terrible as an army with banners?' The little angels hold pink roses (*quasi plantatio rosae*) and white lilies (*lilium convallium*). Pemán suggests that the two kneeling children may have been orphans and the one on the right destined for the priesthood. The inscriptions issuing from the boys and addressed to the Virgin are taken from the Marian litany. See p. 21.

60. BUST OF A YOUNG ECCLESIASTIC. London, Brinsley Ford. 59 × 46 cm. About 1632.   Figure 36

History: Acquired by Richard Ford in Seville, in 1832, from the Aniceto Bravo collection; offered for sale by Ford at Rainey's Auction Rooms, London, June 9, 1836, No. 32: 'Portrait of the Artist, painted by himself', 'By Zurbarán', bought in. The owner is a descendant of R. Ford.

Dating: A date of about 1632 is suggested by comparison with 59, 32, 35, 68–70, and 104.

FIG. 34   Cat. No. 59

FIG. 35   *Cf.* Cat. No. 59

FIG. 36   Cat. No. 60 (detail)

61. SAINT FRANCIS. Buenos Aires, Dr. Alejandro E. Shaw. 114 × 78 cm. Signed: Franco de Zurbaran fac./1632.   Figure 37
History: Perhaps the *St. Francis*, 1⅓ x 1 *vara* (112 × 84 cm.), listed in 1814 as No. 414 in the sixth room of the library in the Royal Palace of Madrid (information about the inventory kindly supplied by F. J. Sánchez Cantón). Jones de Marcille, Nice; Ivan Stchoukine sale, Paris, Hotel Drouot, June 19, 1908, No. 71; Dr. Carvallo, Paris.
Exh: Grafton Galleries, London, 1913/14, No. 91; Buenos Aires 1939, No. 33.
Lit: *Museo Nacional de Bellas Artes*, Buenos Aires, April 1934, I, p. 11.
Probably derived from El Greco's *St. Francis with a Companion.* Zurbarán plunged the face in shadow and cast the figure in a more Baroque diagonal, preserving Greco's pose of the hands, the dry line of the rope, and the slashing folds. Spiritually, the picture is more dramatically realistic than its model. See pp. 22, 32.

62. THE DEAD CHRIST ON THE CROSS. Seville, Museum of Fine Arts, No. 202. 253 × 193 cm. About 1632–4.   Figure 38
History: Guinard suggested that this is the painting seen by Ceán in the church of the College of Master Rodrigo, today the Diocesan Seminary, whence it entered the museum before 1840.
Dating: More three-dimensional and deeper chiaroscuro contrast than in its prototype, *37*, which must be earlier.
Lit: Ceán VI, 50; Cascales, pl. XXIII; Kehrer, pl. 7; G. II, 200.
Painted in greenish ghost-like hues against a dark-green cross. Green crown of thorns. A plastic black shadow accompanies the body and is set off by grey light against the brown background. In comparison to *37*, the feet are turned more sideways to increase plasticity, and the shadow of the head falls below the armpit, not above it. The folds are more involved and petty. See p. 21.

63. THE VEIL OF SAINT VERONICA. Madrid, Angel Avilés. 109 × 77 cm. About 1631.   Figure 40
Exh: Madrid, 1905, No. 36.
Lit: Kehrer, p. 61.
Christ's head suggested in subtle, brownish tints. Small golden pins hold up the white folds. Their rounded fullness and rhythmic arrangement express a deeply religious feeling. The best of several versions of the subject. By the workshop are the examples at Jerez (Church of San Miguel), Seville (San Pedro), and Madrid (Church of San Sebastián and Guillermo Bernstein Collection). See p. 21.

Exh: British Institution, 1853, No. 89; Royal Academy, 1873, No. 113; New Galleries, London, 1895, No. 95 (as 'Portrait of a Spaniard bought by me at Seville in 1832 which was always considered to be that of Francisco Zurbarán. Signed Richard Ford'); Grafton Galleries, London, 1913/14, No. 189.
Lit: Waagen, *Treasures, l.c.*, 1854, II, p. 223.
The identification as a self-portrait is contradicted by the sitter's age, about twenty years old, and by the black garment with narrow white collar, as worn by ecclesiastics. The modelling of the forehead, the eye-sockets, the eyes themselves, the nose, nostrils, mouth, chin, and the outline of the cheek, bear out the master's authorship. Also the distribution and placing of the white highlights and the shadow transitions, at temples and jaw. Cf. *32*, *35*, and *104*.

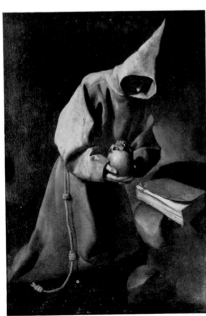

FIG. 37   Cat. No. 61   FIG. 38   Cat. No. 62   FIG. 39   Cat. No. 65

FIG. 40   Cat. No. 63   FIG. 41   Cat. No. 64   FIG. 42   Cat. No. 66

64. THE VEIL OF SAINT VERONICA. Madrid, Heirs of Mariano Pacheco. 101 × 78 cm. Signature: Franco Zurbaran fac 1631.
Figure 41
Condition: Cleaning might give reassurance concerning the authenticity of the doubtful signature.
Exh: Madrid, 1905, No. 35.
Lit: Cascales, pl. LXVII; Kehrer, p. 61.
Christ's face in brown-red sanguine on a light-grey cloak against a black background. Drops of blood streaming down over the forehead and the veil. The fabric is modelled in airy grey shadows. See pp. 21, 191.

64a. THE VEIL OF SAINT VERONICA. Keir, Scotland, William Stirling of Keir. 70 × 51.5 cm. About 1631-6.   Plate 36
History: Standish Collection, Louvre, 1842, No. 183 (as 'Unknown', 42 × 32 cm.); Frank Hall Standish sale, Christie's, May 27, 1853, No. 120, to Sir William Stirling-Maxwell, grandfather of the owner.
Dating: A few years later than 63-64, because of its pronounced mystic quality.
Exh: Manchester, 1857, No. 861; New Gallery, London, 1895-6, No. 174; Spanish Paintings, National Gallery of Scotland, Edinburgh, 1951, No. 43.

65. SAINT AUGUSTINE (?). Bilbao, Felix Valdés. 202 × 105 cm. About 1633.   Figure 39
Collection: Adela Grande Viuda de Barrau, Seville, 1929.
Dating: Although the measurements agree approximately, differences in style and setting make it highly improbable that this is the missing St. Augustine, completing 14-16, of 1626-1628.
Exh: Seville, 1929/30, room VI, No. 5.
Lit: Cascales, pl. II-III (as 'Self Portrait of Zurbarán, dressed as a Bishop').
Lafuente Ferrari suggested, verbally, that St. Leander might be represented. It is probable that this Saint or St. Augustine is meant. Clad in a cope of rich damask bordered in gold and red. White mitre, lined in red with touches of green. See p. 22.

66. THE IMMACULATE CONCEPTION CERRALBO. Madrid, Museum Cerralbo. 200 × 145 cm. About 1632.   Figure 42
History: Marquis of Leganés collection, Madrid, seventeenth century; Marquis of Salamanca sale, Paris, 1867, No. 49, frs. 635, bought in; sold again, 1875, No. 43, frs. 1010. Salamanca seal on stretcher.
Dating: The facial type resembles 67, and a date in the early 1630's is indicated by the relative flatness of the folds of the mantle.

Condition: In Salamanca sale recorded as signed. No signature exists now, but the picture is relined and may have been slightly cut at the bottom.
Exh: Madrid, 1905, No. 78; Royal Academy, London, 1920/21, No. 59.
Lit: Cascales, pl. XXVIII; Kehrer, pl. 53; G. III, 9.
The Virgin, in red and blue, against an orange sky, painted in yellow and vermilion. Below, the serpent of Eve with the apple, and a town with symbols of the Immaculate Conception. See 200, and pp. 19, 21.

67. THE YOUNG VIRGIN PRAYING. New York, Metropolitan Museum of Art, No. 27-137. 117 × 94 cm. About 1632.   Plate 39
Collections: Aureliano de Beruete, Madrid; Dario de Regoyos, Madrid.
Dating: Cascales 'before 1616'; Mayer 'before 11', which he dated 1630-1635, but which actually seems to be before 1629; Kehrer 'in 1638'. Modelling and expression closely resemble 59, of 1632. The drawing of the curtain agrees with many works painted between 1630 and 1634. The suggestion of tenderness in the face foreshadows a more mystic approach which was soon to dominate Zurbarán's style.
Exh: Royal Academy, London, 1920/21, No. 55.
Lit: Cascales, ed. of 1911, pp. 58, 116; Mayer, Sevillaner Malerschule, p. 158; idem, Burl. Mag., 1924, XLIV, p. 212; Kehrer, pl. 54, p. 64; Loga, Malerei in Spanien, p. 267; Wehle, Catalogue, Metropolitan Museum, pp. 234-235; S. I, 45.
White blouse, edged in black; blue bodice; dull-red skirt. Lavender needle-pillow. Faint glory of seraphim. Lilac curtains. Flowers: blue, yellow, white and pink. Pose, expression and costume of Virgin anticipated in 11. The theme is derived from sixteenth-century Bolognese paintings. Cf. also Guido Reni's Sewing Virgin, and an engraving by Jerome Wierix. The apocryphal books place this scene in the Temple. See pp. 2, 22.

68. THE VIRGIN AS PROTECTRESS OF THE CARTHUSIANS. Seville, Museum of Fine Arts, No. 194. 267 × 320 cm. About 1633.
Plates 41, 43
History: One of three (see also 69-70) scenes seen by Ponz and Ceán in the sacristy of the Carthusian Monastery of Our Lady of the Caves, on the outskirts of Seville.
Dating: Cascales '1629'; Marquis of San José gave a date of 1655, untenable both on stylistic grounds and because the document he

FIG. 43   *Cf.* Cat. No. 68

FIG. 44   *Cf.* Cat. No. 70

cited was written only in 1744 (so rightly Hernández Díaz, Sánchez Cantón and Guinard); María Luisa Caturla '1625–1626'. Mayer 'about 1633, but several years earlier' than *69–70*. The technique of modelling employed in the faces, small loaded brush strokes with parallel hatching, is closest to *79–82*, datable in about 1633, a most reasonable date also for *68–70*; for the reddish flesh colour, see *133* and *148*.

Lit: Ponz VIII, 6, 26; Ceán VI, 51; Cascales, pl. LXX; Mayer, *Sevillaner Malerschule*, p. 148; Kehrer, pl. 27, pp. 65–71; idem, *ZfbK*, 1920/21, IV, pp. 248–252; C. Serra y Pickman (Marquis of San José), *Discursos, op. cit.*, pp. 19–20; Hernández Díaz, also in *Discursos*, pp. 45–49; Sánchez Cantón, *La sensibilidad de Zurbarán*, Granada, 1944, pp. 24–25; S. I, 46; Lafuente Ferrari, *Breve historia de la pintura española*, 1945, pp. 165–166; G. III, 1–4; Caturla, *Bodas y obras juveniles de Zurbarán*, Granada, 1948, pp. 34–42; C. Serra y Pickman, *Archivo hispalense*, 1950.

Kehrer found that Zurbarán copied an engraving (fig. 43) by Schelte à Bolswert, a pupil of Rubens. It forms part of a *Life of St. Augustine*, published at Antwerp in 1624. The Virgin, special protectress of the Carthusians, is substituted for the dying St. Augustine. Zurbarán used this book also for *133*. See also pp. 11–2, 16, 23, 30, 191.

69. SAINT HUGH OF GRENOBLE VISITING THE REFECTORY.
Seville, Museum of Fine Arts, No. 203. 262 × 307 cm. About 1633.
Plates 42, 44–45

History, Dating and Lit: See *68*. Also Kehrer, pl. 28; Cascales, pl. LXXIII.

On a Quinquagesima Sunday the cook served, by mistake, meat, forbidden to the Carthusians at all times. They fainted to awake only on Ash Wednesday. Refusing to eat, they sit stiffly erect, resigned to fasting, the very image of the strict monastic life. St. Hugh is shown as he enters to ask where the meat came from. A moment later, it will turn to ashes by the sign of the cross made by the Saint. St. Hugh wears a lavender-blue robe and cape, deep crimson in the shadows. The boy is in light brown-grey, and blue-lavender. His black hat has green tassels. On the table, dishes of red meat, glazed jars in bluish white, and a delicate Chinese porcelain bowl. In the painting on the wall, St. John the Baptist, patron of the Carthusians, in a blue and blue-grey landscape. At the left, a romantic tree with grey-olive bark and salmon wood. The leaves are light brown, light blue-grey and greyish green, all greys being most fluid and glossy. This tree recalls the style of Abraham Bloemaert (1564–1651) and the Virgin and Child are copied in reverse from an engraving after Bloemaert by Boetius Adams Bolswert (1580–1633). The composition as a whole

might derive from Bernardino Passeri's engravings in *Vita et Miracula Sanctissimi Patris Benedicti*, Rome, 1579, pl. 9–C.3, combined with pl. 15–C.9. See pp. 11–3, 22, 191.

70. URBAN II WITH HIS CONFESSOR SAINT BRUNO. Seville, Museum of Fine Arts, No. 204. 272 × 326 cm. About 1633.
Plate 46

History, Dating and Lit: See *68*. Also Kehrer, pl. 29; Cascales, pl. LXXII; S. IV, 254.

Exh: Seville, 1929/30, room VI, No. 4.

The Saint, living only for his inner vision, refuses to be drawn by the energetic Pope into a more active life. Soon afterwards St. Bruno withdrew into a wilderness, where he set up another hermitical community and died among his solitary brethren. He was canonized in 1623. Behind St. Bruno, in black and white, stands a bishop in blue-grey, and another ecclesiastic in brownish carmine. The Pope wears red. Upholstery and hangings in lavender, red, brown, and grey-blue. Rug in vermilion, dark green, and yellow. See pp. 11–3, 22, 191, and fig. 44.

71. STILL LIFE WITH ORANGES. Florence, Count Contini-Bonacossi. 60 × 107 cm. Signed: Franco De Zurbaran faciebt 1633.
Plate 47

Collections: Perhaps identical with the picture in the Mme. J. sale, Hotel Drouot, Paris, May 26–27, 1922, frs. 2600.

Exh: Contini-Bonacossi Exhibition, Rome, 1930, No. 65.

Lit: Mayer, *Burl. Mag.*, 1924, XLIV, p. 212; S. I, 45–46; Seckel, *GdBA*, 1946, XXX, pp. 281–286.

Pewter dish with four large lemons throwing yellow reflections upon the metal; a yellow basket with oranges in red, pink, and yellow; a second pewter dish with a light-pink rose and a white cup filled with water. Brown table. Dark grey background. Mayer praised the picture's monumental simplicity, luminosity, honesty and deep artistic truth. He observed that the objects are not casually placed but deposited devoutly 'like flowers on an altar, strung together like litanies to the Madonna'. Indeed, the objects seem to have a mystical allusion, as a votive offering. Cf. *Deut.* XXVI, 4: 'And the priest shall take the basket out of thine hand, and set it down before the altar of the Lord thy God'. *Deut.* XXVI, 2: 'That thou shalt take of the first of all the fruit of the earth . . . and shalt put it in a basket. . . .' A shop copy on loan at the Fine Arts Gallery, San Diego, California. A later copy with variations in the City Art Museum, St. Louis, Missouri, cannot be connected with Zurbarán. Lacking mysticism, it is conceived as a naturalistic still life not as a religious picture.

FIG. 45   Cat. No. 72   FIG. 46   Cat. No. 76

The soft brushwork lacks precision, while the table throws sharp shadows. One also misses the airiness and the unity of the master's compositions. See pp. 13–4, 24.

72. STILL LIFE WITH NAPKIN. Buenos Aires, Javier Serra. 60 × 79 cm. About 1632–4.   Figure 45
Collections: Ignacio Balanzó, Barcelona.
Dating: The meat cake, painted with the loose brushwork observed in *78a–d*, suggests a date of about 1633. The folds of the napkin compare with those of *52* and *87*. Similar outlines and effects of shading are shown in *34*.
On a grey window sill, a grey pewter plate reflecting in yellow highlights the yellows, vermilions, and light browns of a meat cake. Next, Venetian goblet of transparent glass, embossed in white and gold; a brilliantly white napkin; a glass jar filled with crimson wine. At the right, not visible in the reproduction, a light-grey window jamb. Gudiol suggests, verbally, that the goblet may be dated about 1575 to 1600, and the jar from Cadalso, a village near Madrid, about 1600 to 1630. The technique and design of meat cake and napkin are equivalent to a signature by the artist, here influenced by Van der Hamen's still lifes. See p. 24.

73–74. STILL LIFE WITH FOUR VESSELS. Madrid, Prado, No. 2803. Another version in Barcelona, Museum. 46 × 84 cm. 1633–40.   Figure 47
History: Both canvases were acquired, from different sources, by the late Francisco de Cambó, who donated one to the Prado, and the other to the Museum of Barcelona.
Lit: Mayer, *Burl. Mag.*, 1927, LI, p. 230; Seckel, *GdBA*, 1946, XXX, pp. 287–288; *The Seventeenth Century*, Skira, 1951, p. 101 ill. in colour.
On a brown ledge, a gilded chiselled bronze chalice on a pewter

FIG. 47   Cat. No. 73

dish; a white earthenware amphora; a red earthenware vase with high neck; a greyish-white jar, also on a pewter dish. The shadows form a coherent rhythmic design. The metallic quality of pewter and brass contrasts with the warmth of earthenware, the handmade irregularities of which are carefully observed. The version at the Prado is more subdued in the delineation and vivacity of the objects; it seems more harmonious. The painting at Barcelona has greater life and more plasticity, although each object acts more for itself than in unison. Unless both pictures derive from an unknown original, both may cautiously be accepted as independent, authentic versions. See p. 24.

75. AGNUS DEI. San Diego, California, Fine Arts Gallery. 35 × 52 cm. 1635–40. Inscribed: TANQUAM AGNUS.   Figure 48
History: Perhaps the *Study of a Lamb* sold with the Alphonse Oudry collection, Hotel Drouot, Paris, April 19–20, 1869, No. 129. Sold twice, when in the Arthur Kay, Edinburgh, collection, at Christie's, London, March 22, 1929, and April 8–9, 1943.
Dating: For similarities and subtle differences, compare the ram in *138*.
Lit: S. III, 66–69.

Radiant whites and greys on a grey stone ledge against a dark background. The arrangement, typical of Zurbarán, came to him from Fray Juan Sánchez Cotán, whom he also follows in restricting the picture dramatically to bare essentials. *Acts* VIII, 32: 'Tamquam (ovis ad occisionem ductus est et sicut) agnus coram tondente se sine voce non aperuit os suum.—He was led as a sheep to the slaughter; and like a lamb dumb before his shearer, so he openeth not his mouth.' The classical, similar passage *Isa.* LIII, 7, is so famous that Calderón wrote an allegorical drama 'El cordero de Isaias', the Lamb of Isaiah, that is Christ, 'Ecce Agnus Dei qui tollit peccata mundi' (*John* I, 29; *I Pet.* I, 19). Represented is an ewe lamb, a lamb of atonement serving for a sacrifice for sin (*Num.* VI, 14).

76. A RAM. London, Frank Guymer. 61 × 79 cm. Signed: Franco de Zurbaran facie/1632.   Figure 46
History: Palomino's reference, quoted with *77*, may possibly refer instead to this picture. Recently acquired by a Barcelona collector (?).

Sketchy, spotty modelling. Brush strokes less fused than in the other versions. The author has not seen the painting and can say nothing about the authenticity of the signature. Guinard mentioned still another *Lamb* (72 × 54 cm.), depicted as a walking animal, exhibited by Stanislas O'Rossen, at Madrid, 1905, which may be identical with a *Lamb* by Zurbarán, listed in the *Catálogo de los cuadros de la galería que perteneció al Exmo. Sr. D. Luis de Portilla*, Madrid, 1880, No. 123 (67 × 56 cm.).

SAINT PETER NOLASCO RECOVERING THE IMAGE OF THE VIRGIN. 1630. Cincinnati, Museum (Cat. No. 32)

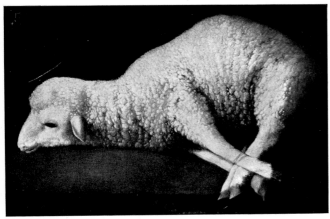

FIG. 48   Cat. No. 75

77. A LAMB. Madrid, Marquise of Socorro. 38 × 62 cm. 1635–40.
Plate 48

History: Perhaps the 'lamb about a year old from the hand of this artist Zurbarán, drawn from life', seen by Palomino at a collector at Seville, who 'says he values it more than one hundred live sheep'. On the back a seal inscribed: REX FERDINANDUS VII, with a key and a trefoil, thus probably given by the king to an ancestor of the owner. Lit: Pal. III, 108; Angulo, *Arch. español de arte*, 1950, pp. 77–78, ill. Yellow horns, pink nostrils. Greenish-grey ledge. Dark background. The woolly coat is painted in creamy whites and browns, stressing three-dimensional effect throughout. Sensitively modelled head. A young ram was used in burnt offerings, that is, offerings of thanksgiving, as in the *Adoration of the Shepherds, 138*, to celebrate the Christ Child's birth.

78. SAINT PETER. Lisbon, Museu Nacional de Arte Antiga, No. 1379. 218 × 111 cm. Signed: Franco de Zurbaran faciebat 1633.
Plates 51, 52

History: The best in quality and the only one signed, of twelve Apostles, transferred to the Lisbon Museum in 1913 from the local church of São Vicente de Fora.
Dating: Formerly erroneously believed to be dated in 1624.
Lit: Museu Nacional de Arte Antiga, O 'Apostolado' de Zurbarán, Lisbon, 1945; R. dos Santos, *Arch. esp. de arte*, 1945, pp. 189–192; Angulo, *ibidem*, pp. 233–235.
Reddish flesh tones, deep-brown shadows, white highlights. Wearing a golden-ochre cloak over a darkish-blue gown. Much repainting in the hands. See pp. 8, 14, 30. An old copy, three-quarter length, in the Greco Museum, Toledo. In order of quality the twelve pictures represent:
(a) Saint Peter.
(b) Saint Mathias (called St. Jude), No. 1369. Forehead plastically modelled in energetic strokes. Powerful hands, in pink with vermilion and with white highlights. Light-grey upper garment, yellow-ochre cloak. The shadowed face in profile against a dark background anticipates some of the Carthusians, *124–130*, at Cadiz. As Angulo suggested, Zurbarán was influenced by Schongauer's engravings of Apostles, here by *St. Matthew*.
(c) Saint Paul, No. 1377. Flesh tones in red-brown earth colour, dark browns, touches of vermilion in the shadows and whitish highlights. Assistants may have collaborated in the green cloak, painted with yellowish lights, and in the vermilion lower garment. The rough, sketchy technique of the head is related to the Hercules series, *93–102*. For the feet and the draperies across the right arm, cf. Schongauer's *St. Paul*.
(d) Saint Philip (perhaps rather Saint Matthew), No. 1374. Simple folds, not without strength. Cleaning may reveal whether Zurbarán painted the ear, nose, and forehead, and possibly the entire head.

(e) Saint Simon, No. 1370. Largely executed by a capable member of the shop: the head is not related organically in its parts and shows too much detail, as do the folds which do not obey a unified pattern. Zurbarán appears to have painted the impressive hands.
(f) Saint James Major, No. 1383. Only the hands are worthy of Zurbarán.
(g) Saint James Minor, No. 1380. This and the two following pictures are essentially shopwork.
(h) Saint John the Evangelist, No. 1381.
(i) Saint Matthew (perhaps rather Saint Philip, resembling Schongauer's engraving of that title in frontal pose), No. 1378.
(j) Saint Thomas, No. 1373. This and the two last ones are of the least quality, and appear to be wholly by the shop.
(k) Saint Bartholomew, No. 1368.
(l) Saint Andrew, No. 1382.
In spirit, pose, and draperies the figures of Zurbarán's *Apostolates* (*78, 144, 145*) recall the engraved series by Callot of 1631.

79. FRAY JERÓNIMO PÉREZ. Madrid, Royal Academy of Fine Arts. 204 × 122 cm. About 1633. Inscribed: M⟨aestr⟩o F⟨ray⟩ GERONIMO PEREZ.
Figure 49

History: See 55. See also 58, 80–83, 85a.
Dating: Later than 55. Stressing the plastic form of the right hand and the distance from the body. Bold effects of foreshortening now used in the left hand. In contrast to 55, no browns are used in the shadows, only light greys, as in *80–82*. The table, not found in 55 but seen in *79–84*, increases the feeling of space. The light, setting off the dark outline of hood and cape, gives the impression of air behind the figure; this device occurs first in *78a*, signed in 1633.
Exh: Madrid, 1905, Nos. 1–4 (together with *80–83*).
Lit: Ceán VI, 49; J. A. Garí y Siumell, *Martyrologium sanctorum Ordinis B.M.V. de Mercede redemptione captivis*, Rome, 1871; idem, *Biblioteca Mercedaria*, Barcelona, 1875; Cascales, pl. XLIX, LI; Sentenach, *Bol. soc. esp. excursiones*, 1913/14, XXI, p. 5; Kehrer, pl. 19, pp. 55–57 ('about 1633'); Mayer, *Historia de la pintura española*, p. 335; S. I, 46; G. II, 174–175; Guinard-Baticle, p. 94 ill. in colour.
Mercedarian writer and professor of theology at the University of Valencia, active a century before Zurbarán. Like *80–81*, not painted from life. See pp. 14, 30.

80. FRAY PEDRO MACHADO. Madrid, Royal Academy of Fine Arts. 204 × 122 cm. About 1633. Inscribed: M⟨aestr⟩o F⟨ray⟩ PEDRO MACHADO.
Plate 49

History, Dating, Exhibitions, and Lit: See 79. Also Kehrer, pl. 21.
Mercedarian writer and professor of theology at Salamanca († 1602). Insistence, force and great plastic power distinguish the modelling of the head and the ample draperies, free and controlled at the same time. The foreshortened head has a three-dimensional quality, a softness and a feeling of volume, as if it were built up in clay. It combines the casualness of a sketch with deliberate plastic shaping of the features. The handling is related to *78a–d*, of 1633. The vermilion table was painted by an assistant.

81. FRAY FRANCISCO ZUMEL. Madrid, Royal Academy of Fine Arts. 204 × 122 cm. About 1633. Inscribed: M⟨aestr⟩o F⟨ray⟩ FRANCISCO ZUMEL.
Plate 50

History, Dating, Exhibitions, and Lit: See 79. Also Cascales, pl. L.
Fray Francisco Zumel (1540–1607) was an outstanding Thomist scholar and professor of philosophy at the University of Salamanca. The collar is so arranged as to lead the eye around the head. Modelled with a very fine brush.

82. FRAY HERNANDO DE SANTIAGO. Madrid, Royal Academy of Fine Arts. 204 × 122 cm. About 1633. Inscribed: M⟨aestro⟩ FR⟨AY⟩ FERNANDO DE(interlaced) S⟨AN⟩. TIAGO PICO DE(interlaced) ORO VERAE(interlaced) FIGIE(interlaced).
Figure 50

FIG. 49   Cat. No. 79   FIG. 50   Cat. No. 82   FIG. 51   Cat. No. 83

History, Dating, Exhibitions, and Lit: See *79*.

Condition: Preservation not as good as of the other portraits, *79–81*, and table covering apparently not by the master.

Fray Hernando (1557–1639) was born and died at Seville, where Zurbarán could have known him. Philip II gave him the nickname 'Pico de oro', that is, 'Golden Tongue', upon hearing one of his moving sermons. After 1631, he was rector of San Laureano, Seville. The words 'VERA EFFIGIES', not occurring on any of the other Mercedarian portraits, suggest that he was painted from life. In contrast to *79–81*

FIG. 52   *Cf.* Cat. No. 82

and *83*, the head has individual character. In Pacheco's *El libro de descripción de verdaderos retratos de ilustres y memorables varones*, a book depicting authentic portraits of distinguished and notable Sevillans, Fray Hernando (fig. 52) looks considerably younger. This book, finished in 1599, remained a manuscript, to which Pacheco added portraits until 1654.

83. SAINT CARMELO, BISHOP OF TERUEL. Madrid, Santa Barbara, Chapel. 198 × 124 cm., enlarged to 213 × 124 cm. About 1633. Inscribed: S. CARMELO OBISPO DE(interlaced) TERUEL.   Figure 51

History: Belonging to the same series as *55, 58, 79–82* and *85a*.

Exh: Madrid, 1905, No. 81.

Lit: See *79*.

Fray Jerónimo Miguel Carmell († 1557) was writing a commentary to the Song of Songs, when, as he arrived at the verse: 'Tota pulchra es amica mea', the Virgin appeared to him (in a glow of golden tones, at the upper right). Saint Carmelo fainted and, coming to, wrote: 'Ita est quoniam ego vidi' ('This is so because I have seen it'). The book in his hands, bearing at the top of the page the words 'De Concepcione', is so inscribed. The Saint wears white draperies; white mitre, lined in red; a blue and red jewelled cross hanging from a red band. Cf. *84*. See p. 22.

84. SAINT CARMELO, BISHOP OF TERUEL. Seville, Museum of Fine Arts, No. 196. 194 × 110 cm. About 1634. Inscribed: S. CARMELO. OBISPO DE TE/RUEL.   Figure 53

History: Mentioned in 1732 in the Sala de Láminas of the Shod Mercedarians, Seville, together with a companion piece. As Guinard proved, this refers to *84–85*, both of which entered the Museum in 1836 coming from the convent.

Dating: About a year after *79–82*, because the lighting is more diffused. In technique, very similar to *68–70* and to *103*.

Lit: See *79*. Also Ponz IX, 3, 48; Cascales, pl. XLVIII; S. II, 132–134 (as by Francisco Reina).

The individualization of the features, indicating the use of a model, distinguishes the head from *83*, depicting the same subject. The face, deeply spiritual, devout and personal, is movingly characterized. Mercedarian shield in red and yellow. Around the neck a vermilion ribbon with a grey and pink cross. In the upper right, the Virgin, clad in blue and light pink, stands on a globe among grey clouds tinged with red. Airy and plastic folds of impressive quality. See p.14.

FIG. 53   Cat. No. 84   FIG. 54   Cat. No. 85   FIG. 55   Cat. No. 85a

85. SAINT PETER PASQUAL, BISHOP OF JAÉN. Seville, Museum of Fine Arts, No. 205. 194 × 110 cm. About 1634. Inscribed: SAN PASQUAL/OBISPO DE(interlaced) JAEN.   Figure 54

History: See *84*.

Dating: Light is surrounding the entire figure and the objects on the table, giving an airy illusion of space. More subtle and painterly than *58*, where to suggest recession, the table is tilted, instead of being foreshortened.

Condition: Disturbing repaint at the front of the habit, and in the hair and gown of the angel.

Lit: See *84*. Also Fray Pedro Cecilio, *Vida y martirio de San Pedro Pascual de Valencia*, Granada, 1629.

Saint Peter Pasqual (1227–1300) was beheaded by the Moors at Granada. He popularized arguments in favour of the dogma of the Immaculate Conception, thus being a fitting companion to *St. Carmelo*. Shortly before Zurbarán painted the picture, a papal investigation, lasting over one hundred years, began of Mercedarian claims that the Saint had been a member of their order. A knife in his neck, he is shown looking up to an angel in vermilion, who holds a gold palm and a green crown of martyrdom. On a green table, a white mitre with vermilion ribbons and a white ink-well. Violet background. The head seems influenced by Ribera. See pp. 14, 22.

85a. FRAY PEDRO DE OÑA, BISHOP OF GAETA. Seville, Museum of Fine Arts (on permanent loan from the Municipality). About 200 × 116 cm. About 1633–4. Inscribed: D⟨on⟩ F⟨ray⟩ PEDRO DE (interlaced) OÑA/ OBISPO DE GAETA.   Figure 55

History: See *55*, also *58*, *80–83*. Discovered in 1951 by the Marquis of Lozoya in the Convent of Mercedarian Nuns at Seville and immediately bought by the Municipality.

Dating: Stylistically closely related to *83*, but by its pose even more designed to lead the eye around the figure.

Lit: See *79*.

Apparently painted from a model. Oña did not sit for it, because he had since 1604 been away in Gaeta where he died in 1626, more than seventy years old. He was a member of the Crown Council, and a writer on Aristotle and on Original Sin.

86. SAINT PETER'S VISION OF THE UNCLEAN BEASTS. Seville, Cathedral, Chapel of St. Peter. 270 × 124 cm. 1633–5.

Plate 53 (Figure 56)

History: One of ten paintings of the altar of St. Peter, still in its original place. Only five, *86–90*, are by Zurbarán, three others by his shop. Of the remaining two, the central *Saint Peter Enthroned* was painted in 1620 or immediately afterwards, long before Zurbarán's pictures for this altar. The tenth, *God the Father*, is an eighteenth-century copy.

Dating: Most controversial. Ceán's date of 1625 was universally accepted, until challenged by Tormo ('strained'), Soria ('1636–1638'), and Lafuente Ferrari ('about 1633'). Guinard first defended the traditional date, then suggested '1625–1630'.

Condition: In need of cleaning and restoration.

Lit: First mentioned by Fernando de la Torre Farfán, *Fiesta de la Santa Iglesia Metropolitana y Patriarcal de Sevilla*, Seville, 1671, p. 155; Pal. III, 108; Ponz IX, 1, 57; Ceán VI, 45, 47–48; Tormo, *Enciclopedia Italiana*, 1937, XXXV, p. 1059; idem, *Bol. soc. esp. excursiones*, 1941, XLIX, p. 7; Mayer, *Sevillaner Malerschule*, p. 148; Kehrer, pp. 33–36; S. I, 156–160; Lafuente Ferrari, *Breve historia de la pintura española*, 1945, p. 165; G. I, 254–257; III, 35; S. VI, 165–173.

Acts X, 11–12: 'And (he) saw heaven opened, and a certain vessel descending unto him, as it had been a great sheet knit at the four corners and let down to earth. Wherein were all manner of four-footed beasts of the earth and wild beasts, and creeping things, and fowls of the air.' The vision of the grey animals lowered in a white sheet taught Peter not to despise the Gentiles but to have them, too, baptized. A subject, rarely shown in art, inspired by Antwerp engravings, e.g., one after Marten de Vos, in the *Acta Apostolorum*, 1579, no. VIII, and another after Stradanus, engraved and published by Philip Galle in 1575, No. 21, where the Saint kneels in profile to the right. The Saint is clad in violet under a brown-orange cloak. The modelling is related to *68–70*, to *78a–d*, of 1633, and to *93–102*, of 1634. See pp. 8, 22, 30, 191.

87. THE REPENTANT SAINT PETER PRAYING. Seville, Cathedral, Chapel of St. Peter. 270 × 124 cm. 1633–5.   Plate 54 (Figure 57)

History, Dating, Condition, and Lit: See *86*.

This was a favourite Catholic Baroque theme aimed at Protestants rejecting confession and penitence. As Kehrer pointed out, like the preceding picture, influenced by an etching of St. Peter by Ribera, dated in 1621 (Kehrer, pl. 2). The head, one of the master's most moving and accomplished, recalls the best heads of the *Mercedarians*, *79–85*, painted about 1633–4. The Saint is modelled with the greatest plasticity. A desire for three-dimensional order animates the drapery folds: enveloping the body, they pull away from it, establishing depth and statuesque roundness. See p. 191

88. THE IMMACULATE CONCEPTION. Seville, Cathedral, Chapel of St. Peter. 323 × 190 cm. 1633–5.   Figure 58

History, Dating, Condition, and Lit: See *86*.

Compare *143*, of 1638. Also related to *68* and *70*, both of about 1633: the folds of the hem of the mantle should be compared to those of Pope Urban's robe, while the face resembles that of the *Virgin as Protectress of the Carthusians*. In comparison to *59*, dated 1632, the draperies are more ample and more High Baroque. Plasticity is stressed to a greater extent; for instance, the hands now open up and let light penetrate between them, and the sleeves show deeper, more dramatic shadows. The Virgin wears a crown, as demanded by Pacheco, *El arte de la pintura*, Seville, 1649, book III, chapter XI. See p. 21, 191.

89. SAINT PETER HEALING THE LAME. Seville, Cathedral Chapel of St. Peter. 76 × 130 cm. 1633–5.   Figure 59

History, Dating, Condition, and Lit: See *86*.

St. Peter, in ochre and lavender-grey, bids the Lame: 'In the name of Jesus Christ of Nazareth rise up and walk' (*Acts* III, 1–10). According to Baronius, thus alone through St. Peter was transmitted the doctrine which heals (i.e., saves). St. John the Evangelist, in pink and green. The Lame, in a very realistic, torn white shirt, a shredded violet garment, and a wavy orange-vermilion mantle, is one of the best small scale figures Zurbarán ever painted. The pose is most closely related to that of *105*, of about 1638. The softly fusing, airy treatment of the picture belongs to Zurbarán at the height of his power. The spatial setting, in an imaginative architecture clearly relating the

FIG. 58   Cat. No. 88

figures to each other and to the front plane, is also characteristic of the mature artist. This is one of his few pictures in which both sides are drawn in perspective, derived (including arches, columns and background figures) from an engraving of the same subject after Marten van Heemskerck, done at Amsterdam in 1572–3. Philip Galle engraved and published it in an *Acta Apostolorum*, Antwerp, 1575, No. 6, (fig. 60). For the main figures, Zurbarán looked at an engraving of the theme after Marten de Vos in another *Acta Apostolorum*, No. II. *89* anticipates the paintings at Guadalupe, *151–158*, of 1638–1639. See pp. 8, 22, 191.

90. SAINT PETER LIBERATED BY THE ANGEL. Seville, Cathedral, Chapel of St. Peter. 235 × 124 cm. 1633–5.

History, Dating, Condition, and Lit: See *86*. S. VI, opp. p. 172, ill.

St. Peter, in violet gray and sienna-ochre, is liberated from Herods' prison by an angel saying: 'Cast thy garments about thee, and follow me'(*Acts* XII, 3–11). The Angel wears pink and green. His head resembles in modelling that of *92*, of 1633–1634. The brushwork of the five paintings Zurbarán did for the Altar of St. Peter is related most closely to that of the Mercedarians, *79–83*, the Carthusians, *68–70*, both of 1633, and to the pictures painted in 1634 at Madrid, *93–103*.

FIG. 56   Cat. No. 86

FIG. 57   Cat. No. 87

FIG. 59   Cat. No. 89

FIG. 60 (Detail)   *Cf.* Cat. No. 89

91. SAINT FRANCIS. Madrid, Maravillas Church. 190 × 110 cm. 1633–4.   Figure 61

Dating: In technique, like its companion piece *92*, related to *68–70* and *79–82*, both of 1633. Comparison with *167*, of 1639, suggests that *91–92* are several years earlier.

Light brown-grey habit against a brown background. See p. 22.

92. SAINT DIEGO OF ALCALÁ. Madrid, Maravillas Church. 190 × 110 cm. 1633–4.   Figure 62

Dating: See *91*.

Holding in his lap white and red roses and standing before a dark wall. For the subject, cf. *54*.

93. HERCULES FIGHTING THE NEMEAN LION. Madrid, Prado, No. 1243. 151 × 166 cm. 1634.   Plate 57

History: One of ten Labours of Hercules, *93–102*, painted together with *103* by Zurbarán at Madrid, between March and November 13, 1634, when he received payment. They were hung in the Hall of Realms of the Buen Retiro Palace, at Madrid.
Lit: Manuel Gallegos, *Obras varias al Real Palacio del Buen Retiro*, Madrid, 1637; Pal. III, 108; Ponz VI, 2, 28; Ceán VI, 52; Tormo, *Bol. soc. esp. excursiones*, 1911, XIX, pp. 215, 307; Cascales, p. 107; Mayer, *Sevillaner Malerschule*, p. 149 ('only four by the artist, the rest by pupils under his guidance'); Kehrer, pl. 36, pp. 77–80 (defended the view, subsequently proved accurate, that all paintings are by Zurbarán, painted close to 1635); Tormo, *Bol. soc. esp. excursiones*, 1941, XLIX, pp. 8, 10 (believed Zurbarán did only three, Nardi the others); S. I, 48 ('all by Zurbarán, painted between March 1634 and 1635'); Lafuente Ferrari, *Breve historia de la pintura española*, 1945, pp. 168–169 (doubted Zurbarán's authorship); Sra. Caturla, *Arch. esp. de arte*, 1945, pp. 292–300 (proved the authenticity of the entire series by publishing Zurbarán's signed receipt, discovered by her); G. III, 29–30; S. V, 75.

By the master, except for the feet which are inferior. The upper body, arrangement in profile, and setting probably adapted, in reverse, from an engraving (fig. 63) by C. Cort, after Frans Floris. The position of Hercules' legs was copied from H. S. Beham's engraving of 1542 representing *Hercules Fighting the Centaurs*. See pp. 8, 11, 14–5, 24, 30, 32.

94. HERCULES KILLING THE HYDRA OF LERNA. Madrid, Prado, No. 1249. 133 × 167 cm. 1634.   Plate 55

History and Lit: See *93*. Also Cascales, pl. LXXVI; Kehrer, pl. 35.
Condition: Appears entirely by Zurbarán, except for the newly painted right foot.

As the second labour, Hercules killed the many-headed Hydra. The animal, in green with yellow and red reflections, flashes its red tongues. Iolaus, holding a torch with vermilion and yellow flames, rushes forward to burn the newly sprouting Hydra heads. A red crab, sent by Hera, bites the hero's right heel, forcing him to bare his teeth in pain. Crushed underfoot, the crustacean transformed itself into the sign Cancer.

95. HERCULES CATCHING THE ERYMANTHIAN BOAR. Madrid, Prado, No. 1244. 132 × 153 cm. 1634.   Figure 65

History and Lit: See *93*.
Condition: In the legs and body, minor collaboration by an assistant.

As fourth labour Hercules snared a wild boar on the slopes of Mount Erymanthos. The hero swings a club at the enraged animal, drawn in brown on the red preparation. In order to concentrate the lights in the centre, Hercules' left foot is hidden behind the head of the boar. Particularly well sketched is the small figure of Hercules in the background.

96. HERCULES CHANGING THE COURSE OF THE RIVER ALPHEUS. Madrid, Prado, No. 1248. 133 × 153 cm. 1634.   Figure 66

History and Lit: See *93*. Also Kehrer, pl. 34.
Condition: Appears to be entirely by Zurbarán.

It is characteristic of the Spanish Baroque that no attempt is made at idealization. The hero, although of extraordinary vigour and virility, is an ordinary citizen whom one might encounter any day in the street. Gushing grey-blue waters, with white highlights, pour through the stables of Augias. Behind, grey rocks with touches of red brown. Particularly exciting and stimulating is the movement of the various planes in the total design. See p. 14.

FIG. 61   Cat. No. 91   FIG. 62   Cat. No. 92

FIG. 63 (reversed)   *Cf.* Cat. No. 93

97. HERCULES SLAYING THE CRETAN BULL. Madrid, Prado, No. 1245. 133 × 152 cm. 1634.   Figure 67 (Plate 59)

History and Lit: See *93*. Also Cascales, pl. LXXVII; Kehrer, pl. 37.
Condition: Face and feet summary in treatment.

Hercules steps vigorously into the path of the grey horns of the brown-skinned bull. A convincing outline defines arms, shoulders, torso, and legs. In the lake (pl. 59), quiet blue waters, with touches of grey and white, reflect the soft variegated greens of the trees. A thin tree with red-brown leaves boldly cuts across the water and the clear grey sky. In purity and contemplative stillness the landscape reminds one of the best paintings by Corot. See p. 14.

98. HERCULES KILLING KING ERYX. Madrid, Prado, No. 1242. 136 × 167 cm. 1634.   Plate 56

History and Lit: See *93*. Also Kehrer, pl. 38.

Erroneously interpreted as Hercules killing the 'Spanish' king Geryon. Neither is Geryon identical with a Spanish ruler Geronte of Tartessus, nor is he Hercules' victim in this painting. Geryon was a three-headed North-African tyrant whom Hercules killed with an arrow, thereupon stealing his cattle and driving it back to Greece. In Sicily, on the way home, Hercules was challenged by King Eryx, a renowned pugilist. Hercules killed Eryx by throwing him thrice to

the ground. Zurbarán painted the hero as he quietly awaits Eryx' last gasp. The pose was derived perhaps from Frans Floris' *Hercules Obtaining the Apples of the Hesperides*, engraved 1563 (fig. 64).

99. HERCULES SEPARATING THE MOUNTAINS CALPE AND ABYLA. Madrid, Prado, No. 1241. 136 × 167 cm. 1634.   Figure 68

History and Lit: See *93*.

On the way to his eleventh task, the finding of the apples of the Hesperides, Hercules separated the mountain linking Europe and Africa into two, Mount Calpe (Gibraltar) and Mount Abyla (opposite it on the Moroccan coast), which became known as the Pillars of Hercules. The hero, holding in each hand an iron bar, pulls the mountains apart. At the lower right lies his attribute, the club, which appears in all ten paintings.

100. HERCULES LIFTING UP ANTAEUS. Madrid, Prado, No. 1248. 136 × 153 cm. 1634.   Figure 69

History and Lit: See *93*.

Condition: The toes of the right foot, the upper arm, and the hair of Antaeus may not be by Zurbarán.
Trying to accomplish his eleventh labour, Hercules defeated the giant Antaeus by lifting him up from the ground. Thus depriving the giant of the source of his strength, he crushed him to death. Hercules' face, in brown-reds, browns, blacks and whites, is very bold and sketchy in execution, and one of the best of the series. The central motif, especially the position of Hercules' arms and legs and of the right arm and leg of Antaeus, is copied from an engraving by H. S. Beham, of 1545. Although relying on the one-hundred-year-old German print, Zurbarán intensified the Baroque energy, violence, and tension of the scene.

101. HERCULES FIGHTING THE THREE-HEADED CERBERUS. Madrid, Prado, No. 1247. 132 × 151 cm. 1634.   Figure 70

History and Lit: See *93*.

Hercules binds Cerberus, the watch-dog of the underworld, painted in grey with light-beige tones. Red reflections around the snout and eyes give more fierceness to the monster. At the left, vermilion and yellow flames are leaping against dark rocks. Behind Hercules, a red fire glows below a grey-blue sky. His wreath of green olive leaves symbolizes the successful execution of this twelfth and last labour, while the yellow-grey skin of the Nemean lion girding his loins recalls the first task.

102. HERCULES SEARED BY THE POISONED ROBE. Madrid, Prado, No. 1250. 136 × 167 cm. 1634.   Plate 58

History and Lit: See *93*.

For having attacked his wife Deianira, Hercules shot the centaur Nessus. The dying centaur made Deianira an unwitting tool of his vengeance by advising her to dip a robe in his poisoned blood and to give it to Hercules. In the distance, Nessus, mortally wounded by an arrow, was copied from H. S. Beham's engraving of 1542. In the centre, the dying Hercules writhes in torment as he tries in vain to pull off the searing robe. From the white cloth, fire leaps up with yellow and vermilion flames. The landscape is darkened by its smoke. Face, hands and body are excellently modelled. The figure is probably inspired by Torrigiani's famous statue of *St. Jerome* (at Seville, then in San Buena Vista, today in the Museum), and by a French woodcut, by Gabriel Salmon, done at Nancy in 1528 (fig. 71). In reverse, it resembles Zurbarán's hero in the pose, the painfully distorted head looking upward, one hand pulling off the robe, one leg thrust out toward the observer. For the position of the left foot, Zurbarán may have thought of Velázquez's *Don Juan Calabazas* (Prado, No. 1205), which on stylistic grounds should be dated in 1634, precisely when Zurbarán was painting the Hercules series and in daily contact with Velázquez. See p. 14.

FIG. 64   *Cf.* Cat. No. 98

FIG. 65 Cat. No. 95

FIG. 66 Cat. No. 96

FIG. 67 Cat. No. 97

FIG. 68 Cat. No. 99

FIG. 69 Cat. No. 100

FIG. 70 Cat. No. 101

FIG. 71   *Cf.* Cat. No. 102

103. THE RELIEF OF CADIZ. Madrid, Prado, No. 656. 302 × 323 cm. 1634.

Plates 60–61

History: See *93*. A companion piece, the *Expulsion of the Dutch from the Island of St. Martin*, is lost.

Lit: Since Ponz VI 27 attributed to Caxés. R. Longhi, *Vita artistica*, 1927, II, p. 8, suggested Zurbarán as the painter. S. I, 43, 47–48 gave detailed reasons for his authorship. Lafuente Ferrari, *Breve*

historia de la pintura española, 1945, p. 168, tended to agree. M. L. Caturla, *Arch. esp. de arte*, 1945, pp. 292–300, reproduced Zurbarán's signed receipt, discovered by her.

Condition: The faces may have suffered through old cleaning. Hands and draperies are better preserved.

On November 1, 1625, the English under Lord Wimbleton disembarked at Cadiz, trying in vain to seize that town. The defender, Fernando Girón, in black with a marshal's red baldric, is seated because of his gout. Behind him, a Knight of Santiago in black wears the red cross. In the centre, the Duke of Medinasidonia (?) in dark armour, red baldric, violet pantaloons. To the right, a commander in half-armour, a jacket of violetish claret slashed with green and embroidered with the cross of Santiago, green sleeves edged in gold, and green hose. Another officer has a grey jacket, red baldric, plum and silver sleeves, and claret hose. A younger officer in grey jacket, blue sleeves, and blue hose. Beyond the pink flag and yellow and rose soldiers of the middle ground, red ships are engaged in a naval action. In the background, lightly sketched figures in black-brown with touches of red and blue. See pp. 7, 14–5, 24, 30, 32.

104. ALONSO DE VERDUGO DE ALBORNOZ. Berlin, Kaiser Friedrich Museum, No. 404c. 185 × 103 cm. Signed: Franc^{co} de Zurbaran f. Inscribed: AETAS 12 A⟨nno⟩s, thus painted in 1635.

Figure 72

History: Oudry sale, Hotel Drouot, Paris, April 16–17, 1869, No. 155, frs. 2400, to Emperor Napoleon III; his sale, Christie's, May 9, 1872, No. 327, £178 to Holloway. Acquired in 1906 from Alfred Morrison, London.

Lit: Cascales, pl. LXVI (as 'Prince Balthasar Carlos'); Kehrer, pl. 44, pp. 84–85 ('not Prince Balthasar Carlos'); Marquis of Saltillo, *Investigación y Progreso*, 1928, II, pp. 33–34, identified the boy by the escutcheon; S. I, 48.

The sitter (1623–1695), later first Count of Torrepalma, was born at Carmona, near Seville. The green cross of the order of Alcántara decorates his half-armour and his escutcheon. Red baldric, plum-coloured slashed pantaloons with pink rosettes, white hose, black shoes. The only undoubted child portrait by the master, although documents show that he did others, it excels by sensitive characterization, and by sharp delineation of draperies. The curiously hesitant, unbalanced stance was to be repeated in Velázquez's *Balthasar Carlos*, of about 1641, at Vienna. While Zurbarán's shadows emphasize shallow space, Velázquez accentuated depth. See pp. 7, 14–5, 30.

FIG. 72   Cat. No. 104   FIG. 73   Cat. No. 105   FIG. 74   Cat. No. 109

FIG. 75   Cat. No. 110

FIG. 76   Cat. No. 111

105. SAINT JOHN THE BAPTIST IN THE WILDERNESS. Seville, Cathedral, Chapel of the Antigua (Old Sacristy). 166 × 158 cm. About 1638.   Figure 73

History: According to a letter to Ponz, of 1779, a gift by Pedro Curiel. Until about 1800 atop a door in the Baptistery.
Lit: Matute, *Archivo hispalense*, 1887, III; Ceán VI, 48; idem, *Descripción de la catedral de Sevilla*, 1804, p. 80 and appendix p. IX; *González de León, op. cit.*, II, p. 81; *Arch. esp. de arte*, 1929, V, p. 174 (letter to Ponz); S. I, 158, 161 ('about 1638'); G. I, 258–259 ('about 1638'); III, 36.

Draped in brown camel-hair skin and a rose cloak. The pose, lighting, mood, strong chiaroscuro and firm modelling are anticipated in Zurbarán's predella painting from the Retable of St. Peter, *89*, which can be only a few years earlier at most. The pose of the legs may have come from a painting of *St. John* by Guido Reni, and was repeated by Zurbarán's pupil Antonio del Castillo in an unpublished painting at the New York Historical Society, there attributed to Velázquez.

106. SAINT BRUNO.

107. SAINT DOMINIC.

108. SAINT FRANCIS.

109. SAINT PETER MARTYR.   Figure 74

Seville, Archbishop's Palace. Life size. About 1636.

Having not been shown these four paintings, the author cannot express an opinion as to whether they are by the master himself, although photographs might lead one to a favourable view. The *St. Dominic* may be compared to the same subject, done by studio assistants, at Castellón de la Plana and at the Convent of the Good Death, at Lima (*171i*). The four paintings probably once formed part of an altar.

110. SAINT CATHERINE. Bilbao, Museum, No. 107. 124 × 100 cm. About 1636.   Figure 75

Companion to *111*. Wearing a vermilion cloak with whitish highlights, and a light-blue bodice slashed and puffed with green and embroidered in gold. Lavender sleeves with yellow highlights. Venetian-red belt; gold neck-chain; gold crown, and red hair ribbon. Grey background. Distinguished colour harmonies, design and modelling speak for Zurbarán's authorship. See pp. 23–4.

111. SAINT ELIZABETH OF THURINGIA (?). Bilbao, Museum, No. 108. 124 × 100 cm. About 1636.   Figure 76

Dating: Comparison with *112* indicates an approximate date for *110* and *111*.
Lit: Gaya Nuño, *Zurbarán*, 1948, pl. XLVIII.

Companion of preceding. Yellow bodice of brocade, patterned in silver and vermilion, pink skirt, green cloak edged in gold. Venetian-red streamers. In her hair a gold crown and a green ribbon bow; around her neck, pearls and a gold chain with dark-grey stones. A sienna book and a yellow palm in her left. Dark- and light-grey background. The attributes may point to St. Elizabeth (1207–1231), one of the most popular Saints in Zurbarán's Seville. See pp. 23–4.

112. THE VIRGIN IN CLOUDS. Llerena, Parish Church. 186 × 103 cm. 1636–8.   Figure 77

History: One of probably fifteen paintings for the High Altar of the church, commissioned on August 8, 1636, and finished before 1641. Discovered by the author. See *113–114*.
Dating: See *110–111* and *146*.
Condition: Poor, much paint having been lost in horizontal streaks, although the face is intact, except for slight damage at the left cheek and temple and the right eye and upper cheek.
Lit: López Martínez, IV, p. 223; G. III, 25 (citing the document of 1636, found by M. L. Caturla).

FIG. 77   Cat. No. 112 (detail)   FIG. 78   Cat. No. 113

Full length, life size, clad in a rose gown and a blue cloak, white kerchief around the neck. The Virgin stands among clouds, her head surrounded by a blue halo, and by an orange-yellow sky turning into carmine-grey clouds. The hands are crossed over her chest and the delicately modelled features suggest tenderness and compassion. The subject is apparently the Virgin of Sorrows. Two paintings, one of the same theme and the other of Christ, resembling *112–113* in pose, complete an Apostolate, of about 1638, at Lima, *144a–o*. See pp. 9, 31–2.

113. CHRIST BLESSING. Badajoz, Provincial Museum. 51 × 26 cm. 1636–8. Panel.   Figure 78

History, Dating, and Lit: See *112*.
Condition: Essentially undamaged, except for the loss of paint at the mouth, lower cheeks, chin and neck.

FIG. 79   Cat. No. 115

The Resurrected Christ, with stigmata on hands and feet, is clad in a grey gown under a vermilion and pink cloak. In his left is a large brown cross. The pose recalls that of *Christ Crowning St. Joseph, 120,* of 1636–7. *113* was the ciborium door of the High Altar. See p. 9.

114. THE DEAD CHRIST ON THE CROSS. Llerena, Parish Church. Life size. 1636–8. Panel.

History, Dating, and Lit: See *112*. Discovered by the author.
Condition: Badly damaged, probably in the fire that swept the church in 1936. At both sides are broad strips of blackened burnt pigment and much loss. These areas affect particularly the arms and hands. Head, body and feet are in relatively good condition, except for part of the left cheek and the entire left ear.

Resembling somewhat two other versions, *62, 170*, but more turning in the sideward tilting movement of the head. The drapery folds are bolder and more blown up than in any other version, but recall *37*. Once probably the pinnacle of the High Altar, the panel is now set high into the top of an eighteenth-century side altar. See p. 9, 21.

115. SAINT EUPHEMIA. Madrid, Dr. C. Jiménez Díaz. 83 × 73 cm. About 1636–40.   Figure 79

History: Bought from a dealer at Cadiz.
Condition: Probably cut from full-length size, since the blue cloak continues to the edge of the relined area, and since Zurbarán seldom painted less than entire figures.

Saint Euphemia was martyred in 307 not far from Byzantium. Soon afterwards a picture of her was painted. It was described two generations later by Asterius as showing the Saint 'with eyes cast down from modesty'. Zurbarán followed this description, giving the Saint an expression that suggests inner contemplation. She wears a crimson-violet gown under a dark-blue cloak changing to a pale greenish-blue in the lights. Pale rose-carmine lips. Brownish-grey background, lighter at the right.
In the version of this subject at the Palazzo Bianco at Genoa, the folds are less ample, the features are prettier, less plastic, and possess less inner life. The left fingers are not formed into a fist. The cloak appears to be green instead of blue, but cleaning may change that colour and may prove that the very dirty painting at Genoa is authentic. At present one might assume it was painted with considerable assistance by the workshop. See pp. 23–4.

116. SAINT URSULA. Genoa, Palazzo Bianco. 172 × 105 cm. About 1636.

History: Perhaps one of ten Virgin Martyrs once in the sacristy of a church belonging to a convent at Seville. Perhaps, together with its companion piece, *St. Euphemia*, and *179–180*, among the ten Virgin Martyrs, ascribed to Bernabé de Ayala, Alcazar, Seville, 1810, no. 327. From there all four pictures were taken to Paris by Marshal Soult, at whose sale, in 1852, the two Genoa paintings were bought by the Duchess of Galliera; bequeathed by her in 1884.
Lit: W. Suida, *Genua*, 1906; S. I, 167; S. IV, 256.

Clad in a green bodice, gold-edged and with pink cuffs, and a greenish-grey skirt. A vermilion cloak trimmed with gold lace falls down over her back. At the lower right, the green hem of an underskirt. Gold crown, ear-rings, necklace and belt. Holding a book in her left and an arrow in her right. The modelling is, throughout, more convincing than that of the companion piece. The features recall perhaps Zurbarán's second wife and resemble those of other Virgin Saints by the master. See pp. 23–4.

117. SAINT LAWRENCE. Leningrad, Hermitage, No. 349. 292 × 226 cm. Signed: Franco de Zurbaran facie/1636.   Figure 80

History: Once in the right transept of San José, church of the Barefooted Mercedarians, at Seville, dedicated in 1636. Companion piece of *118*, which faced it. Alcazar, Seville, 1810, No. 219; taken to

FIG. 80   Cat. No. 117

FIG. 81   Cat. No. 118 (from Reveil)

Paris by Marshal Soult; his sale, 1852, bought for frs. 3000, by Nicholas I.
Lit : Ponz IX, 3, 50; Ceán VI, 47, 49; Cascales, pl. IX; Kehrer, pl. 39; G. II, 180–181.

The sainted deacon wears a richly embroidered chasuble, showing St. Paul in a circular frame set in an elaborate square-edged floral design. The background is developed in bands parallel to the picture surface. See pp. 15, 31.

118. SAINT ANTHONY ABBOT. Unknown collection. 282 × 221 cm.
Signed: Franco de Zurbaran facbat 1636.   Cf. Figure 81

History: See 117. Soult sale, 1852, No. 26, fr. 1000, bought in; sold again Soult sale, 1867, No. 4, and unrecorded since, but perhaps identical with a painting seen by August L. Mayer in a collection belonging to heirs of Napoleon's Marshal Bertier, at Paris.
Lit: See 117. Also Reveil, Musée de Peinture et de Sculpture, Paris, 1828, II, p. 130.

Walking toward the left, holding a rosary to exorcize evil spirits and accompanied by his faithful pig. Not identical with 173 and 186.

119. SAINT APOLLONIA. Paris, Louvre, No. 1740. 113 × 66 cm.
About 1636. Inscribed: s. POLO/NIA.   Plate 68

History: See 120. Alcazar, Seville, 1810, No. 322; taken to Paris by Marshal Soult; his sale, 1852, No. 32, frs. 1200, bought in; Soult sale, Paris, April 17, 1867, No. 5, bought for frs. 6000.
Dating: The date appears to be about the same as that of 117–118, dated in 1636, the year the church was dedicated.
Condition: Owing to a change made by the artist, the underside of the left hand looks too bulky.
Lit: Ceán VI, 49; Kehrer, pl. 62; G. II, 178–179; S. IV, 256–257.

St. Apollonia, patron saint of dentists and protectress against tooth-aches, holds in her right a pair of tongs with a tooth. Clad in a lemon

skirt, a sleeveless rose overdress, and a grass-green mantle. Wreath of claret and vermilion flowers. Vermilion-pink cheeks, rose mouth. The facial type and pose are anticipated in 46 and 56. See pp. 15, 23–4.

120. CHRIST CROWNING SAINT JOSEPH. Seville, Museum of Fine Arts, No. 198. 248 × 166 cm. About 1636–7.   Plates 63–64

History: Guinard suggested that it was the centre of the High Altar of San José belonging to the Barefooted Mercedarians, at Seville (see 117–119, 121–122, 163 from the same church). It would have been flanked by 119 and a St. Lucy, and topped by 121. Alcazar, Seville, 1810, No. 184 (as by Bernabé de Ayala). Entered the Museum before 1840 from San José (or from the Carmelite College of the Good Angel).
Exh: Madrid, 1905, No. 8.
Lit: Ponz IX, 3, 50; Ceán VI, 47–49; Cascales, pl. XXVII; Kehrer, pl. 57; S. I, 162; G. II, 177–180; III, 37–38.

In a yellow and orange sky, God the Father, in rose and white, and the Holy Dove. Christ, in a pink robe and a light-blue cloak, places a wreath of pink, light-blue and white flowers on St. Joseph, in traditional violet and gold-brown. St. Lucy, companion piece of 119, is almost entirely by the shop. After leaving the Soult collection it entered the Museum of Chartres. See p. 15.

121. GOD THE FATHER. Seville, Museum of Fine Arts, No. 207. 240 × 277 cm. About 1636–7.   Figure 82

History: See 120. Alcazar, Seville, 1810, No. 73. Guinard disproved the assumption that the picture was once part of the altar of St. Peter in the Cathedral of Seville. Entered the Museum before 1840 from San José.
Lit: Ponz IX, 3, 50; Ceán VI, 47–49; Kehrer, pl. 1; G. II, 177–178.

Clad in a violet cloak worn over a pink robe. At the lower left, a large blue globe. Yellow and orange sky. Particularly majestic is the outstretched right hand.

FIG. 82   Cat. No. 121

122. THE VIRGIN OF MERCY WITH TWO MERCEDARIANS.
Madrid, Duchess of Montpensier. 166 × 129 cm. About 1638. Figure 83

History: Ceán saw the picture in the sacristy of San José of the Barefooted Mercedarians, at Seville; Galerie Espagnole, Louvre, 1838, No. 337; Louis Philippe sale, Christie's, 1853, No. 62, £65 to Colnaghi for the Duke of Montpensier, in whose Palace of San Telmo, at Seville, it appears in 1866, No. 190. Subsequently for many years at Castle Randan, Auvergne.

Dating: The modelling of the faces and the formation of the folds corresponds to the late 1630's.
Lit: Ceán VI, 49; Cascales, pl. XXXII; R. Ford, *Athenaeum*, London, 1853; A. J. Conte, *Boletín Museo Provincial de Cádiz*, 1925, no. 9, pp. 33–39 (pointed out confusion with *134*); S. I, 160; G. II, 184–185.

The Virgin, crowned with flowers, wears the shield of the Mercedarian Order at her neck. The two angels strewing flowers anticipate, with few variations, the two angels at the lower right of *161*, painted for Guadalupe in 1639. Of the two Mercedarian monks, standing below in adoration, the right one wears a cardinal's red hat. Two much inferior school copies with variations exist, one in the Gardner Museum, Boston, the other in the Lázaro Foundation, Madrid. See pp. 15, 31.

123. THE PENTECOST. Cadiz, Museum of Fine Arts, No. 65. 160 × 116 cm. 1635-7.   Figure 84

History: Provenance unknown, before entering the Museum about 1835.
Dating: In comparison with *124–142*, all from the Carthusian Monastery at Jerez, looks slightly earlier. Recalls *59* and *78a-d*.
Condition: Much obscured by dirt, so that some heads are at present not entirely convincing as work by the master himself.
Exh: Madrid, 1905, No. 13.
Lit: G. III, 20.

Chiaroscuro effects and warm reds give the desired supernatural force to this scene. The Virgin is clad in pink, painted over a dark-blue cloak, which once covered her lap. Around her neck a transparent yellow scarf. The Apostle in the foreground, extreme left, wears vermilion; the next a light-green robe and a yellow cloak. In the foreground at the right, one Apostle in whitish robe and green cloak, the other in a green robe and a light-lavender-blue mantle. In the

FIG. 83   Cat. No. 122

FIG. 84   Cat. No. 123

THE ADORATION OF THE MAGI. 1638. Grenoble, Museum (Cat. No. 139)

FIG. 85   Cat. No. 124   FIG. 86   Cat. No. 125   FIG. 87   Cat. No. 126

middle ground, Apostles in lavender; green; deep blue-green and sienna-ochre; vermilion; and sienna. Red sky, painted in vermilion, yellow ochre, and white.

124. SAINT HUGH, BISHOP OF GRENOBLE. Cadiz, Museum of Fine Arts, No. 71. 120 × 64 cm. 1637–8. Panel.   Figure 85

History: One of eight panels seen by Ponz in the corridor to the sanctuary, directly behind the High Altar in the Carthusian Monastery, at Jerez. Transferred to the Museum in 1835. See *125–132*. One panel, probably *St. Artald*, is lost.
Dating: Zurbarán worked for the Monastery in 1637, 1638 and 1639. *123–132* seem slightly earlier than the High Altar, *133–141*, of 1638–9.
Exh: Madrid, 1905, No. 18.
Lit: Ponz XVII, 6, 16; Ceán VI, 51; E. Romero de Torres, *Boletín Comisión Provincial de monumentos históricos y artísticos de Cádiz*, I, 1908, pp. 98–99; Tormo, *Época*, February 13, 1909; Kehrer, pl. 32; López Martínez, II, 25; S. I, 163; G. III, 14–20; Pemán IV, 223–227.

Forewarned by a vision of seven stars (appearing at the upper right in a pink-carmine sky and signifying the coming of St. Bruno with six companions) St. Hugh in 1084 gave the plot of land near Grenoble whereon the Carthusian Order was founded two years later. The Saint wears a blue cape over white Carthusian robes, and on his head a white and gold mitre. See pp. 8, 15–6, 23, 31.

125. SAINT ANTHELMUS. Cadiz, Museum of Fine Arts, No. 70. 120 × 64 cm. 1637–8. Panel.   Figure 86

History, Dating, and Lit: See *124*.
Exh: Madrid, 1905, No. 17.

The first General of the Carthusian Order and Bishop of Belley is shown as an old man, shortly before his death in 1178. His withered face, with carmine lips, is in the shadows. It is painted very thinly directly on the brown preparation. On a blue ribbon around his

neck is a gold cross set with black jet. At the right a table covered with carmine fabric edged in gold. Dark background.

126. SAINT BRUNO HOLDING A CROSS. Cadiz, Museum of Fine Arts, No. 72. 122 × 66 cm. 1637–8. Panel.   Figure 87
History, Dating, and Lit: See *124, 127*.
Exh: Madrid, 1905, No. 19.

The dark profile against a dark blue background is a *tour de force* of chiaroscuro painting. White garments contrast with the airy darkness of the sombre brown foreground and of the grey, cloudy sky. See p. 22.

127. THE BLESSED JOHN HOUGHTON. Cadiz, Museum of Fine Arts, No. 73. 122 × 66 cm. 1637–8. Panel.   Plate 65
History, Dating, and Lit: See *124*. Like *126* and *131–132*, two cm higher and wider than the other panels and with a rounded top. *126* and *127* faced each other and flanked the sanctuary. *131* and *132*, also facing each other, were originally opposite them on the back side of the High Altar, but Ponz saw them in the church proper on the doors leading through the High Altar to the sanctuary. *124* and *125* were set into the left wall (Gospel side) of the corridor, turned in the same direction as *126*; *128–130* were set into the right wall (Epistle side), turned in the direction of *127*.
Exh: Madrid, 1905, No. 20.

The prior of the London Charterhouse was martyred by Henry VIII in 1538. He stands in profile in a brown cave. With his right hand he offers his heart. Around his neck falls the brown-yellow rope of his martyrdom.

128. THE BLESSED CARDINAL NICHOLAS ALBERGATI. Cadiz, Museum of Fine Arts, No. 74. 120 × 64 cm. 1637–8. Panel.
     Figure 88

History, Dating, and Lit: See *124;* Guinard-Baticle, p. 95 ill. in colour.
Exh: Madrid, 1905, No. 21.

FIG. 88   Cat. No. 128   FIG. 89   Cat. No. 130   FIG. 90   Cat. No. 132

The Carthusian Cardinal (1375–1443) looks up in an ecstatic vision. Over white Carthusian habits he wears the rose cape and carmine hat of his dignity. In the background at the right, rectangular areas in light grey represent architecture in an interesting abstract pattern. The face is modelled in pink-yellow lights and transparent dark grey shadows; the mouth is brown-carmine. The pose may be compared to *117* and *194*. Jan van Eyck painted Albergati from life, 1431 (Vienna).

129. SAINT HUGH, BISHOP OF LINCOLN. Cadiz, Museum of Fine Arts, No. 68. 120 × 64 cm. 1637–8. Panel.   Plate 66

History, Dating, and Lit: See *124*.
Exh: Madrid, 1905, No. 15.

The famous builder of Lincoln Cathedral wears a bishop's blue cape. He holds a golden chalice with the small figure of the nude, blessing Christ Child standing in it. Behind the Saint appears his symbol, the white swan of Stowe, friend of the Bishop and guardian of his sleep. To the right, against a blue sky, a turreted building. See p. 191.

130. UNKNOWN CARTHUSIAN BISHOP. Cadiz, Museum of Fine Arts, No. 69. 120 × 64 cm. 1637–8. Panel.   Figure 89

History, Dating, and Lit: See *124*.
Exh: Madrid, 1905, No. 16.

Perhaps St. Ainald, Bishop of S. Jean de Maurienne and prior of Portes (1132–56). St. Ainald was, however, canonized only in the nineteenth century. The Carthusian stands in bold chiaroscuro against light-grey buildings and a light-blue sky. At the left, dark-brown ruins. The dark upper body is set against a light background, while the white habit is framed by deep darks. The bishop's cape is painted in carmine and blue giving an effect of lavender.

131. ANGEL WITH CENSER. Cadiz, Museum of Fine Arts, No. 75. 122 × 66 cm. 1637–8. Panel.   Plate 67

History, Dating, and Lit: See *124*, *127*. Also S. IV, 257.
Exh: Madrid, 1905, No. 22a.

Bright-yellow gown, crimson bodice, blue streamer, blue leggings with gold ornaments. Gold chain around the waist and gold censer (*Revel.* 8, 3). Blue wings with much white and red. Light-grey background. Three-dimensional space stressed by placing one hand and one foot in darkness, and by the curving streamer. In comparison with the companion piece, *132*, the pose is firmer, the drapery folds more forceful and plastic. The costume and poses of both Angels derive from Flemish sixteenth-century prints, recalling in the stance the cut-out borders, tassels and leggings, for example, the engraving of *Dan*, of 1575, by Pieter de Jode after Crispin van den Broek. (⁴⁴)

132. ANGEL WITH CENSER. Cadiz, Museum of Fine Arts, No. 76. 122 × 66 cm. 1637–8. Panel.   Figure 90

History, Dating, and Lit: See *124*, *127*, and *131*.
Exh: Madrid, 1905, No. 22b.

Clad in a light-pink robe, a light-green bodice with gold buttons and tassels, and light-green leggings with vermilion lining and gold ornaments. His wings, painted in grey with blue and a little red, are most feathery and inviting to the touch by their realistic texture. The blond hair is painted in whitish colours on brown. He wears a pearl diadem with a small cross. The folds are more subdued than in the companion piece, *131*, and partly weak and indecisive. Slight collaboration by an assistant is possible. See p. 191.

133. THE BATTLE OF EL SOTILLO. New York, Metropolitan Museum of Art, No. 1920–104. 335 × 191 cm. 1638.   Plate 62

History: Rallón (died 1689), cited by Guinard, described the composition of the High Altar of the Carthusian Monastery of Our Lady of Protection at Jerez. It consisted of *133*, *135–140*, and possibly *134* or *141*. *133* was the centre of the altar. The later collocation of *133–134* in the Lay choir, where Ponz saw them, appears to be due to an early eighteenth-century rearrangement. Galerie Espagnole, Louvre, 1838, No. 355; Louis Philippe sale, Christie's, 1853, No. 405, £160 to Lord Taunton; Bought from his heirs in 1920.

Dating: *138* is signed and dated in 1638, and *140* in 1639. By their style most of the paintings for the High Altar were painted in 1638.
Lit: Fray Esteban Rallón, *Historia de Xerez de la Frontera*, partly published in 1926, pp. 139 ff; B. Gutiérrez, *Historia de Xerez de la Frontera (1787)*, Jerez, 1886, I², pp. 231–232; Ponz XVII, 6, 20; Ceán VI, 51; Ford, *Atheneum*, 1853 ('the picture of the day'); Cascales, 1911, p. 89; idem, 1918, pp. 43, 54; Kehrer, p. 71; H. B. Wehle, *Bulletin, Metropolitan Museum*, 1920, XV, pp. 242–245; Loga, *Malerei in Spanien*, p. 275; C. Pemán, *Boletín Museo de Bellas Artes de Cádiz*, 1922, IV, No. 5, note p. 12; H. B. Wehle, *Catalogue, Metropolitan Museum*, 1940, p. 235; S. I, 45, 154; G. III, 14–20; Pemán IV, 203–227.
The battle of El Sotillo, 1370, was won through the intercession of Our Lady of Protection, who by a heavenly light uncovered to the Christian defenders the Moors waiting in ambush. A hermitage, erected on this spot and still existing, appears in the background. The Carthusian monastery was built nearby two hundred years later and dedicated to Our Lady of Protection. The soldier, serving as a repoussoir figure at the left, is clad in brown, with a black hat, white collar, and lavender hose. Otherwise the picture is mostly derived from an engraving by Schelte à Bolswert, *St. Augustine Appearing to Francesco Gonzaga, Duke of Mantua* (fig. 91), in the *Life of St. Augustine*, Antwerp, 1624, used also for *68*. The Virgin, in lilac and blue, replaces the St. Augustine of the print. Zurbarán took over the dark diagonal of the lower left against a lighter background. As in the print, profile heads of soldiers and a battery of lances appear above the large halberdier. The two riders nearest him are faithfully copied from the two heads above the horse, which is also used in the painting. The dark half-length soldier, at the right, in the Bolswert print wears a large moustache and is reversed in position. See pp. 8, 16, 24, 31.

134. THE VIRGIN OF THE ROSARY WITH CARTHUSIANS.
Poznań, Muzeum Wielkopolskiego, Raczynski Collection. 325 × 190 cm. 1638.   Figure 92

History: See *133*. Seen by Ponz in the Lay Choir, but because of measurements, subject and composition perhaps originally in the second tier, centre, of the High Altar of the Carthusian Monastery at Jerez (see, however, Pemán IV, 216–218). Galerie Espagnole, Louvre, 1838, No. 331; Louis Philippe sale, Christie's, 1853, No. 142, £165 to Count Raczynski.
Dating: Mayer, at one time, suggested 1626, but stylistic similarity and former physical proximity to *133* point to 1638.
Lit: See *133*. Also Kehrer, pl. 30, pp. 70–71 ('1635').

The Christ Child is blessing the world. Crowned with a wreath of roses and a golden crown, the Virgin, clad in a pink gown, is receiving a rosary from a little angel. Yellow and rose sky. Below, on a colourful

FIG. 91   Cf. Cat. No. 133

FIG. 92   Cat. No. 134

Oriental rug strewn with roses, Carthusians kneel in adoration. Although their poses derive from those of *68*, of 1633, the space is now more clearly indicated by the shadows and the drapery folds are more enveloping and softer.

135. SAINT JOHN THE BAPTIST. Cadiz, Museum of Fine Arts,
No. 66. 61 × 81 cm. 1638.   Plate 86
History: See *133*. Entered the Museum from the Monastery in 1835.
Dating: See *133*.
Exh: Madrid, 1905, No. 14.
Lit: See *133*. Ponz, XVII, 6, 16; Kehrer, pl. 31; Cascales, pl. LXXIV.
St. John the Baptist was included in the High Altar as the patron of the Carthusians. See *69*. He wears a crimson-violet cloak, turning to dark violet in the shadows. The head, excellent in modelling, shows fat pigments, thin shadows, and transparent hair. The hands are more sketchy and hurried in execution, and the silvery lamb is somewhat feeble. Note the chiaroscuro of the body and the contrast against the brown rocks at left and the grey boulders at the right.

The four *Evangelists* at the Museum of Cadiz, cited by Ponz as part of the High Altar and as from the hand of Zurbarán, although probably designed by the master, were executed by his assistants to judge by their style. Pemán IV, 220–221, indicates hypothetically the original location of these pictures. See p. 22.

FIG. 93   Cat. No. 136

136. SAINT LAWRENCE. Cadiz, Museum of Fine Arts, No. 67.
61 × 81 cm. 1638.   Figure 93

History, Dating, and Lit: See *133*. See also *135*, the companion piece.
C. Pemán suggested that St. Lawrence was included in the High
Altar because of the special cult devoted to him by the Carthusians.
Clad in a richly gold-embroidered, vermilion cope, worn over a
white surplice. Leaning against him is the huge grill of dark-blue-grey
iron on which he suffered martyrdom. The hands recall in the bold,
sketchy technique the art of Ribera. The trees are a liquid green, with
fine detail and minute stippled leaves in yellowish-green and dark
green. On the left, beyond the brown earth of the foreground, a lake
reflects the colour of the trees. Dramatic effects are produced by
sharply delineated dark silhouettes.

137. THE ANNUNCIATION. Grenoble, Museum, No. 559. 261 ×
175 cm. 1638.   Plates 69, 71

History: See *133*. In the side aisles of the High Altar. Brought to the
Museum at Cadiz upon the secularization of the Carthusian Monastery
at Jerez in 1835, it was acquired with at least six other Carthusian
paintings in an underhanded way by Baron Taylor for the Galerie
Espagnole, Louvre, 1838, No. 325; Louis Philippe sale, Christie's,
1853, No. 157, £1700 (together with *138–140*) to Colnaghi for the
Duke of Montpensier; his collection, 1866, No. 186. Gift of General
de Beylie, who bought *137–140* in 1904.
Dating: See *138, 140*.
Exh: Boston, Museum of Fine Arts, 1874, Nos. 1–4 (with *138–140*).
Lit: See *133*. Ponz XVII, 6, 16; Cascales, pl. XIX; Kehrer, pl. 48;
S. I, 156–158.
The Virgin is clad in a rose-claret gown, a blue cloak, and a sienna
veil. Saint Gabriel wears a slate gown, painted over a dark preparation
and giving the effect of lavender. This gown is covered almost
entirely by a vermilion garment highlighted in yellow. Yellow scarf,
in the shape of a streamer, at the left shoulder. Blue wings with touches
of greys and browns. Above, reddish-brown clouds against a yellow
sky serve as a heavenly balcony for pink seraphim, a small nude angel
and two large angels, one in blue, the other rose. The cloudburst
relates heaven and earth. A typical Baroque version of the theme,
derived from Antwerp prints, cf. the engraving in Geeraard de Jode's
Thesaurus sacrarum historiarum, 1579, p. 66. See p. 16.

138. THE ADORATION OF THE SHEPHERDS. Grenoble, Museum,
No. 560. 261 × 175 cm. Signed: Franco de Zurbaran Philipi/IIII
Regis Pictor faciebat/1638.   Plates 70, 72

History: See *137* (also *133*); Galerie Espagnole, Louvre, 1838, No. 327;
Louis Philippe sale, No. 159; Duke of Montpensier, *Catalogue*, 1866,
No. 179.

Exh: See *137*, also Seville, 1896, No. 26.
Lit: See *133* and *137*, also Cascales, pl. XX; Kehrer, pl. 49; *Bulletin,
Musées de France*, VII, 1935, p. 28.
On top of a brown saddle-bag of coarse wool embroidered in yellow,
red, and green, the Christ Child rests on a white sheet. The gesture of
the Virgin showing the Child to the shepherds signifies the first
recognition of Christ by man, and was so traditionally represented at
least since 1550. St. Joseph wears violet and ochre-orange. To the left,
a boy in brown and a grinning girl in white and vermilion. Behind
them, a singing angel in light green with yellow. Another, in white
painted with a phosphorescent effect over a dark preparation, plays
a light-brown guitar. The shepherds are in lavender grey, olive-green,
and brown, respectively. Dark night sky. The top vaguely recalls
that of Raphael's *St. Cecilia*, at Bologna. The harp-playing angel wears
vermilion, slate, and pink. See pp. 16, 21.

139. THE ADORATION OF THE MAGI. Grenoble, Museum, No. 561.
261 × 175 cm. 1638.   Figure 94

History: See *137* (also *133*); Galerie Espagnole, Louvre, 1838, No. 328;
Louis Philippe sale, No. 160; Duke of Montpensier, *Catalogue*, 1866
No. 189.
Exh: See *137*.
Lit: See *133* and *137*, also Kehrer, pl. 50; Guinard-Baticle, p. 93, ill. in
colour.
One of Zurbarán's most colourful paintings, particularly rich in blue.
The Virgin wears an intensely blue cloak over a pink claret gown. The
Christ Child is in white and grey. Caspar has an ermine-collared
mantle of rich gold damask woven with carmine. His gold crown has
a light-blue peak. A page, in dark blue, holds up his train. Melchior
wears a rose-grey jerkin, with a gold tassel and edged with pearls,
over a dark-blue brocade woven with a floral pattern in gold and
green. His sleeves are dark blue, and a green cloak hangs from his left
shoulder. Gold jewelry at neck and waist. His gold crown fits over a
red peaked cap with a yellow feather and a blue neck veil. Balthasar,
the Moorish king, is clad in rich rose. His turban, in white with green
stripes, contrasts with dark-red feathers above. Behind a dark architecture, the sky is a luminous blue, the horizon light yellow. See p. 21.

140. THE CIRCUMCISION. Grenoble, Museum, No. 562. 261 ×
175 cm. Signed: Franco de Zurbaran faci/1639.   Figure 95

History: See *137* (also *133*); Galerie Espagnole, Louvre, 1838, No. 329;
Louis Philippe sale, No. 140; Duke of Montpensier, *Catalogue*, 1866,
No. 174.
Exh: See *137*.
Lit: See *133* and *137*, also Cascales, pl. XXII; Kehrer, pl. 51.
The legend says that Rabbi Simeon in his translation of *Isaiah*
foretold the Virgin birth of Christ. (See also *Luke* II, 25–35.) Here,
clad in a violet cloak over a blue gown, he holds up the Child to the
high priest. The faces of both old men are strongly influenced by
Ribera. The high priest wears elaborate, multi-coloured garments
(see *Exod.* XXVIII, 2–39), inspired by Flemish art: a golden helmet
with a half-moon and blue earcaps; a rose shawl; a violet upper robe
embroidered in gold, blue and light brown-yellow; a blue under-robe
edged in gold and pearls, enriched at the lower border with the
traditional golden bells and pomegranates; and under all this a white
habit visible below and at the sleeves. St. Joseph is at the right, next
to a man holding a candle, whose eyes are hidden by a vermilion
peaked cap worn over a white mantle edged in blue. The page has
tan shoes, blue hose, a violet slashed jacket, woven with silver thread,
and a green upper-garment bordered in yellow. The crimson tablecloth in the centre is edged in gold. At the left, a woman in a white
kerchief, then Anna the Prophetess (*Luke* II, 36) in a vermilion cape
and yellow coif, and two men, one in blue, the other in vermilion
and green. The light-grey arcade in the background rises against a
light-blue sky. The colour contrasts are of great refinement, for
instance, in the very centre, the blue, white, violet and crimson. The
orthogonal lines meet above the high priest's head. Movement into
depth is minimized.

FIG. 94 Cat. No. 139

FIG. 95 Cat. No. 140

FIG. 96 Cat. No. 141 FIG. 97 Cat. No. 142 FIG. 98 Cat. No. 143

141. SAINT BRUNO IN PRAYER. Cadiz, Museum of Fine Arts, No. 64. 341 × 195 cm. About 1638. Figure 96

History: Ponz and Ceán saw a *St. Bruno* and a *St. Christopher*, both by Zurbarán, in the Sacristy of the Carthusian Monastery at Jerez, from which this picture entered the Museum in 1835. The *St. Christopher*, unrecorded since and presumably lost, would have been a very large picture as is customary for this subject, and thus a fitting companion piece to the *St. Bruno*. Pemán believes this picture occupied the centre space in the second storey of the High Altar.
Dating: Agrees in style with *133–140*.
Exh: Madrid, 1905, No. 12.
Lit: Ponz XVII, 6, 22 (?); Ceán VI, 51; G. III, 14–20; Pemán IV, 217.
The Founder of the Carthusian Order receives a crown of roses from angels with pink and blue streamers. On the ground, a white mitre and a yellow crozier. Red chair and crimson tablecloth. Sensitively painted landscape in greys and greens. See p. 22.

142. SAINT BRUNO WITH CROSS AND SKULL. Cadiz, Museum of Fine Arts, No. 17. 108 × 82 cm. 1638. Figure 97

History: Entered the Museum from the Carthusian Monastery at Jerez in 1835.
Lit: Ponz XVII, 6, 23 (?); Ceán VI, 51; S. I, 158; Pemán IV, 217–218.
Listed in the museum's catalogue of 1876 as by Placido Costanci, an Italian painter of 1750, because Ponz mentioned, as by Costanci, a *St. Bruno* in the Sacristy. It is not clear whether this is the same picture, but Zurbarán's authorship is certain and would become more evident by careful cleaning. Perhaps cut down from a full-length figure. The modelling, excellent throughout, should be compared with *56, 119, 140* and *165*. A copy, in the National Museum, Havana, Cuba, is there attributed to the master. See pp. 22, 31.

143. THE IMMACULATE CONCEPTION WITH SAINTS JOACHIM AND ANNE. Edinburgh, National Gallery of Scotland, No. 340. 251 × 172 cm. 1638. Figure 98

History: Almost agreeing in size and closely related in style to *133–134* and *137–140*, all from the High Altar of the Carthusian Monastery of Jerez, it may have been originally one of the two 'excellent' paintings seen by Ponz in small retables of the Lay Choir. Galerie Espagnole, Louvre, 1838, No. 332; Louis Philippe sale, 1853, No. 143, £90 to Hickman; Lord Elcho and Wemyss, 1857; acquired, probably from him, in 1859.
Exh: Manchester, 1857, No. 793; Spanish Paintings, National Gallery of Scotland, Edinburgh, 1951, No. 41.
Lit: Ponz XVII, 6, 20; Ceán VI, 51 (?); Cascales, pl. XXIX; S. I, 156; Pemán IV, 218–219; *Studio*, vol. 140, Nov. 1950, p. 141, ill. in colour.
The unadorned Virgin is clad in very light wine-red and light blue. In the clouds beneath her, the pale whitish horn of the moon. St. Joachim wears a green cloak over a deep-carmine robe, visible at the neck and wrists. His dark-crimson turban is striped in sienna. Technique and pose recall *86*. St. Anne wears a beige head-veil and a lavender cloak over a carmine gown. The landscape, in greys and greens, contains some of the symbols of the Immaculate Conception. Yellow sky with pink cherub heads. See p. 21.

144. SAINT BARTHOLOMEW. Lima, San Francisco, Sacristy. 181 × 94 cm. 1637–8. Figures 99, 100

History: One of thirteen 'Apostles, a Christ and a Virgin', listed in 1785 as new addition to the Sacristy in the *Libro Inventario de la Sacristía de Nuestro Padre San Francisco de Jesús de Lima*, p. 42 (manuscript in the Archive of San Francisco, Lima, as quoted by Gento Sanz). This is the chief monastery in the Franciscan Province of the Twelve Apostles.
Dating: The modelling, poses and design of draperies relate to other works of about 1637–8. The landscape background, absent in the earlier Lisbon Apostle series *78a–l*, is typical of the late 1630's.
Condition: All paintings are more or less damaged and some are repainted in parts.

Lit: J. M. Peña Prado, in *Lima Precolombina y Virreinal*, Lima, 1938, pp. 157–159 (as close to Ribalta); Marquis of Lozoya, *Mercurio Peruano*, XXIV, January 1942; idem, *Arch. esp. de arte*, 1943, no. 55, pp. 1–6 ('St. Bartholomew is entirely by the hand of Zurbarán' . . . 'all pictures are (*at least*) from the workshop of Zurbarán, but some are careless and weak work of pupils or . . . almost totally wrecked'); B. Gento Sanz, *San Francisco de Lima*, Lima, 1945, pp. 252–261; E. Marco-Dorta, *Historia del arte hispano-americano*, Barcelona, 1950, II, pp. 476–7.
In order of quality:

(a) Saint Bartholomew. Entirely by Zurbarán. Rose tunic, blue-grey mantle. Great plasticity. Rough, sketchy brushwork in face and hands.

(b) Saint James Major. Entirely by Zurbarán. Lilac tunic, green mantle.

(c) Saint Andrew. By Zurbarán, especially head, hands and landscape. Red tunic, green mantle. No repainting.

(d) Saint Matthew. Face and hand mostly by Zurbarán. Well designed green draperies. Landscape background much retouched.

(e) Saint Philip. Face and right hand by Zurbarán. Brownish draperies.

(f) Christ. Face and light-violet tunic by Zurbarán, rest much repainted. Vermilion mantle.

(g) Saint Thomas. Excellent head by Zurbarán, much repaint in draperies. White tunic, red mantle, sienna book.

(h) Saint Paul. Only the face seems by Zurbarán.

(i) Saint Mathias. The face seems by Zurbarán, the hands are poor and the draperies shop work. Green tunic, red mantle.

(j) Saint Simon. Face and draperies seem partly by Zurbarán and partly by the shop. Green tunic, brown-red mantle.

(k) Saint Jude Taddeus. Entirely a good shop product. Dark-red tunic, blue mantle. No repainting.

(l) Saint James Minor. A good shop work. Red tunic, yellow mantle.

(m) Saint Peter. By the shop. Blue tunic, ochre mantle. Much damaged.

(n) Saint John the Evangelist. By the shop. Green tunic, red mantle.

(o) The Virgin. Shop work, greatly damaged. Red tunic, blue mantle.

Repetitions by local painters in San Francisco at Arequipa; La Almudena at Cusco; Santiago at Pomata; and elsewhere in Peru. Also influenced a series at San Martín, Potosí, Bolivia. See pp. 19, 31, 191.

145. SAINT MATHIAS. Guatemala City, Sto. Domingo, Sacristy. 177 × 105 cm. About 1637–9. Inscribed: S. MATIAS XII. Inscribed on reverse of Saint Simon: Este Apostolado eceptuando a S. Andrés qᵉ es del Maestro Merlo en Guatemala, S. Bartolomé, el Salvador y la Virgen por Rosales todos los demas son del insigne Dn Francisco Surbaran en Sevilla qᵉ murió en Madrid el año de 1662. A solicitud del R. P. Fray Luis de la Puente los reparó Rosales año de 1804 en la N⟨ueva⟩ Guatemala a 1º de Marzo.   Figure 101

History: One of 'twelve paintings of the Apostles which came to Antigua from Cadiz by way of Mexico' (*Notas cronológicas de estas Indias, Tesoros de Sto. Domingo*, manuscript quoted by Díaz); saved in the earthquake of July 29, 1773 which destroyed the church of Sto. Domingo in Antigua, and brought to Sto. Domingo, Guatemala City; displayed there since 1804.
Dating: The modelling recalls the works for Jerez and Guadalupe.
Condition: All paintings are more or less damaged, dirty, and half of them largely repainted.
Lit: V. M. Díaz, *Las bellas artes en Guatemala*, Guatemala, 1934, pp. 313–316; Angulo, *Arch. esp. de arte*, 1949, no. 86, pp. 169–70; idem, *Historia del arte hispano-americano*, Barcelona, 1950, II, pp. 436–8, 440.

Arrestingly quiet, monumental figures, in contrast to the more pathetic mood of the Lima series. See pp. 19, 31.

FIG. 99   Cat. No. 144a   FIG. 100   Cat. No. 144b   FIG. 101   Cat. No. 145b

In order of quality:

(a) Saint Philip. V (ill. by Angulo, p. 170). Entirely by Zurbarán and best of series. Brown garment, white sash embroidered in red and green. Red and blue touches in flesh. Loose brushwork. Powerful, plastic hands and head. Profile.

(b) Saint Mathias. XII (ill. by Angulo, p. 170). Face, hand, and draperies by Zurbarán. Grey-blue tunic, light-tan mantle.

(c) Saint Thomas. VII. Face by Zurbarán. Dark-green tunic, red mantle. Faces right. Right hand holds staff. Pose related to 144g.

(d) Saint Simon. XI (ill. in Díaz, p. 479). Hands and part of light-grey garment by Zurbarán. Face repainted by Rosales.

(e) Saint Peter. I (ill. in Díaz, p. 478; Angulo, p. 170). Only the right foot by Zurbarán, the rest much repainted by Juan José Rosales in 1804. Blue tunic, orange-brown cloak, red sash. Pose similar to 144m.

(f) Saint John the Evangelist. IV. Good product of Zurbarán's shop. Not much repaint. Not by the Mexican painter Ramírez as stated by Díaz. Green tunic, red mantle, gold cup. The pose is repeated in the St. John, by Zurbarán's shop, in the Museum at Cordova.

(g) Saint James Major. III. A good shop piece. Sky-blue garment, light-brown cape. Walking to left, looking to right, right hand stretched out.

(h) Saint Matthew. VIII. Good shop work. Light-brown cloak. Wears glasses, carries a square rule. Pose similar to 144d.

(i) Saint Paul. (ill. Angulo, p. 170.) Shop piece. Face repainted. Blue tunic, sienna-brown mantle. Pose related to d and to 171g.

(j) Saint Andrew. II. Face and part of the draperies by Zurbarán's shop, the rest repainted by Thomas de Merlo who died in 1739, although the inscription on d states that j is entirely by Merlo. Green-brown garment.

(k) Saint James Minor. IX. The hands are by Zurbarán's shop, the rest entirely repainted by Rosales. Red tunic, light-grey cloak.

(l) Saint Jude Taddeus. X. Completely repainted by Rosales.

(m) Saint Bartholomew. VI. By Rosales. The original picture must have perished in the Antigua earthquake, 1773. Rosales also added a painting of Christ and one of the Virgin.

146. CHRIST AS SAVIOUR OF THE WORLD. Barcelona, Felix Millet. 100 × 73 cm. Signed: Franco de Zurbaran/faciebat 163⟨8⟩. The last digit has been somewhat repainted but seems to be an 8.

Plates 74–76

History: For many years owned by the Duchess of Parcent, Madrid.
Exh: Royal Academy, London, 1920/21, No. 58.
Lit: Cascales, pl. LXII; Kehrer, pl. 58, p. 96; S. I, 162.

Over a pink robe, Christ wears a grey cloak with touches of violet, thus the same colours as in 113. The flesh is very light with much rose; touches of pink at the eyes and in the shadow of the nose; bluish eye-balls. Tender shadow transitions give the face a feeling of holiness. In contrast, the hands are strong and energetic, painted in flesh colour and pink, with white touches at the nails. The blue globe has yellowish lights and violet reflections. Golden-brown background turning to gold around the head. Comparing the face to 55 and 56, one notices remarkable progress in Zurbarán's ability to model in the round, to fuse planes, and to suggest form and spirit.

147. THE VEIL OF SAINT VERONICA. London, A. Ruck. 100 × 82 cm. About 1638–40.   Figure 102

History: Sands Johnson sale, Christie's, May 19–20, 1926, No. 314, £47 to R. Ward; Unnamed sale, Christie's, May 28, 1926, £47 to Morson; owned by A. Ruck in 1929, unrecorded since.
Dating: The classic severity of the drapery folds as compared to 63–64, and the plastic, yet mellow and softly fusing painting of Christ's head suggest a date of about 1638–40.
Lit: A. L. Mayer, Apollo, 1928, VII, p. 180 (in colour); S. I, 170.

Frontal view of Christ's head on a plain, flat expanse of white drapery, relieved only at the top and sides by most pure and precise folds, inviting in their harmony to religious devotion. See p. 21.

148. SAINT ROMANUS AND SAINT BARULAS. Chicago, Art Institute of Chicago, No. 1947–793. 246 × 185 cm. Inscribed: 1638.

Plate 77

History: Once the centre of the High Altar of the church of San Román, Seville; Alcazar, Seville, 1810, No. 11; taken to Paris by

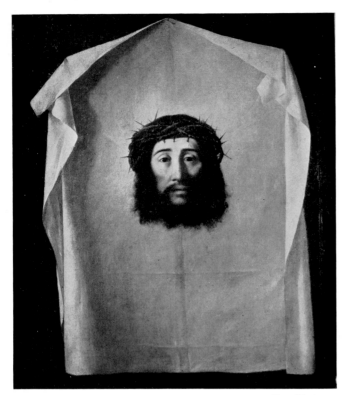

FIG. 102   Cat. No. 147

Marshal Soult; his sale, 1853, No. 28, frs. 5700, bought in; second sale, 1867, No. 6, frs. 5330; Ivan Stchoukine, Paris, about 1910; Dr. Carvallo, Paris, 1913; Charles Deering, Chicago; given by his heirs, 1947.
Exh: Grafton Galleries, London, 1913/14, No. 98; Chicago, 1933, No. 186; Chicago, 1934, No. 84.
Lit: Ceán VI, 48; Matute, *Archivo Hispalense*, 1887, III; Kehrer, pl. 40, pp. 82, 145; *Bulletin, Art Institute of Chicago*, 1922, XVI, p. 58; *Revista de Arquitectura*, 1922, p. 54; Kehrer, *Spanische Malerei*, p. 202; S. I, 155; G. I, 263.

St. Romanus, an early martyr at Antioch, incited the Christians to resist the desecration of their churches. Condemned to the stake, he was temporarily saved by a heavenly rain which put out the flames. This scene is alluded to in the background. Thereupon, for mocking his tormentors, his tongue was torn out, but he miraculously continued to preach. He holds an open book, inscribed: 'Beatus Romanus orabat dicens, Domine Iesu Christe osten virtutem tuam, ut magnificetur nomen sanctum tuum, quod est benedictum in secula. Ora pro nobis Beate Romane, ut digni efficiamur promissionibus Christi.' He wears a reddish-brown garment under a reddish cope richly embroidered in gold and with a figured border of the Prophets, in violet, yellow ochre, rose, olive green, red, blue, white, and vermilion. At the left is St. Barulas, with his throat cut. As a boy of seven he was among the converted spectators of St. Romanus' preaching and both were martyred together. He is clad in a blue blouse, a red garment, and grey shoes. At the horizon the low, lavender hills of Extremadura. Very luminous light-grey and yellow sky. Monumental triangular design set against a radiant background. See p. 31.

149. THE BLESSED HENRY SUSO. Seville, Museum of Fine Arts No. 197. 209 × 154 cm. About 1638. Not signed. Inscribed: ENRIQUE.   Figure 103

History: Together with *150*, done for the left transept of the Dominican church of Santo Domingo Porta Coeli, just outside of Seville. *149* was

at the east side, and *150* opposite it at the west side. Both in the Alcazar, Seville, 1810, Nos. 67–68.
Dating: López Martínez found the contract, but cannot locate it at present. Guinard felt that both canvases, usually dated 1640–1645, could be somewhat earlier.
Exh: Royal Academy, London, 1920/21, No. 60.
Lit: Ponz IX, 5, 3; Ceán VI, 50; Cascales, pl. VIII; Kehrer, pl. 42; G. II, 187–188.

The Dominican Henry Suso, or Heinrich Seuse (1295–1366), was, with Eckart and Tauler, one of the great German mystics. He was famous for his visions and ecstasies. Wearing the black and white habit of his Order, he scratches into his skin with a bloody grey nail an 'H', the symbol of Christ's name. The sky is light-grey and above yellowish. At the left, Suso seated on the ground in contemplation, oblivious to a Dominican talking to him. An angel, in lavender-pink, leads a saddle horse toward the Beato. On the right, Suso is seated by a spring. See pp. 15, 18, 22, 31.

150. SAINT LOUIS BERTRAM. Seville, Museum of Fine Arts, No. 201. 209 × 155 cm. About 1638.   Plate 78

History, Dating, and Lit: See *149*. Kehrer, pl. 41; idem, *Spanische Malerei*, p. 203; Cascales, pl. XLVII.

Saint Louis Bertram (1525–1581) was a great preacher and missionary in Colombia and Panama, before returning to his native Valencia. On the Leeward Islands one of the heathen Carib priests attempted to poison him, but divine intercession helped exorcize the venom. A green and red dragon, symbolizing the poisoned wine, issues from the grey cup. The Saint's deadly pale, grey-yellow face and lavender lips strongly contrast with those of *149*. In the background at the left,

FIG. 103   Cat. No. 149

FIG. 104   Cat. No. 151 FIG. 105   Cat. No. 152 FIG. 106   Cat. No. 153

the Saint with a companion burns idols before two kneeling Indians; at the right he preaches, inspired by the Dove of the Holy Spirit. A grey landscape extends to the blue-green trees, animated by succulent green leaves to the left, and inky brown-red and green leaves to the right.

151. THE PREMONITION OF BROTHER PETER OF SALAMANCA.
Guadalupe, Jeronymite Monastery, Sacristy. 290 × 222 cm. 1639.
Figure 104

History: One of eight Jeronymite miracles in the Sacristy still in their original location (*151–158*), listed in clockwise order beginning at the epistle side. *151* is closest to the altar. *151–153* are at the window (epistle) side, *154–158* opposite them on the gospel side (facing the windows). See Cascales, pl. LXXX. Cf. Figure IX on p. 17 above.
Dating: *157* is dated 1638; *152, 155, 156* and *158* are dated 1639.
Condition: Now almost monochrome and much darker than the reproduction would indicate. Cleaning would reveal the whites and dark brown violets of the monks' habits against the greys of the architecture.
Lit: Ponz VII, 4, 18; Ceán VI, 51–52; Tormo, *El monasterio de Guadalupe y los cuadros de Zurbarán*, Madrid, 1905; Kehrer, pp. 91–99; Fray Germán Rubio, *Historia de Ntra. Sra. de Guadalupe*, Barcelona, 1926, pp. 407–408; G. III, 21–22; Pemán, *B.S.E.E.* 1951, pp. 155–187.

Brother Peter of Salamanca († 1479) points out to a companion a heavy grey-blue sky with pink clouds, as an ominous premonition of the Moorish wars. Reflected light falls on the faces and habits of the two friars. The chiaroscuro contrast increases the drama and mystery of the night scene. The architecture at the left is almost in true perspective. See pp. 8, 15–6, 31.

152. BROTHER JOHN OF CARRIÓN AWAITING DEATH IN PRAYER.
Guadalupe, Jeronymite Monastery, Sacristy. 290 × 222 cm. Signed: Fran^{co} de Zurbaran fac/1639.
Figure 105

History and Lit: See *151*.

Forewarned of his imminent death, which took place in 1416, the Brother kneels in the choir. He is surrounded by the other monks, of whom he has already taken leave. Only three colours are used: white and brown-violet in the habits, dark and light-grey in the architecture. Like *151* and *153–158* designed with moving simplicity and truthfulness, free from pathos.

153. THE CHARITY OF BROTHER MARTIN OF VIZCAYA.
Guadalupe, Jeronymite Monastery, Sacristy. 290 × 222 cm. Signed: Fran^{co} de Zurbaran facie / 1639.
Figure 106

History, Dating, and Lit: See *151*.

Brother Martin († 1440), famous for his charity, distributes bread to the poor. In the foreground, a Riberesque old man clad in a violet-grey jacket and a brown and yellow-ochre cloak.

154. THE TEMPTATION OF BROTHER DIEGO OF ORGAZ.
Guadalupe, Jeronymite Monastery, Sacristy. 290 × 222 cm. 1639.
Figure 107

History, Dating, and Lit: See *151*.

To tempt the friar († 1465), the devil took the shape of a lion, a black bear, and a woman. Looking somewhat boyish, she has a long red tongue and claws, and is dressed in dark green with a dark-red mantle. At the upper right, the Virgin of Guadalupe, in yellowish red against an orange sky, appears to the kneeling friar. Night setting. The animals resemble the style of *93–102*.

155. CHRIST REWARDING BROTHER ANDREW OF SALMERÓN.
Guadalupe, Jeronymite Monastery, Sacristy. 290 × 222 cm. Signed: Fran^{co} de Zurbaran faciet/1639.
Figure 108

History and Lit: See *151*. Also Kehrer, pl. 56; Cascales, pl. XXVI.

The friar († 1408) had made vows of perpetual kneeling. To reward him for this self-inflicted penance, Christ appeared to him one night in the church of Guadalupe. Brother Andrew is painted in white and violet, while Christ wears light pink under a light-blue cloak. Resembling the heavenly musicians in *138*, an angel, in white, and winged putti look on from the upper right. The scene recalls *Christ Appearing to St. Norbert*, an engraving in the *Vita S. Norberti*, Antwerp, 1605, which Zurbarán used also for *24, 26* and *70*. See p. 16.

156. GONZALO OF ILLESCAS, BISHOP OF CORDOVA.
Guadalupe, Jeronymite Monastery, Sacristy. 290 × 222 cm. Signed: Fran^{co} de Zurbaran f/1639.
Plate 79

History and Lit: See *151*. Also Kehrer, pl. 55; Cascales, pl. XXV.
Condition: As in *154–155, 157–158* and *159*, all facing the windows, the colours have paled somewhat from constant exposure to light.

Gonzalo of Illescas († 1464), confessor of John II and co-regent of Castille, wears a white habit and the blue mozetta of his dignity, and

FIG. 107   Cat. No. 154   FIG. 108   Cat. No. 155   FIG. 109   Cat. No. 158

is seated on a light-olive chair. The tablecloth is bluish-grey-violet in the shadows, and claret-pink in the lights. At the lower right, a black and brown dog. A pink-red curtain discloses dark-grey columns. Beyond, the Friar is seen, standing in the very door of Guadalupe and distributing alms to four cripples on a tilted platform. The main figure, the curtain and the objects on table and window-sill are arranged along parallel curves. Medieval vanishing axis perspective.

157. THE MASS OF FATHER PETER OF CABAÑUELAS. Guadalupe, Jeronymite Monastery, Sacristy. 290 × 222 cm. Signed: Francᵘˢ de Zurbaran/faciebat 1638.   Plate 80 (Figure 154)

History and Lit: See *151*.

Father Peter († 1441) is said to have once doubted whether the consecrated bread and wine were the body and blood of Christ. Thereupon these disappeared from the altar during Mass and, to the profound wonderment of the Father, the Host materialized in mid-air exuding drops of blood falling into the chalice. His companion remained unaware of the vision, which was completed by a heavenly voice saying: 'Tace quod vides, et inceptum perfice' (Keep silent what you see, and perform what you have begun). Father Peter wears a pink chasuble edged in gold and with a dark-brown and gold damask centre. The Host, painted as a white disc resting on a red one, is surrounded by a yellow circle of light turning to orange at the periphery. The Persian rug on the floor is green, with yellow, rose, and light blue. The play of light and shadow and the modelling of the flesh portions, as well as the design of the architecture, recall *86–90*, painted only a few years earlier. The perspective, while drawing the spectator deep into space, establishes lines of emotional tension in planes parallel to the picture surface.

158. PRIOR FERNANDO YAÑEZ DE FIGUEROA BEFORE HENRY THE SECOND. Guadalupe, Jeronymite Monastery, Sacristy. 290 × 222 cm. Signed: Francᵒ de Zurbaran fat/1639.   Figure 109

History and Lit: See *151*. Also Cascales, pl. VI.

Under Fray Fernando Yáñez de Figueroa, the first prior of Guadalupe (from about 1389 till his death in 1412), the principal existing buildings were constructed, including the big cloister, the cells and the renovated church. Shown is the prior's refusal to accept the archbishopric of Toledo offered him by the King of Castille, who vainly tries to place a crimson cap on the friar's head. The prior wears black. Henry the Second's grey costume is embroidered with pearls and gold and

slashed with pink. His small cape is violet and he has pink hose, pink sleeves with yellow lights, a pink baldric, and mouse-grey shoes. The nobleman behind him cannot be a self-portrait of the artist, as has been suggested, for he wears the red cross of the Order of Santiago.

159. THE FLAGELLATION OF SAINT JEROME. Guadalupe, Jeronymite Monastery, Sacristy Chapel. 235 × 290 cm. 1638–9.   Plates 81, 84

History: One of three large paintings by Zurbarán in the Sacristy Chapel, immediately adjoining the Sacristy (see *160–161*). See also *151–158, 162*.

Lit: See *151*. Also Ramón Mélida, *El Correo de Madrid*, March 11, 1908 (believing *159* by Ribera, but *160* by Zurbarán); Cascales, pl. LXXI.

Condition: *159*, facing the window, has paled more than its opposite, *160*. Neither painting shows any repainted areas. A small speck of paint has fallen from Christ's forehead, baring the canvas. Repairs should prevent further damage.

In a letter to St. Eustochium, St. Jerome told how, sick with fever, he dreamed to be before Christ's throne and to be questioned about his faith. Proclaiming himself a Christian, the Saint was rebuked by Christ, who accused him of being a follower of Cicero and condemned him to hard punishment by the angels. Christ wears a light-blue mantle over a gown of very light lavender. St. Jerome's deep-black hair contrasts with the brilliant white of the cloth hanging from his loins. One chastising angel is in deep blue with a plum-coloured belt, the other in yellow with tan shadows. The kneeling angel at the left is one of Zurbarán's best. His garment is light pink and his mantle grey-blue. His companions are yellow ochre, light green and dark green, and in rose and vermilion, respectively. The composition has been criticized as not sufficiently conventional. It is spacious and free, appealing to modern eyes. The solids maintain subtle relationships throughout the picture. The general arrangement is derived from Mannerist prints similar to Heemskerck's *Story of Job*, No. 2, by Ph. Galle, 1563. Both *159* and *160* are entirely by Zurbarán. See p. 18, 191.

160. THE TEMPTATION OF SAINT JEROME. Guadalupe, Jeronymite Monastery, Sacristy Chapel. 235 × 290 cm. 1638–9. Plates 82–83, 85
History, Condition, and Lit: See *159*.

St. Jerome wrote to St. Eustochium: 'Often in the vast solitude of the desert I dreamed I was amidst the pleasures of Rome. While my companions were but scorpions and wild beasts, I imagined taking part in the dances of young ladies. Gaunt from fasting, my fantasy boiled over with desires.' The Saint's cloak is a sensuous vermilion. A vermilion-looped bow dangling from the neck of a guitar marks the centre of the painting. Playing this instrument is one of Zurbarán's most alluring feminine figures, in an orange jacket with blue baldric, a violet skirt edged in gold, a blue petticoat, and a pearl necklace tied by a red ribbon. Next to her a girl in green, another, playing a harp, in vermilion, light green and blue edged with gold. Throughout, strong chiaroscuro contrasts and dramatic plasticity, stressed to the utmost, enhance the great realism of the picture. Noticing the powerful influence of Ribera in the figure of St. Jerome, Tormo in 1905 saw 'nothing of Zurbarán in brushwork and colour'. Today, after comparison with *137–140*, no doubt is justified, and the picture must be considered one of the master's best. See pp. 18, 22.

161. SAINT JEROME CARRIED UP TO HEAVEN. Guadalupe, Jeronymite Monastery, Sacristy Chapel. 145 × 103 cm. 1638–9.
Figure 110

History: See *159*. In the top centre of the altar, above a sculpture.
Lit: See *151*. Also Cascales, pl. XXIV.

At the top centre, the figure of Christ is faintly visible amidst rose and yellow clouds. St. Jerome is borne up by nude angels, here and there decorated with a pink, blue or olive streamer. One carries the Saint's red cardinal's hat. The putti show Italian influence and those at the lower right repeat the angels in *141*. The Saint's face is derived from Ribera and the pose of his left hand also from *141*. The most interesting portion of the picture is the landscape below, in blue and grey tones and airy distances.

162. JERONYMITE SAINT. Guadalupe, Jeronymite Monastery, Sacristy Chapel. 34 × 16 cm. 1638–9.   Figure 111

History: One of ten Jeronymite Saints in the predella of the altar which contains *161* at the top. The two outer ones, measuring 34 × 18 cm., were stolen over fifty years ago and are unrecorded since. The other eight are in place, each 34 × 16 cm., except *d* and *e* which measure 34 × 45 cm.
Condition: All are in need of proper cleaning and restoration; *a*, *f*, and *h* are better in preservation and quality than the remainder.
Lit: See *151*.

Several Saints faithfully repeat poses of *124–130*, at Cadiz, painted about a year earlier, or of other contemporary paintings by the artist. From left to right they are:
(*a*) Friar reading, to left, cf. *125*.
(*b*) Bishop reading, frontal, cf. *130*.
(*c*) Friar in profile, to left, cf. *127*.
(*d*) Seated Friar, in profile, cf. *St. John the Evangelist*, Museum, Cadiz.
(*e*) Kneeling Friar, to left.
(*f*) Friar holding a cross in his left hand, looking up to right.
(*g*) Virgin Martyr with palm, cf. *112*.
(*h*) Friar looking up, cf. *128*. This Friar shows the finest, most minute brushwork of the series.

163. FRAY GUILLERMO DE SAGIANO. London, Tomas Harris. 61 × 41 cm. 1636–7.   Figure 112

History: One of thirty-eight Mercedarian Martyrs, painted for the lower cloister of the Barefooted Mercedarians, whence they passed to the Alcazar, Seville, 1810 (listed as Nos. 179, 337, 362 and 380); sixteen of these, marked *, were later in the Galerie Espagnole, Louvre, 1838, Nos. 364–379; and in the Louis Philippe sale, Nos. 213–217, 260–264, 448–453.
Dating: Contemporary with *117–122*, also painted for the Barefooted Mercedarians at Seville.
Exh: Tomas Harris, London, 1938, No. 14.
Lit: Pal. III, 108; Ponz, IX, 3, 50; Ceán VI, 49; *Catálogo Galería Manuel López-Cepero*, Seville, May 15–30, 1860, Nos. 238–9. E. Harris, *From Greco to Goya*, London, 1938, p. 44 (first suggested

FIG. 110   Cat. No. 161

the derivation of the series and published *163a*); Guinard, *Hommage à E. Martinenche*, 1939, p. 33 (*b–d*); Angulo, *Arch. esp. de arte*, 1941, pp. 365–373 (*b–n*); idem, *l.c.*, 1944, p. 9 (*o–p*); idem, *l.c.*, 1947, p. 146 (*q–s*); G. II, 185–187 (*t–u*); Pemán III, 208–209 (*v–w*).

Angulo and Guinard rightly stressed that the series was executed by Zurbarán's workshop, although apparently based on designs by the master. See pp. 15, 31. The following pictures have been published:

*(*a*) Fray Guillermo de Sagiano.
*(*b*) San Serapion, Coll. Jacques Lifschitz, New York.
*(*c*) Fray Arnaldo de Arenchs. On loan Fogg Museum, Cambridge, Mass.
*(*d*) Fray Pedro de Armengol, Duchess of Montpensier, Madrid.
(*e*) Fray Pedro de San Dionisio, Coll. Adanero, Madrid.
(*f*) Friar at the stake, Coll. Adanero, Madrid.
(*g*) Friar at the stake, Coll. Adanero, Madrid.
(*h*) Friar shot by arrows, Coll. Ceballos, Madrid.
(*i*) Crucified Friar, Coll. Viuda de Gonzalo Bilbao, Madrid. Exh: Madrid, 1905, No. 28.
(*j*) Kneeling Friar, Greco Museum, Toledo.
*(*k*) Martyr with his hands cut off, Pereire sale, Hotel Drouot, January 30–31, 1868, No. 65, frs. 300.
*(*l*) Martyr holding his tongue in his right hand, Pereire sale, No. 66, frs. 314.
(*m*) Martyred Friar, Coll. Pérez Asensio, Jerez, Cascales, pl. LIII.
(*n*) Martyred Friar kneeling, Coll. Pérez Asensio, Jerez, Cascales, pl. LII.
*(*o*) Martyr, Laperlier sale, Paris, Feb. 20–21, 1879, No. 198.
*(*p*) Martyr, Laperlier sale, Paris, Feb. 20–21, 1879, No. 199.
(*q*) Seated Martyr, Priv. Coll., Seville.
(*r*) Standing Martyr, Priv. Coll., Seville.
(*s*) Martyr holding the Mercedarian standard, Priv. Coll., Seville.
*(*t*) Hanging Friar killed by arrows, on loan to the Wadsworth Atheneum, Hartford, Conn.

FIG. III   Cat. No. 162h   FIG. 112   Cat. No. 163a   FIG. 113   Cat. No. 164   FIG. 114   Cat. No. 165

*(u) Martyred Bishop, resembling *124*, W. E. Duits, London.
*(v) Martyr embracing a cross, Dealer, London.
*(w) Martyr kneeling before a cloudburst, Schaeffer Galleries, New York. 61 × 39 cm., enlarged to 63 × 42 cm. Exh: New Gallery, London, 1895-6, No. 83, owned by Sir Charles Turner.

164. SAINT AUGUSTINE. Mexico City, School of Plastic Arts, No. 324. 204 × 108 cm. About 1638.   Figure 113

History: Together with *165* once part of a series of Founders of Monastic Orders, in Mexico probably since the seventeenth century. Angulo found four copies (one after *164*, three after lost originals) in the Franciscan monastery of Tlalnepantla, on the outskirts of Mexico City. *St. Jerome* and *St. Elias*, excellent shop pieces, in the Museum, Guadalajara, Jalisco, probably belonged to this series.
Dating: The modelling and three-dimensional depth suggest a date late in the thirties. The silhouette repeats *6*, of about 1626.
Lit: H. von der Gabelentz, *Rep. für Kunstwissenschaft*, 1926, XLVII, p. 152; Angulo, *Arte en América y Filipinas*, 1935, I, pp. 56-60; S. I, 163.

The Saint, clad in black and wearing a white mitre with yellow embroidery, is walking beside the seashore. The figure forms a dark hulking mass against the grey-blue sky. In the background, the Saint is told by the Christ Child he would never penetrate the mysteries of the Holy Trinity. See pp. 22, 31.

165. SAINT JOHN OF GOD. Mexico City, School of Plastic Arts, No. 323. 202 × 107 cm. About 1638.   Figure 114

History, Dating, and Lit: See *164*.

The founder of the Hospitalers (Brothers of Charity), clad in a grey habit, is outlined against a light-grey sky, yellow toward the horizon. In the background, the Saint carries a sick man. These small figures are in the master's best manner.

166. SAINT FRANCIS KNEELING. London, National Gallery, No. 230. 152 × 99 cm. About 1639.   Plate 87

History: Galerie Espagnole, Louvre, 1838, No. 346; Louis Philippe sale, 1853, No. 50, £265 to the National Gallery.
Dating: Related stylistically to *146*, *167* and *176*.
Lit: Ford, *Atheneum*, 1853; Kehrer, pl. 74, p. 119; MacLaren, pp. 84-5.

St. Francis, in a brown garment with patches of sienna, kneels stiffly upright on the bare ground. Light falls dramatically on the nose, the lips, the upper arm, side and hands. The shadowed portion of the face is almost invisible and much darker than in *61*, of 1632. Kehrer called attention to the statuesque character of the figure, resem bling in spirit Spanish seventeenth-century sculptures, such as Mena's *St. Francis*. For the past hundred years the picture, more than any other, has represented Zurbarán's art, giving critics and the public the impression that his mood was sinister, tormented, dark, unhappy and morose. See pp. 18, 22.

167. SAINT FRANCIS KNEELING. London, National Gallery, No. 5655. 162 × 137 cm. Signed: Franco de Zurbaran/faciebat/1639.
                    Plate 88

History: Heirs of S. G. de la Huerta, Madrid, to Sir Arthur Aston, British Envoy from 1840 to 1843; his sale, August 6, 1862, No. 5 to Agnew for Sam Mendel; his sale, Christie's, April 23, 1875, No. 348, to Agnew and sold immediately to Mrs. Wood; bequeathed by her son, Major C. E. W. Wood, in 1946.
Exh: Royal Academy, London, 1872, No. 93; Spanish Exhibition, London, 1946, No. 24, and 1947, No. 40.
Lit: MacLaren, pp. 86-7.

The Saint's cloak is brown with patches of white. The pale face is relieved by touches of blue near the ear, and of Venetian red at the eye and mouth. Dark-grey rocks, before a very dark cave. Dark-blue sky with touches of pink. The trees are dark green. The bluish tones in the flesh occur also in *170* and *176*. See pp. 18, 22, 31.

168. SAINT FRANCIS KNEELING. Aachen, Suermondt Museum, No. 137. 133 × 104 cm. About 1635-40.   Figure 115

History: Bequeathed to the Museum, sometime before 1914, by Frau Weber van Houten.
Dating: The pose is similar to *167*, of 1639, but the lighting and modelling are less generalized and less fused, so that the date is probably earlier.
Lit: Kehrer, pl. 73, pp. 118-119.

The garments are in browns and whites.

169. SAINT FRANCIS KNEELING. Düsseldorf, Municipal Art Collection, No. 773. 164 × 123 cm. About 1637-9.   Figure 116

FIG. 115   Cat. No. 168   FIG. 116   Cat. No. 169   FIG. 117   Cat. No. 170

Collections: Countess de la Paz (?), Madrid; Otto Mündler, Paris; Wesendonck, Bonn, No. 87; Provinzial Museum, Bonn, No. 336.

Dating: Anticipating *167* more closely, particularly also in the drawing of the draperies, than does *168*. Kehrer's date, shortly before 1659, would appear too late.

Lit: Kehrer, pl. 78, p. 124.

The Saint wears a brownish-yellow habit, mended with yellowish patches. In the Vienna Museum, No. 6770, a variant by a follower.

170. THE DEAD CHRIST ON THE CROSS WITH A DONOR.
Bilbao, Lezama-Leguizamón Collection. 246 × 169 cm. Signed: Fran^co de Zur/baran faciebat/1640.   Figure 117

Collections: Hueto and Sons, Vitoria, Spain, 1924.

The figure of Christ was copied, with few variations, from *62, 114*, the two prior *Crucifixions* latest in date. Better in quality is the half-length of a donor, clad in black doublet, stiff white collar and cuffs. He is about twenty-five years old. The hands show touches of red and blue to indicate the veins, just like the hands of Christ in *176*, of 1639. See pp. 21, 31.

171. SAINT BERNARD OF CLAIRVAUX.
Lima, Monastery of San Camilo de Lelis (Buenamuerte). 184 × 103 cm. About 1640.   Figure 118

History: One of Thirteen Founders of Monastic Orders, 'probably bequeathed by Doña Gertrudis de Vargas to Father Laguna on February 1, 1769', according to Lozoya.

Dating: Related to the works from Jerez.

Condition: All dirty and damaged, some repainted in part.

Lit: Marquis of Lozoya, *Arch. esp. de arte*, 1943, No. 55, pp. 5–6; Marco Dorta, *Historia*, II, pp. 477–479. Schenone, *Anales*, 1951, p. 61.

The poses are somewhat similar to those of the Ten Founders of Monastic Orders, all shop work, at Castellón de la Plana. That series includes Saint Benedict, but lacks Saints Anthony Abbot, Bernard, Francis de Paul, and John of God. See pp. 19, 31. In order of quality, the Lima series comprises:

(*a*) Saint Bernard of Clairvaux. Zurbarán painted the head, the hands and the landscape; he may have had very slight assistance in the draperies. Excellent quality.

(*b*) Saint Augustine. The hands and landscape seem by the master, the rest good shop work.

(*c*) Saint Bruno. Good shop work, possibly with aid by Zurbarán in the face and draperies.

(*d*) Saint Ignatius. Good shop work, possibly with touches by the master in the face.

(*e*) Saint Francis de Paul. Good shop work, and so is the next one.

(*f*) Saint Elias. A similar version, also by the shop, in the Museum at Cordova.

(*g*) Saint Jerome. Hands perhaps by Zurbarán, rest by shop, repaint in face.

(*h*) Saint Francis. Hands possibly by Zurbarán, face repainted. Derived from a *Saint Francis* destroyed in 1936 at Villalba del Alcor, Huelva. Colonial copies of *h, i* and *k* in Sucre, Bolivia.

(*i*) Saint Dominic. Left hand and landscape possibly by Zurbarán, face and rest by the shop.

(*j*) Saint John of God. By the shop, as are the three following ones.

(*k*) Saint Peter Nolasco.

(*l*) Saint Basil.

(*m*) Saint Anthony Abbot. After the original, *186*.

172. SAINT FRANCIS KNEELING.
Bogotá, San Francisco. 164 × 111 cm. About 1640. Inscribed on reverse: El S⟨eño⟩r D⟨oct⟩or D⟨o⟩n Ant⟨oni⟩o Verástegui Oidor de esta R⟨ea⟩l Audiencia de S⟨an⟩ta Fé por su especial devoción de las Llagas de N⟨uest⟩ro P⟨adr⟩e S⟨a⟩n Fran⟨cis⟩co dió a este su Conv⟨en⟩to esta Pintura para que cada año se ponga en el Altar mayor en los dias del Quinario para beneficio de los Fieles año de 1768.   Figure 119

History: According to the inscription, given to San Francisco in 1768 by Antonio Verástegui, a Basque who resided at Bogotá as President of the Supreme Court of New Granada.

Lit: Reproduced in colour in the magazine *Vida*, Bogotá, 1943.

The Saint, full-length kneeling to right, wears a brown garment patched in grey. In the upper right Christ with four rose wings. In the light-grey landscape appear at the left a grey hermitage and brown trees. A copy with variations, by the shop and measuring 153 × 110 cm., is in the collection of Doña Mercedes Bessabé, Viuda de Manuel Taramona, formerly of Bilbao, now Madrid. See p. 22.

173. SAINT ANTHONY ABBOT.
Florence, Count Contini-Bonacossi. 162 × 120 cm. About 1639.   Figure 120

Collections: Yves Perdoux, Paris, 1925.

Dating: Done according to Mayer after 1640; a date of about 1639 is here suggested by comparison with *124–143*, and especially *167* and *186*.

Exh: Galerie Charpentier, Paris, 1925, No. 111; Contini-Bonacossi Exhibition, Rome, 1930, No. 66 (edited by A. L. Mayer).

Lit: G. II, 182.

FIG. 118   Cat. No. 171a   FIG. 119   Cat. No. 172   FIG. 120   Cat. No. 173

The Saint is attired in a white and brown habit. He holds a grey stick marking his age and feebleness and is accompanied by a black pig representing the demon of temptation. The foreground is brown and the distances light green, turning to light blue at the horizon. At the left, a brown tree with green leaves below and brown ones higher up. The pose and composition follow, with few changes, *118*, of 1636.

174. SAINT MARY MAGDALENE. Mexico City, School of Plastic Arts, No. 746. 146 × 111 cm. Doubtful signature: Fra⟨n^co⟩ . . . baran. About 1640.   Figure 121

History: Perhaps the 'Magdalena' seen by Palomino in the church of Santa Magdalena at Pallarés, Badajoz. General John Meade (British Consul at Madrid) sale, London, March 6, 1851, to Richard Ford; his descendant, Captain Richard Ford sale, Christie's, June 14, 1929, No. 25, £241 to Savile Galleries; Tomas Harris, London; bought by Alberto Pani for the Mexican Museum, 1934.
Dating: The drawing of the draperies, and the subject, meditation on death, related to the death of the painter's wife, suggest a date about 1640.

Condition: Very poor. Some new repainting on the forehead; but the entire face is probably old repaint rather than the work of Zurbarán. Some later repaint in the draperies and hands. In the signature, the letters 'Fra' may be new; they do not agree in colour and thickness of brushstroke with 'baran'. Moreover, 'baran' could even be read as 'aciebat'.
Exh: British Institution, London, 1852, No. 46; New Gallery, London, 1895/96, No. 39; Tomas Harris, London, 1931, No. 7.
Lit: Palomino III, 108 (?); Waagen, *Art Treasures*, II, p. 223; Borenius, *Burl. Mag.*, 1931, LIX, pp. 33–34; S. I, 164; G. III, 27.

The Saint, clad in black, at a table covered by a rich yellow velvet with red floral pattern and lined in green. On the table a red hour-glass, skull, and pewter candlestick. At the lower left, a red pillow. Blackish background. It is not entirely certain that Zurbarán, and not one of his better pupils, is the author.

175. POTTERY AND A CHOCOLATE MILL. Kiew, Museum of Art. 48 × 75 cm. Signed: Juan (or Fran^co) de Zurbaran. Date unknown.   Figure 122

Collections: Khanenko, St. Petersburg, until 1918.
Lit: V. Voinov, *Apollon*, St. Petersburg, 1916, p. 1; Sir Robert Witt, *Burl. Mag.*, 1924, XLV, pp. 43, 52; Ghilarov, *Burl. Mag.*, 1938, LXXII, pp. 190–191; Seckel, *GdBA*, 1946, XXX, pp. 289–290.

FIG. 121   Cat. No. 174   See pp. 24, 25.

FIG. 122   Cat. No. 175

176. CHRIST AT EMMAUS. Mexico City, School of Plastic Arts. 228 × 154 cm. Signed: Fran de/Zurbaran/1639.

History: Probably since the seventeenth century in the Monastery of San Agustín, Mexico City, whence it entered the Museum in 1861.
Condition: An anonymous engraving (fig. 123), pulled by Federico Cantú from the eighteenth-century plate for the author, shows details no longer visible in the painting: a much lighter background with a stone wall and a tree against an evening sky. Most of St. Simon's profile and his left hand are lost and newly painted in. At the right, Cleopas' nose, eyes, and cheek were recently restored.
Lit: Revilla, *El arte en Mexico*, 1895, p. 147; Alvarez, *Las pinturas de la Academia*, Mexico, 1917, p. 35; Icaza, *Mundial*, November 2, 1922;

H. von der Gabelentz, *Rep. für Kunstwissenschaft*, 1926, XLVI, p. 151; Angulo, *Arte en América y Filipinas*, 1935, I, pp. 54–56; S. I, 162; A. Carrillo Gariel, *Las galerías de pintura de la Academia de San Carlos*, Mexico, 1944, pp. 44, 69; S. V, 74.

Christ is clad in a greyish-blue jacket with dark-blue collar, a lavender cloak and a brown hat. His face and hands have light-blue shadows and pink lights. At the left, St. Simon (or St. Peter by confusion with Simon Peter of *Luke* XXIV, 34), in a sienna garment and a green cloak with yellowish lights. Cleopas wears a red shirt. On the table, a gray cloth over a dark-blue one visible at the lower edge; and a knife; a dish with bread and parsnips; another with brown olives; a brown water jar glazed grey and blue; a light-brown loaf of bread. Zurbarán's composition was apparently inspired by Dürer's woodcut (B. 48). See p. 31.

177. SAINT AUGUSTINE. Kingston Lacy, Wimborne, Dorset, Ralph Bankes. 180 × 102 cm. Before 1640 (?).

History: Said to have come from the chapterhouse of the Cathedral of Plasencia (about 100 miles from Guadalupe) and to have been owned by Philip, Duke of Savoy, before entering the Bankes Collection, formed mainly about 1800.
Condition: In need of cleaning.
Lit: Waagen, *Art Treasures*, IV, p. 382 (as by Murillo); Ch. B. Curtis, *Velazquez and Murillo*, Boston, 1883, No. 261 (as by Murillo).

The Saint, full length and life size, clad in black, is seated at a table, on which are some books. He holds a pen, and, turning his head, looks at the spectator and up as if hearing a voice from heaven. The author sees no reasons for the present attribution to Murillo and believes that closer study and cleaning might establish Zurbarán's authorship. See p. 22.
A half-length copy, of about 1800, is engraved as by Murillo in the catalogue of the Lucien Bonaparte collection, 1812, sold at London in 1816. Bought by Charles X, in 1829, given to the Louvre, and since 1872 in the Ingres Museum, Montauban.

178. PEARS AND FLOWERS. Chicago, Art Institute of Chicago, Walker Fund, No. 1947–511. 81 × 107 cm. 1633–44.   Figure 124

History: José de Madrazo, Madrid, 1856, No. 449; Marquis of Salamanca († 1883), Madrid; Countess of Montarco, Madrid, 1905; Knoedler & Co., New York, 1935; Joseph Brummer, New York; acquired in 1947.
Exh: Madrid, 1905, No. 48; Knoedler, Newport, Rh. I., 1935, No. 1.
Lit: Balsa de la Vega, *Ilustración española y americana*, May 22, 1905, p. 302; Cascales, 1911, p. 93; Kehrer, p. 147; S. I, 164; S. II, 128–129; Seckel, *GdBA*, 1946, XXX, pp. 288–289; P. T. Malone, *Bulletin, Art Institute of Chicago*, 1948, XLII, no. 2, p. 17.
See pp. 19, 24, 191.

FIG. 123   *Cf.* Cat. No. 176   FIG. 124   Cat. No. 178

FIG. 125   Cat. No. 179   FIG. 126–7   Cf. Cat. Nos. 179–81   FIG. 128   Cat. No. 181

179. SAINT ELIZABETH OF THURINGIA. Montreal, Van Horne Collection. 171 × 107 cm. 1638–42.   Figure 125

History: See *116*. Soult sale, Paris, May 19–22, 1852, No. 35, to Count Duchatel, frs. 3200; Ehrich Galleries, New York, before 1913, to Sir William van Horne.
Exh: Montreal, 1933, No. 23.
Lit: Cascales, p. 94 (as St. Casilda); Loga, *Art in America*, 1913, I, p. 101 (as St. Casilda); Kehrer, pl. 66, p. 107; Mayer, *Arts and Decoration*, 1916, VI, p. 221; idem, *Cicerone*, 1916, VIII, p. 6; Kehrer, *Spanische Malerei*, p. 205; Mayer, *Historia de la pintura española*, p. 249; S. I, 167; II, 130–131; IV, 256.

Clad in a gown of brown sienna woven with a red and light-bluish-grey floral motif, embroidered below with pearls and stones in dark blue and red. Vermilion sleeve with yellow high-lights; lilac mantle edged in lace; red watered damask skirt; dark-brown shoes. Adornments, consisting of a gold diadem and strings of pearls in her hair; a vermilion ribbon; a pearl necklace with a silver shield; a gold bracelet at the upper arm. Grey background. See figs. 126–7 and pp. 23–4. Fig. 127, Saint Emmerentia, after D. Teniers the Elder.

180. SAINT RUFINA. New York, Hispanic Society of America, No. A1891. 172 × 105 cm. 1638–42.   Plate 89

History: See *116* and *179*. Soult sale, Paris, May 19–22, 1852, No. 36, frs. 3300, to Count Duchatel; Ehrich Galleries, New York, before 1913, to Archer M. Huntington; his gift, 1925.
Lit: Cascales, pl. XXXVII; Kehrer, pl. 68, pp. 107, 148; Mayer, *Arts and Decoration*, 1916, VI, p. 220; Trapier, *Hisp. Soc. of America, Catalogue, Paintings (Sixteenth to Eighteenth Centuries)*, New York, 1929, pp. 136–137; idem, *Handbook*, 1941, p. 21; S. I, 166–167; II, 131; IV, 256.

Described in the Soult sale as 'Another female Saint, standing figure, turned in profile supported by a symbolic book and her eyes raised heavenward. Her costume consists of a green silk robe over which she wears an upper garment of silk woven with gold and silver, and to which is attached a pink mantle falling to the floor.' The upper garment is grey, a transparent white scarf is thrown around her neck, and two lumps of clay resting on the book identify her as a Sevillan pottery worker. A misprint in the Soult catalogue ('levier' instead of 'livre') has veiled the true provenance of the picture. See figs. 126–7 and pp. 23–4.

181. SAINT CASILDA. Madrid, Prado, No. 1239. 184 × 98 cm. About 1640.   Figure 128

History: First recorded, in 1814, in the Royal Palace at Madrid, whence it later entered the Prado. It may have come to Madrid from Seville during the War of Independence.
Dating: The broader, less linear handling of the face and draperies, in comparison to *179–180*, suggests a slightly later date.
Lit: Cascales, pl. XXXV; Kehrer, pl. 61, p. 107 (believed *181* to be earlier than *179*); Sánchez Cantón, *Catálogo, Museo del Prado*, 1949, p. 745; S. IV, 256; Gómez Castillo, *Discursos*, 1950, p. 64 ('by Ayala'); Guinard-Baticle, p. 97, ill. in colour.

St. Casilda, the daughter of a Moorish ruler of Toledo, suffered martyrdom for helping imprisoned Christians. One day, on her way to the gaol with a loaf of bread, it was miraculously changed into flowers. The Saint wears a plum-coloured upper skirt edged with pearls; a dark-green lower skirt; an intense vermilion sleeve; a light-blue jacket, lined in green and edged with gold and pearls; and a yellow and orange mantle. In her hair, a gold and ruby diadem, pearls and a violet ribbon. Gold chains at the neck, waist, and upper arms. She holds roses and some yellow and orange flowers. See pp. 23–4, 32 and figs. 126–7.

182. VIRGIN AND CHILD WITH A DISH OF FRUIT. New York, Hon. Oscar B. Cintas. 142 × 109 cm. 1640–5.   Figure 129

History: Anonymous sale, Christie's, July 14, 1939, £18, to Koetser, New York.
Dating: Stylistically between *179–181* and *199*.
Lit: S. I, 165; II, 126–131.

The Christ Child is dressed in white and blue. The Virgin in a light-red tunic and deep-blue cloak, a blue ribbon at the nape of her neck and a transparent white veil. On a table covered by dark-red velvet, a pewter dish with yellow fruits, some with green leaves. Chair backed in green. Light-grey background. See pp. 19, 21.

183. SAINT FRANCIS STANDING. Lyon, Museum. 197 × 106 cm. 1640–5.

History: In a convent at Lyon before 1793, the picture disappeared during the Revolution, was bought by a junk dealer in 1802 at a public sale for 18 francs and acquired by the city in 1807.
Lit: *Lyon, Notice des tableaux, Catalogue*, 1808, p. 16 (as by Ribera);

PEARS AND FLOWERS. About 1633–44. Chicago, Art Institute (Cat. No. 178)

FIG. 129   Cat. No. 182

M. Raymond, *Le Musée de Lyon*, 1887, p. 46; Kehrer, pl. 76, pp. 121–123 ('about 1645'); idem, *Spanische Malerei*, p. 214; S. I, 166.

This representation is frequently found in Spanish art and explained by E. Mâle, *L'art religieux d'après le Concile de Trente*, Paris, 1932, pp. 480–483. Chest and hands are without wounds, and the lips, cheeks and nose are red, while in *184* the face has the pallor of death, and there are stigmata on hand and chest. The effect of a sculptured statue is created by a stiff, frontal pose, by the plastic vigour of the

draperies, and the placing in front of a niche. Kehrer saw the essential meaning of this dematerialized figure, all death, ecstasy, and love for God. See pp. 19, 22.

184. SAINT FRANCIS STANDING. Boston, Museum of Fine Arts, No. 1938–1617. 207 × 106 cm. 1640–5.   Figure 130

History: Bought by the British Ambassador in Madrid, in 1823, Baron Heytesbury; Lady Heytesbury sale, Heytesbury, Wiltshire, April 27–May 1, 1926, No. 1358, £21; Tomas Harris, London, 1931; bought from Böhler & Steinmeyer, Lucerne, 1938.
Lit: Waagen, *Art Treasures*, IV, p. 389; *Bulletin, Museum of Fine Arts*, 1939, XXXVII, pp. 4–5; S. I, 162, 166.
Exh: Tomas Harris, London, 1931, No. 5; Hamburger Kunstverein, 1935, No. 27.

In comparison to *183* the facial expression is less ecstatic, the mouth not opened as wide, and the modelling a little more precise and harder. The niche is delineated more clearly, and distinct horizontal and vertical planes are introduced at the bottom. The habit is painted in hues of brown and grey.
A copy, from the Galerie Espagnole, Louvre, 1838, No. 349 and the Louis Philippe sale No. 207, was exhibited at the Galerie Charpentier, Paris, 1925, No. 115.

185. SAINT FRANCIS STANDING. Barcelona, Museum. 181 × 111 cm. 1640–5.

Another original replica of *183*. The colour of the habit is light grey. *184* is better in condition and quality. See p. 191.

186. SAINT ANTHONY ABBOT. Madrid, Marquis of Casa Torres. 204 × 110 cm. 1640–5.   Figure 131

History: Unknown. Not identical with *118*.
Dating: Resembles stylistically *187–188*, but is larger in size. There is no evidence that *187–188* were ever cut down.
Exh: Madrid, 1905, No. 37.
Lit: G. II, 181–182.

In white and brown habit and cowl, looking up to the blue Tau cross appearing in the sky (*Revel.*, 14, 1). The sky is dark grey with pinkish hues, the landscape in greens and greys. In view of a shop copy *171m*, one of a series of Thirteen Founders of Monastic Orders, Guinard rightly suggested that *186* also once formed part of such a series. Another copy at the Museum, Málaga. See p. 31.

FIG. 130   Cat. No. 184   FIG. 131   Cat. No. 186   FIG. 132   Cat. No. 187   FIG. 133   Cat. No. 188

187. SAINT BENEDICT. New York, Kleinberger & Co. 185 × 100 cm. 1640–5.   Figure 132

History: Same as *184*. Lady Heytesbury sale, No. 1329, £40; Julius Böhler, Lucerne.
Exh: Royal Academy, London, 1875, No. 197; 1890, No. 130; Hamburger Kunstverein, Hamburg, 1935, No. 26.
Lit: Waagen, *Art Treasures*, IV, 388; Mayer, *ZfbK*, 1927/28, LXI, p. 289 ('about 1635–1640'); S. I, 166.

The Saint is dressed in black. Mayer explained the earthenware pot in his left hand as a wine jar, 'a measure which the Saint permitted to his brethren when he returned, at their request, from his hermitage to direct the monastery again as an abbot. One of the brethren was dissatisfied with the measure and put poison into the Saint's cup, which burst into a hundred pieces before any damage was done.' In the background, the Saint kneels in prayer, holding a crozier symbolic of his bishopric. Companion piece to *188*. Both belonged to a series of Founders of Monastic Orders. A shop copy at Castellón de la Plana. See p. 22.

188. SAINT JEROME. San Diego, California, Fine Arts Gallery. 185 × 103 cm. 1640–5.   Figure 133 (Plate 93)

History: Same as *184*; Lady Heytesbury sale, No. 1357, £22; Böhler & Steinmeyer, Lucerne; Kleinberger & Co., New York; bought in 1929.
Condition: The lion seems mostly repainted, and the landscape shows much loss. A little repaint in the habit, apron, and right hand.
Exh: Royal Academy, London, 1875, No. 200; 1890, No. 140; Fine Arts Gallery, San Diego, 1935, No. 590; Golden Gate International Exposition, San Francisco, 1939, No. 102; World's Fair, New York, 1940, No. 113; Museum of Art, Toledo, 1941, No. 72 ('about 1645'); Durlacher Brothers, New York, 1945, No. 12.
Lit: Waagen, *Art Treasures*, IV, p. 388; Mayer, *ZfbK*, 1927/28, LXI, p. 289; R. Poland, *Fine Arts Gallery*, *Bulletin*, January 1930; *Pantheon*, 1930, V, p. X; S. I, 162–163.

The founder of the Jeronymites, companion piece of *187*, wears over his Jeronymite white habit and brown apron the pink mozetta and carmine hat of a Cardinal. His hand points to the pinkish sky, where a trumpet appears, calling men to the Last Judgement, a vision of the Saint in the Syrian desert. The pleading eyes and half open mouth (pl. 93) underline the insistent appeal to the observer to be ready at all times to meet the Creator. The face is particularly impressive, with soft but firm shadows. The complexion is ochre, the lips wine-red. See *193*, of 1644, and shop copies at Castellón de la Plana and Málaga.

189. THE VIRGIN GIVING THE CHASUBLE TO SAINT ILDEPHONSE. Zafra, Parish Church. About 290 × 180 cm. 1643–4.   Figure 134

History: Centre piece of an altar commissioned in 1643–4 as sepulchre for Alonso (Ildephonse) de Salas Parra and his wife Gerónima de Aguilar Guevara Figueroa. The altar is in its original location at the Epistle side in the chapel of St. Ildephonse (now re-dedicated to Our Lady of Los Remedios), founded on May 16, 1643. The altar comprises also eight other paintings by Zurbarán, *190–197*, arranged as follows:

pinnacle		190	
second storey	192	189	194
first storey	191		193
predella	195	196	197

Dating: A stone tablet, placed next to the altar at the time of its completion, reads: ESTA CAPILLA AI AL/TAR ES ONROSO SEPULCRO ADŌDE/ YACEN ALONSO DE (interlaced) SALAS PARAL PRO/CURADOR G⟨eneral⟩ SINDI/CO I REGIDOR PER/PETUO DE(interlaced)STA VILLA DE(interlaced) CAFRA Y D⟨oñ⟩A (interlaced) GEZO(interlaced)/ NIMA DE (interlaced) AGUILAR GUEVARA SU MU/G⟨er⟩ I LOS Q⟨ue⟩ SUCEDIE/ REN POR SU TES/TAMENTO QUE (interlaced) M⟨an⟩DA(interlaced)RŌ HA(interlaced)CER ESTE RE/TABLO AÑO DEL S⟨eño⟩R DE 1644.
Lit: Caturla, Conjunto de Zurbarán en Zafra, *ABC*, Madrid,

FIG. 134   Cat. No. 189

April 20, 1948; eadem, A Retable by Zurbarán, *Burlington Magazine*, 1952, XCIV, pp. 44–49, ill.

Discovered in 1945 by Sra. Caturla. Only three ensembles by Zurbarán are still in their original place: this one and *86–90* and *151–162*. *189–197* are the only datable paintings between 1640 and 1653. The Virgin, in red and blue, turned almost in profile to her left, gives a gold, red and green chasuble to St. Ildephonse who kneels at the right. He is dressed in dark crimson over a white surplice and faces nearly in profile to his right. Behind him stand two Angels in white. This is the last known narrative scene by Zurbarán. From now on he painted single figures or at most the Virgin with the Two Children. See pp. 19, 31.

190. THE DOUBLE TRINITY. Zafra, Parish Church. About 125 × 135 cm. 1643–4.   Figure 138

History, Dating and Lit: See *189*.

The Christ Child walking between St. Joseph, at the left, and the Virgin, at the right. Above Him, in the yellow sky, the dove of the Holy Spirit and a faint indication of God the Father. Murillo painted the subject at the same time, but with the Virgin at the left and St. Joseph at the right, in the Karl Bergsten Collection, Stockholm (reproduced in Mayer, *Murillo*, Berlin, 1923, p. 3). See p. 22.

FIG. 135   Cat. No. 191   FIG. 136   Cat. No. 192   FIG. 137   Cat. No. 193

191. SAINT JOHN THE BAPTIST. Zafra, Parish Church. About 200 × 80 cm. 1643–4. Figure 135

History, Dating and Lit: See *189*.

Full length, standing and turned three-quarter to his left. He wears a vermilion cloak and holds a lamb on his right arm, while his left hand grips a cross. In the background at the left, rocks are piled to the top. See p. 22.

192. SAINT MICHAEL CASTING OUT LUCIFER. Zafra, Parish Church. About 200 × 100 cm. 1643–4. Figure 136

FIG. 138   Cat. No. 190

History, Dating and Lit: See *189*.

Full length and frontal, the Saint wears blue half-armour, a flaring green skirt and a floating red sash. His large and symmetrically spreading wings are white with a red border. Wielding a sword he stands upon the fallen Lucifer. Below Lucifer are torn-off dragon wings and his tail. Yellow fore- and background.

193. SAINT JEROME. Zafra, Parish Church. About 200 × 80 cm. 1643–4. Figure 137

History, Dating and Lit: See *189*.

The Saint is turned to his right almost in profile and writes in a book which is lying next to a piece of paper on a ledge. His bright red garment is cast in deep folds. At his feet rests a lion. Dark rocks extend along the left edge to the top. A trumpet appears at the upper right. See p. 22.

194. SAINT NICHOLAS OF TOLENTINO. Zafra, Parish Church. About 200 × 100 cm. 1643–4. Figure 138a

History, Dating and Lit: See *189*.

Frontally posed, the young Saint is dressed in black against a yellow sky. The pose recalls that of *149*, while the right hand is placed on his chest as in *117*. Landscape background with trees. See p. 22.

195. ALONSO DE SALAS PARRA. Zafra, Parish Church. About 50 × 75 cm. 1643–4.

History, Dating and Lit: See *189*.

Almost half-length, turned to his left, his hands joined in prayer, resembling in pose the donor in *170*. He wears a black garment, a white stiff collar and starched white cuffs. According to the inscription (see *189*), he was Representative of the people of Zafra and Alderman for life. His coat of arms, atop the altar at the left, party per chevron: first, lion of or; second, five lilies of gules; third, castle of argent.

FIG. 138a   Cat. No. 194   FIG. 139   Cat. No. 196   FIG. 140   Cat. No. 197

196. SAINT ANDREW. Zafra, Parish Church. About 50 × 23 cm. 1643–4.   Figure 139

History, Dating and Lit: See *189*.

197. SAINT BARNABAS. Zafra, Parish Church. About 50 × 23 cm. 1643–4.   Figure 140

History, Dating and Lit: See *189*.

The Saint is dressed in red and grey. He holds a book.

198. SAINT JEROME WITH SAINT PAULA AND SAINT EUSTOCHIUM. New York, Samuel H. Kress Foundation. 247 × 174 cm. About 1638–40.   Plate 73

History: Perhaps from the Sevillan convent Sta. Paula of the Jeronymite Nuns, where between 1635 and 1642 documented work on altars, paintings and sculptures was carried out by A. Cano, the older Herrera, the sculptor Montañés, Murillo's teacher Juan del Castillo, and lesser artists. Standish Collection, Louvre, 1842, No. 161 ('Zurbarán, St. Dominique et deux religieuses, 246 × 174 cm.'); Standish sale, Christie's, May 27–8, 1853, No. 105, £21; Alphonse Oudry sale, Drouot, April 16–17, 1869, No. 157 ('Zurbarán, Evêque introduisant deux religieuses, 252 × 180 cm.'), frs. 500, bought in; idem, April 10, 1876, Drouot, No. 60, frs. 715; M. Knoedler & Co., New York, 1951. Dating: Influenced by *137–140* and *151–158*, both painted 1638–9, years corresponding to the peak of activity at Sta. Paula (see above). Lit: Mrs. Jameson, *Sacred and Legendary Art*, London, 1857, third edition, I, under 'St. Jerome'.

St. Jerome was accompanied from Rome to Bethlehem by several noble Roman ladies, among them the widow Paula and her daughters Marcella and Eustochium. Paula built two monasteries, one for men, and one for women, the latter headed by herself. At her death in 404 she was succeeded by St. Eustochium, and St. Jerome became St. Paula's biographer. In the men's monastery St. Paula had built, St. Jerome translated the Old Testament from the Hebrew. The Saint and the nuns wear white robes and loose raw umber panels. His cape is glazed in madder over white and grey underpainting. The nuns have beige wimples and black hoods. Venetian red chair with gold nails. Red cardinal's hat at the right. A lion is hiding under the saint's chair. The sky and architecture at the left are in delicate pale blues, pinks and greens over a dark ground, and the background behind the saint discloses a dark door. This is a capital painting, entirely by Zurbarán, but difficult to reproduce. Composition, types, poses, draperies, lights and darks, brushwork, and background architecture prove the master's authorship. For the profile head of St. Paula, cf. the kneeling Dominican in *5, 91* and *136*; for the younger nun, cf. *46, 56* and *199*; for St. Jerome, cf. *15* and the head of Rabbi Simeon in *140*; for the background, cf. also *140*.

199. THE VIRGIN AND CHILD SEATED IN CLOUDS. Seville, Museum of Fine Arts. 181 × 102 cm. About 1645.   Figure 141

History: entered the Museum from the Hospital de la Sangre, Seville.

Dating: The figures are in the same position, but slightly more *en face*, as in *182*. Cf. the arm and hands of the Virgin and the folds at the bottom of her skirt. In *199* the expression of the face has become more gentle, the painting is apparently later.

Lit: Cascales, pl. XXXIII; S. II, 131.

The Christ Child is nude but for a lavender cloak. He holds a green branch. The Virgin wears a darkish-blue mantle over a pink gown, and a white scarf striped in light green and red. A strand of golden round stones around her neck. Below, grey-white clouds, and behind a sky in yellow and red. See pp. 19, 21.

200. THE IMMACULATE CONCEPTION. Seville, Town Hall, Mayor's Room. 198 × 120 cm. 1645–50.   Figure 142

History: Formerly in the Sevillan Convent of Our Lady del Pópolo, dissolved in 1868.

FIG. 141 Cat. No. 199   FIG. 142 Cat. No. 200   FIG. 143 Cat. No. 201

Dating: Done fifteen to twenty years after *66* and showing less contrasty, more transparent chiaroscuro, gently blending transitions, as well as fuller, more plastic and more spacious drapery folds. The face, with eyes now looking up, is painted in the softly fusing style of *199*.

Lit: G. III, 9 (believed that the style does not entirely exclude a date of 1630 and that *200* was a first study, preceding *66*).

The moon, snake and dove are omitted. See pp. 19, 21.

201. SAINT DIEGO OF ALCALÁ. Madrid, José Lázaro Foundation. 110 × 84 cm. About 1650.   Figure 143

Lit: Mayer, *Sevillaner Malerschule*, 1911, p. 160 (as by Zurbarán, earlier given by him to Juan Rizi); Kehrer, pl. 67, p. 147 (late work); Cascales, pl. LVIII; S. I, 169.

Shown in a light brown-yellow habit against a luminous sky. In his lap pink roses. See the earlier versions of this theme, *54* and *92*. Formerly held to be by Murillo. See p. 22.

202. SAINT ANTHONY OF PADUA. Seville, Alfonso Grosso. 148 × 108 cm. About 1650 (?).   Figure 144

History: At least since the eighteenth century in a private collection, at Manzanilla, near Seville; Salvador Cumplido, Seville, 1905.

FIG. 144 Cat. No. 202   FIG. 145 Cat. No. 203   FIG. 146 Cat. No. 205

Dating: The faces show a greater softness than earlier paintings.
Exh: Madrid, 1905, No. 41; Seville, 1929/30, Room VI, No. 17.
Lit: Identical (?) with a *St. Anthony with the Christ Child*, in the Julian Williams Collection, Seville, mentioned by J. Amador de los Ríos, *Sevilla pintoresca*, 1844, p. 473; S. I, 170; G. II, 202.

St. Anthony in grey; the Christ Child nude but for a transparent white gauze fabric. At the right, a greyish-silver basilica before green cypress trees. To the left, near a body of grey water, a green plant with rose buds, a rosary and a brown book with red ends. Predominant colours: greys and browns. See pp. 19, 22, 25.

203. SAINT SEBASTIAN. Seville, Museum of Fine Arts (on loan from Adela Grande de Barrau). 200 × 105 cm. 1640-50.   Figure 145

History: Acquired in 1868 from the Monastery of San Agustín, Seville.
Dating: There are similarities with *149-150*, as well as with *204, 206*.
Exh: Seville, 1929/30, Room VI, No. 3.
Lit: S. I, 169.

The twisting body suggests the tortures inflicted on the Saint. Violetish-white loincloth, soft in feeling. Airy landscape in grey, brown, and green, under a wide light-blue sky.

204. CHRIST CARRYING THE CROSS. Orléans, Cathedral, Sacristy. 195 × 108 cm. Signed: Franᶜᵒ de Zurbar⟨an⟩/1653.   Plate 91

History: In the Cathedral since about 1810, having been carried away from Spain by the troops of Napoleon.
Exh: Orléans, 1876.
Lit: G. III, 28-29. (See Ponz V, 6, 29; Ceán VI, 51.)

Christ wears a purple robe, his face has a greenish cast, and his hands are reddish. Brown cross. Light-blue and pinkish sky. The modelling of face and drapery corresponds closely to *206*. In the church of the Barefooted Carmelites, at Madrid, Ponz and Ceán saw two versions of this theme, one half length and the other signed in 1661, thus neither identical with *204*, painted five years before Zurbarán moved from Seville to Madrid. See pp. 20, 21, 31.

205. SAINT PETER REPENTANT. Marseilles, Museum, No. 838. 134 × 96 cm. After 1650 (?).   Figure 146

History: Possibly Galerie Espagnole, Louvre, 1838, No. 340; King Louis Philippe sale, 1853, No. 64, £4 to Bigge. Acquired by the Museum in 1869 through the exchange Talabot. Found by the author among pictures not exhibited.
Condition: Very dirty and in need of cleaning.
Lit: *Marseilles, Musée, Catalogue*, 1908, No. 838 (as 'attributed to Ribera'); Charles Sterling (in a letter of 1949) saw the picture in 1938 and believed it to be probably by Zurbarán.

The Saint, three-quarter length and seated before a dark cave at the left, wears a blue-green robe and an orange cloak. His flesh is brown with white highlights. A small portion of his white shirt may be seen at the neck. A black key lies on his lap. The landscape is brown with touches of vermilion, grey and green. The sky turns to dark grey-blue at the upper right, and toward the horizon to yellow and pink. Final confirmation of authenticity must await cleaning.

206. THE VIRGIN AND CHILD WITH SAINT JOHN. San Diego, California, Fine Arts Gallery. 137 × 104 cm. Signed: Franᶜᵒ de Zurbaran/1658.   Plate 96

History: Counts of Altamira, Madrid, sale, London, June 1, 1827, No. 55, £42, to the Marquess of Stafford; his descendant, the Duke of Sutherland, Stafford House, London, sale, Christie's, July 11, 1913, No. 143, £525, to Cureau; Dr. C. Guettler, Munich; Reinhardt Galleries, New York; acquired in 1935 from Lilienfeld Galleries, New York.
Exh: British Institution, London, 1838, No. 10; Lilienfeld-Van Diemen Galleries, New York, 1934, No. 24; Fine Arts Gallery, San Diego, 1935, No. 591; Los Angeles Art Association, 1937, No. 114.

FIG. 147   Cat. No. 208

Lit: Waagen, *Kunstwerke in England*, 1833, p. 63; idem, *Works of Art and Artists in England*, London, 1838, II, pp. 250-251; idem, *Treasures*, II, p. 67; Stirling-Maxwell, *Annals of the Artists of Spain*, new ed., III, pp. 927-928; Head, *Handbook of the History of Spanish . . . Painting*, 1848, p. 131; Tormo, in Cascales, p. 219; Mayer, *Sevillaner Malerschule*, 1911, p. 159; Kehrer, pl. 72, pp. 117-118; *International Studio*, October 1926, p. 20 (in colour); Trivas, *Apollo*, June 1941; S. I, 169-170; Seckel, *GdBA*, 1946, XXX, p. 297; *Fine Arts Society of San Diego, Catalogue*, 1947, pp. 86-87 (lists signature wrongly).

The Christ Child in white; the Virgin in red and blue, wearing an embroidered Spanish shawl. St. John in red and brown. Pewter dish with yellow apples at the left. Wine-red curtain. Landscape in greys and greens under a pink and blue-grey sky. See pp. 20-1, 32.

207. THE VIRGIN NURSING THE CHRIST CHILD. Moscow, Pushkin State Museum of Fine Arts. Measurements unknown. Signed: Franᶜᵒ de Zurbaran 1658.

Lit: K. Malitskaya, *The Spanish Painting of XVI-XVII Centuries*, Moscow, 1947, pp. 113-114, ill.

The Virgin, three-quarter length, is seated almost in frontal pose but turned slightly to her right. She wears a red tunic and around her neck a whitish veil. From her right breast she nurses the Christ Child whom she holds and who lies on an expanse of white draperies. Her head bends toward the Child. At the lower right is a small table or stool on which a pewter dish with small fruits, and a rounded whitish jar. Compare Dürer's engraving *The Virgin Nursing*, of 1519 (Bartsch 36). See pp. 21, 32.

208. THE VIRGIN WITH THE SLEEPING CHRIST CHILD. Madrid, Marquis of Unzá del Valle. 120 × 98 cm. Signed: Franᶜᵒ de Zurbaran/1659.   Figure 147

Exh: Madrid, 1905, No. 49.
Lit: Kehrer, pl. 82, pp. 125-126; Angulo, *Arch. esp. de arte*, 1944, pp. 8-9.

The Christ Child is wrapped in relucent white. The Virgin wears a vermilion-red raiment, and a wine-red kerchief around her neck. Very little can be seen of her blue cloak. On a brown table, a pewter plate with apples of greenish-yellow hue tinged with rose. Brown background. Behind the head ot the Virgin, a reddish-brown glow, and a red transparency beneath her veil. Rose-tinged fingers. Angulo has shown that the composition derives from Dürer's engraving *Madonna with the Monkey*, of 1498 (B. 42). See pp. 21, 32.

209. THE HOLY FAMILY. Budapest, Museum of Fine Arts, No. 2536. 121 × 97 cm. Signed: Fran^{co} de Zur/baran f./1659.   Plate 95

History: Painted in Madrid and surely not the painting of this theme, done probably in the early 1630's, seen by Ponz and Ceán in the Carthusian Monastery at Seville. Probably in the sale of an aristocrat, Paris, June 27, 1825, No. 99. Perhaps in the Count of Altamira sale, London, at Stanley's, June 1, 1827, No. 39. That picture was sold in the Viscount Clifden sale, Christie's, May 6, 1893, No. 32 (121 × 94 cm., signed and dated 1659, from the Altamira sale) £24 to Colnaghi & Co., London. Porges, Paris; bought from Kleinberger & Co., Paris, 1904, for frs. 7672.
Lithographed by Florentino de Craene at Paris in 1825, printed by the Real Establecimiento litográfico de Madrid.
Exh: Hamburger Kunstverein, Hamburg, 1935, No. 25.
Lit: Mayer, *Monatshefte für Kunstwissenschaft*, 1908, I, pp. 520, 522; idem, *Sevillaner Malerschule*, 1911, p. 160; idem, *Geschichte der Spanischen Malerei*, 1922, pp. 324–326; Kehrer, pl. 81, p. 125; Loga, *Malerei in Spanien*, p. 283; G. III, 4–5.

The Virgin in pink and blue. The Christ Child in a long yellowish-grey garment and in white. Yellowish-grey drapery below the Christ Child. The brown wall of the background discloses a deep-blue sky and yellow horizon. This painting is very Murillesque. See pp. 22, 32.

FIG. 148   Cat. No. 212 (detail)

210. THE ANNUNCIATION. Philadelphia, Philadelphia Museum of Art, Wilstach Collection, No. 1900-1-16. 213 × 314 cm. Signed: Fran^{co} de Zurb⟨aran faci⟩ebat. Not dated. 1658.   Plate 99

History: Painted in 1658 at Madrid, because given in that year by Gaspar de Bracamonte to the parish church of Peñaranda de Bracamonte, Salamanca Province, according to documents found by Sra. Caturla; seen there, before 1724, by Palomino; removed in 1824 and a copy, still *in situ*, put in its place; Valentín Carderera, Madrid; sold to Marquis of Salamanca; his sale, Paris, June 3–6, 1867, No. 48, frs. 20,000 to the Earl of Dudley; his sale, Christie's, June 16, 1900, No. 54, £231, to Colnaghi & Co.; from them purchased October 2, 1900.
Exh: Leeds, 1868, No. 2933; Royal Academy, London, 1871, No. 405.
Lit: Pal. III, 108; Ceán VI, 52; Tormo, in Cascales, p. 219; *Catalogue, Wilstach Collection*, 1913, No. 486; Mayer, *Historia de la pintura española*, 1926, p. 149; *Bulletin, Philadelphia Museum*, November 1940, XXXVI; S. I, 158 (believed the picture to be a copy and dated it too early); Soria, *Boletín Soc. esp. excursiones*, 1948, LII pp. 149–51 (fully accepted the picture); G. III, 31–32.

The Virgin wears red and blue, and a yellow scarf. She kneels at a green prie-dieu. The angel is dressed in white under a dalmatic painted in grey, gold, red and black. Over his shoulder a green drapery. Wine-red curtain. Grey and brown architecture. Chiaroscuro contrasts are minimized and one senses a melancholy mellowness. The composition repeats curved lines. The door stops movement into depth and separates the two figures. They are, however, united at eye level by the panelling which, twisted at the lower edge, exaggerates the orthogonal. A variant (160 × 254 cm.), apparently not by Zurbarán, was exhibited as by the master in *Siete obras maestras*, Sala Parés, Barcelona, 1949–50, pls. LXXIV–LXXIX. The author has not seen it. See p. 32.

211. THE YOUNG VIRGIN PRAYING. Leningrad, Hermitage, No. 328. 75 × 54 cm. About 1660.   Plate 92

History: Acquired in 1814 from the Banker W. G. Coesveldt at Amsterdam.
Dating: Stylistically related to *210* and *222*.
Lit: A. Somof, *Ermitage Catalogue*, 1909; Kehrer, pl. 80, pp. 124–125.

The Virgin, a young child, wears a deep-blue mantle and a red tunic embroidered at neck and cuffs. Brown chair. Deep-green sewing pillow with a piece of white material. Mellow and mystic expression. See pp. 20, 22.

212. THE YOUNG VIRGIN PRAYING. Madrid, Manuel Gómez Moreno. 80 × 54 cm. About 1660.   Figure 148

History: From a convent at Medina del Campo, near Valladolid.

Wine-red tunic, very intense blue and green. Brown background. Resembling *211* quite closely, where the expression of the head is more moving and more convincing in modelling. However, in *212* the draperies seem more interesting. See pp. 20, 22.

213. SAINT JAMES OF THE MARCHES. Madrid, Prado, No. 2472. 291 × 165 cm. About 1658. Signed: Fran^{co} de Zurbaran.   Figure 149

History: Painted, together with three pictures by Alonso Cano and Bartolomé Román, for the chapel of San Diego at Alcalá de Henares, near Madrid; removed to the Museo de la Trinidad, Madrid, then to San Francisco el Grande, Madrid.
Date: Tormo and Kehrer suggested 1660–1661, but the picture may be two years earlier, since Cano was at Madrid in 1658. Román died there in 1659.
Exh: Madrid, 1905, No. 53; Exposición Franciscana, Madrid, 1927, No. 32 (facsimile of signature, pl. 61).
Lit: Mayer, *Sevillaner Malerschule*, p. 156 (after 1639); Kehrer, p. 126.
The Saint (1391–1476) wears a light-brown habit, grey sandals and a sienna cord. In his left a rose-coloured scarf edged in gold lace and a chalice filled with red wine. In the background, the Saint and

three other Franciscans welcome back to life a little boy who had died. A dark-brown curtain at the left. Airy architecture of grey hues and interesting space divisions. Subtle harmonies of greys and browns. See p. 32.

214. A DOCTOR OF LAW. Boston, Isabella Stewart Gardner Museum. 194 × 103 cm. 1658–60.   Plate 90

History: Marquis of Leganés, Madrid, before 1700; Marquis of Salamanca, Madrid, sale, Paris, June 3–6, 1867, No. 207, frs. 500 (as by Velázquez); Ivan Stchoukine sale, Paris, Hotel Drouot, June 19, 1908, No. 70; bought from the Ehrich Galleries, New York, in 1910. Dating: The advanced and airy style suggests a late date. Compare the much harder, block-like head of *60*, of about 1632, and *104*, of 1635. The brushwork of the collar, resembling *222* of 1661, and the execution of the hands may be explained best by Zurbarán's renewed contact with Velázquez, from 1658 onward at Madrid. The diffused, fairly even lighting of the right side of the face does not seem to occur before that year and is similar to the style of *220*.
Lit: Mayer, *Arts and Decoration*, 1916, p. 219; Kehrer, pl. 43, p. 84 ('about 1638'); Loga, *Malerei in Spanien*, p. 284; Hendy, *Gardner Museum, Catalogue*, 1931, p. 428; Tormo, *Enciclopedia Italiana*, 1937, XXXV, p. 1059 ('1633'); S. I, 166, 169.

FIG. 150   Cat. No. 216

The young scholar of the University of Salamanca wears a red-brown robe, a broad collar of brilliant cinnabar, and a green cap. Black sleeves, olive-green gloves. Dark-green curtain. Grey ground and background. The pose and glove derive from the portraits of *Philip IV* and of the *Infante Carlos* (Prado, Nos. 1182 and 1188), painted by Velázquez at Madrid between 1625 and 1627. This was noticed also by Kehrer. See pp. 7, 20.

215. SAINT FRANCIS IN MEDITATION. Munich, Old Pinacotheca, No. 504. 64 × 53 cm. About 1658–60.   Plate 94

History: In the eighteenth century in the Gallery at Mannheim; brought to Munich in 1799; entered the Museum in 1836 from the Hofgartengalerie.
Lit: Kehrer, pl. 75, pp. 120–121 (about 1653–1659).

Typifying the melancholy mood and the broadly fusing palette of late Zurbaráns. Kehrer pointed out that the picture is painted in a unified accord of brown-grey fabrics against a blue and grey evening sky, brownish in tonality. The brownish-yellow skull harmonizes with these colours. This vision is subdued and gentle, intimate and undramatic. The draperies are modelled with breadth and fullness. Even the pose of the right hand, the index finger becoming part of the figure's silhouette, is integrated with the total design. See p. 22.

216. SAINT FRANCIS KNEELING. Bilbao, Felix Valdés. 127 × 97 cm. Signed: Franco de Zurbaran/1659.   Figure 150

Collections: Aureliano de Beruete, Madrid, 1905.
Exh: Madrid, 1905, No. 44; Royal Academy, London, 1920/21, No. 62; Exposición Franciscana, Madrid, 1927, No. 34 (facsimile of signature, pl. 61).
Lit: Cascales, pl. LVI; Mayer, *Sevillaner Malerschule*, 1911, p. 159; Kehrer, pl. 79, p. 124.

A three-dimensional feeling is emphasized by the pose, turned toward the observer and holding the skull in front. Also by the small cross

FIG. 149   Cat. No. 213

leaning against a parchment book and pointing toward the observer. These foreshortenings are rare in Zurbarán's art. By exception, the texture in the fabric of the habit is indicated. There are no marked contrasts of light and shade. A light-grey, airy landscape and a very light sky create a 'blond' mood. See pp. 22, 32.

217. SAINT PETER REPENTANT. Puebla, Mexico, José Luis Bello y Zetina. 159 × 124 cm. Signed: Franco de Zurbaran fec/1659.

History: The picture must have entered Mexico in the seventeenth or eighteenth century, since several old copies are there, one in the Museum of Querétaro. Bought in Mexico City about 1864 from a dealer, José Pérez, by José Luis Bello González, grandfather of the owner.
Condition: Not good. Face and hands are entirely altered and repainted.
Lit: J. L. Bello and G. Ariza, *Pinturas poblanas*, Mexico, 1943, p. 111, ill.; S. I, 171.

Seated, full length, resting his head upon his folded hands and looking upward to his left. Greenish-blue garment. Golden key at the waist. Behind the Saint, his yellow-ochre cloak. At the right, the cock on a column. See pp. 22, 32.

218. VIRGIN AND CHILD WITH SAINT JOHN. New York, Paul O. Berliz. 130 × 100 cm. About 1660.   Figure 151

History: Photographed about 1920 by Vicente Moreno, Sr., in a private collection at Madrid, as by an 'anonymous author'.
Dating: Iconographically and stylistically close to *207*, *208* and *223*, all derived from Dürer's prints.

The blond Christ Child in white. The Virgin in red and blue, wearing a beige scarf and in her hair a red ribbon. At left in front of St. John is a dark grey ledge on which are his reed cross; a band inscribed: EC⟨CE⟩AGNUS D⟨EI QUI TOLL⟩IS PECATA . . ; and a pewter dish with yellow apples and red cherries. Dark background. Of the late versions of the Madonna theme, this is the most realistic and the one most interesting compositionally. See p. 21.

FIG. 151   Cat. No. 218

FIG. 152   Cat. No. 223

219. SAINT LUKE BEFORE THE CRUCIFIED. Madrid, Prado, No. 2594. 105 × 84 cm. 1635–40.   Plate 98

History: Perhaps once in the royal collections at Madrid, since it belonged to the Infante Sebastian Gabriel, at Pau, who died in 1875 and was a great-grandson of Charles III; acquired in 1936 from Cristóbal Colón, married to an heiress of the Infante.
Exh: Madrid, 1905, No. 29.
Lit: *Catalogue . . . des tableaux . . . Don Sebastian de Bourbon et Bragance*, Pau, 1876, No. 284 ('Christ et St. Luc'). Kehrer, pl. 83, p. 126; Sánchez Cantón, *Museo del Prado, Catálogo*, 1949, pp. 748–749.

It has been suggested that not St. Luke but Zurbarán himself is represented, because the subject of the Saint before Christ is not known elsewhere. It may, however, have been invented by Zurbarán or by the donor of the picture. Cranach repeatedly painted three-quarter-length figures next to the Crucified. The face of the figure holding a palette looks too idealized to have been painted from life. 'St. Luke' wears a pink-lavender tunic and a dark green cloak, a costume not of Zurbarán's time, but contemporary with the apostles. The identity of this figure with Zurbarán can be proved only by finding an unrefutable likeness of the artist. None is known for sure at present (see, however, *224*, fig. XIV). See pp. 20–1, 191.

220. ET PONIT VESTIMENTA SUA. Jadraque, Parish church. 167 × 107 cm. Signed: Franco de Zurbaran 1661.   Plate 97

History: Jadraque, in Guadalajara Province, is 45 miles North East of Alcalá (see *213*). The picture may have been commissioned for the church from Zurbarán then living at Madrid.
Exh: Madrid, 1905, No. 27.
Lit: Mayer, *Sevillaner Malerschule*, 1911, p. 160; Cascales, pl. LXXIX; Kehrer, pl. 84, pp. 126–127; S. I, 171.

'He riseth from supper, and laid aside his garments; and took a towel, and girded himself. After that he poureth water into a basin, and began to wash the disciples' feet, and to wipe them with the towel wherewith he was girded' (*John*, XIII, 4–5). The painting is thus a symbol of Christ's humility, and by implication, of the artist's own humility toward Christ. Zurbarán still possessed sobriety and capacity for design, although the modelling has become very gentle. Kehrer pointed out that the foreground melts into the background, and that the figure itself fades into the surrounding atmosphere without the sharp outlines of Zurbarán's earlier work. See pp. 20, 32.

221. CHRIST AFTER THE FLAGELLATION. Wroclaw (Breslau), Museum, No. 119. 179 × 123 cm. 1661.

History: Since before 1852 in the Berlin Museum (Nagler, *Künstlerlexikon*, XXII, 1852); loaned by it to the Silesian Museum since about 1906. Never owned by A. Morrison, London.
Lit: Kehrer, pl. 86, p. 141; Angulo, *Arch. esp. de arte*, 1945, pp. 234–5.
A white loincloth; a purple garment on the ground. Brown column and brown background. Along the outlines, particularly along the shoulders, numerous pentimenti may be observed where the painter changed the silhouette. Angulo rightly suggested that the body was adapted from an engraving, widely copied in Spain and Spanish America, by Lucas Vorstermanns, after G. Seghers.

222. THE IMMACULATE CONCEPTION. Budapest, Museum of Fine Arts, No. 800. 136 × 102 cm. Signed: Franco De Zurbaran/facie 1661.   Plate 100

History: Listed in an inventory of the Esterházy collection, Budapest, in 1820, and given to the Museum in 1871 by Prince Nicolaus Esterházy. Perhaps identical with an *Immaculate Conception*, signed and dated 1661 on a paper, once in the Aniceto Bravo collection, Seville (see J. Amador de los Ríos, *Sevilla pintoresca*, 1844, p. 422).
Lit: Mayer, *Monatshefte für Kunstwissenschaft*, 1908, I, p. 522; idem, *Sevillaner Malerschule*, p. 160; Kehrer, pl. 85, pp. 127–128; Loga, *Malerei in Spanien*, p. 283; Cascales, pl. LXXVIII; S. I, 171.
The Virgin, unlike all other versions of the theme by the master, is opening her arms as if welcoming heaven. She wears a white gown and around her waist a pink scarf. No jewelry. Around her head, a grey-blue halo changing to white-yellow, then to orange-red. The sky is pink-orange turning to grey-blue. Below, a silvery, dream-like landscape, wholly ethereal, of the Marian symbols. The flaring mantle, in blue, is characteristic of Late Baroque grandiloquence. The folds are merely calligraphic and have lost the rugged medieval strength of Zurbarán's earlier draperies. There exists a feeling of lightness and liberation not reached by the artist before. See pp. 20–1, 32.

223. THE VIRGIN AND CHILD WITH SAINT JOHN. Bilbao, Museum, No. 441. 165 × 127 cm. Signed: Franco de Zurbaran/1662.
Figure 152

Collections: Countess of Canillas, Madrid; José de Madrazo, Madrid, 1856, No. 450; Marquis of Salamanca, Madrid, sale, Paris, June 3–6, 1867, No. 50, frs. 1700; Marquis of Camarines, Madrid; his heir, the Marquis of Nerva, Madrid; bequeathed by his heir, María Martín de Oliva, in 1936.
Lit: Madoz, *Diccionario geográfico estadístico e histórico de España*, Madrid, 1845, X, p. 861; Mayer, *Apollo*, 1928, VII, p. 181; Angulo, *Arch. esp, de arte*, 1944, pp. 7–9.

The brown-haired Virgin has a vermilion dress, a blue cloak and a sienna-brown neck veil. A white diaper half covers the Christ Child. St. John wears a dirty-brown and sienna camel skin. The lamb is cream-coloured with white and brown spots. Green tablecloth. Pewter dish with yellow and red apples and salmon-coloured pears. Limp and diffuse modelling of faces and hands. Angulo has shown that the composition is derived from Dürer's engraving *The Madonna with the Monkey* (B. 42). See *207, 208, 218*, and pp. 21, 32.

224. FRANCISCO DE ZURBARÁN. Paris, Louvre. 12·6 × 9·5 cm. 1650–60. Red chalk drawing.   Figure XIV

Collections: The third Count del Aguila († 1808), Seville (?); Frank Hall Standish († 1841), Duxbury Hall, Lincolnshire; bequeathed by him to King Louis Philippe, Louvre, 1842, No. 492; Standish sale, Paris, December 6, 1852, to the Louvre.

Bust portrait, possibly from life. Conforming in pose, lighting and details of modelling to Zurbarán's style, but the expression and the hesitant execution point to a pupil. A further argument against Zurbarán's authorship is the omission of "Francisco de" in the inscription "Retrato de Zurbaran", which is apparently by the same hand as the drawing. The drawing may be cautiously accepted as a true likeness of the aged master, and thus would refute the identification of the figure in *219* with Zurbarán.

A copy by Valentín Carderera (1797–1880) and inscribed: "Retrato de Zurbaran." Sacada de un dibujo del mismo tamaño de lapiz rojo de la coleccion Standish" is in the Biblioteca Nacional, Madrid. From this copy Federico de Madrazo (1815–94) made a vigorous woodcut published in *Seminario pintoresco español*, Madrid, November 5, 1848, p. 357, accompanying an article by Carderera on Zurbarán.

FIG. 154.   Zurbarán's Signature, 1638 (detail from Plate 80, Cat. No. 157)

FIG. 155   Cat. No. 226   FIG. 156   Cat. No. 228   FIG. 157   Cat. No. 236

225. THE DEAD CHRIST ON THE CROSS. Chicago, Art Institute of Chicago. 290 × 168 cm. Signed Franco De Zurba(ran)/fat. 1627.

Plates 20–21

History: Not mentioned in the contract of January 17, 1626, but placed in the oratory of the sacristy of San Pablo, Dominican church at Seville, presumably in 1627 and at any rate before June 1629, remaining there probably until 1808–10; most likely in Alcazar, Seville, room 7, No. 224, 336 × 168 cm., 1810; taken to France (?); given by the Duke of Alba to Father Dulac for the Jesuit College, Canterbury, 1880; Jesuit College, Isle of Jersey; Jesuit College, Chantilly, until 1951; A. Fankhauser, Basel, 1952, who sold it to the Art Institute.

Lit: Pal. III, 108; Ponz IX, 3, 24; Matute, *Anales eclesiásticos y seculares*, I, 177; Ceán, VI, 47, 50; F. González de León, *Noticia artística de Sevilla*, II, p. 178; Gestoso y Pérez, *Ensayo de un diccionario*, II, p. 124; Kehrer, p. 36; G. II, 193–194, 198–199; S. VI, 169; José Milicua, *Arch. esp. de arte*, 1953, No. 103, pp. 177–186.

Violent light, like lightning, strikes Christ's heavy body from His left, and is abruptly swallowed up by the blackish background. The head, almost torn from the left shoulder, has sunk deep unto the right upper arm. A single pain-racked movement, unified in an arc, runs from the right hand to the hip. The resplendent whites of the loincloth counteract in their liveliness, agitation, short angles and crumpled intersecting planes the quiet stillness of the large body. Thus the dead Saviour looms more massive and awesome, yet plain and bare of rhetoric. The flesh tones are rendered in whites, grays and ochre, slightly greenish in the face, hands and feet. Tiny streams of blood trickle from the bluish nails which tear into the flesh. Milicua, in a masterly description, stresses the unique serenity of this *Crucifixion*, its hallucinating superhuman and yet extremely human quality. Zurbarán's poetic transcript of reality has a sobriety and depth of religious feeling that seems as close to Caravaggio as it is to Velázquez, Champaigne and Georges de la Tour.

This is the master's most important picture up to June 1629, when it was singled out for praise by Seville's city counsellor Rodrigo Suárez. Palomino, Ponz and Ceán lauded its 'stupendous' plastic effect resembling sculpture. Milicua emphasized Zurbarán's originality as compared to the carved *Crucifixions* by Montañés, and found in *225* iconographic elements derived from Michelangelo, Battista Franco, Orazio Borgianni and the Greco pupil Luis Tristán. Being earlier than any *Crucifixion* by Velázquez or Cano, *225* and the much smaller *8* are the first versions by Zurbarán of *Christ on the Cross*.

226. THE IMMACULATE CONCEPTION BANDARÁN. Seville, Colegio de Esclavas Concepcionistas del Divino Corazón. 139 × 104 cm. About 1629–32.

Figure 155

History: Discovered in 1953 by Father José Sebastián y Bandarán.
Lit: J. Sebastián y Bandarán, *Archivo hispalense*, 1954, No. 64–65.
A small, exquisite version of a theme greatly favoured by the artist. In the pose of the hands, the sleeves, the outline of the mantle and other details closest to *59*, of 1632. Bandarán noticed the influence from Velázquez' *Immaculate Conception Frere*.

227. THE DEAD CHRIST ON THE CROSS. Marchena, Parish church, Sacristy. 181.5 × 107 cm. 1635.

History: Discovered in the original location together with *228–235* in 1953 by José Hernández Díaz.
Date: Commissioned in 1635 from Zurbarán who was paid 90 ducats for the nine paintings according to a document of 1637 found by J. Hernández Díaz.
Condition: *227–235* are in mediocre condition, needing relining and cleaning. Until then it is difficult to assess the participation of the studio, perhaps Bernabé de Ayala, in one or the other painting.
Lit: G. III, 24 note 2; J. Hernández Díaz, *Los Zurbaranes de Marchena, Arch. esp. de arte*, 1953, No. 101, pp. 31–36, plates I–VIII.
The draperies, praised by J. Hernández Díaz, as well as the pose repeat *62*, painted three to five years earlier.

228. THE IMMACULATE CONCEPTION. Marchena, Parish church, Sacristy. 183 × 107 cm. 1635–7.

Figure 156

History and Lit: See *227*.
Salmon tunic, blue mantle studded with stars and gilt-lace-edged. Below is a landscape with the Marian symbols. The pose and the arrangement of the draperies disclose a new iconographic type, not otherwise seen in the master's oeuvre. Also unique is the halo of rays instead of the customary stars.

229. SAINT JOHN THE BAPTIST. Marchena, Parish church, Sacristy. 183 × 107 cm. 1635–7.

History and Lit: See *227*.
Derived from a print also often copied in Peru. Perhaps by the studio. Salmon mantle and greenish-gray fur.

230. SAINT JAMES MAJOR. Marchena, Parish church, Sacristy. 180 × 107 cm. 1635–7.

History and Lit: See *227*.

Greenish-blue tunic and crimson mantle. Enlarges Rubens' half-length version in the Prado, No. 1648, of 1603, seen by Zurbarán during his visit to Madrid in 1634. Another copy of Rubens' picture, at San Francisco, Lima, is there attributed to the circle of Ribera (!).

231. SAINT PETER. Marchena, Parish church, Sacristy. 182.5 × 108 cm. 1635–7.

History and Lit: See *227*.

Green tunic and dark ochre mantle. Possibly by the studio. The pose slightly related to *78a*.

232. SAINT PAUL. Marchena, Parish church, Sacristy. 181.5 × 107 cm. 1635–7.

History and Lit: See *227*.

Green mantle and lilac-purple tunic. Interesting pose, the left foot considerably higher than the right one, thus originating a twisting spiral movement coming to a stop in the bold profile of the patriarch's head.

233. SAINT BARTHOLOMEW. Marchena, Parish church, Sacristy. 178 × 107 cm. 1635–7.

History and Lit: See *227*.

White mantle, gray-violet tunic. One of the most successful creations of this altar series. Volumes, shapes, and light and dark counteract one another in a lively, monumental, yet controlled rhythm.

234. SAINT JOHN THE EVANGELIST. Marchena, Parish church, Sacristy. 183 × 106.5 cm. 1635–7.

History and Lit: See *227*.

Olive green tunic, cadmium red mantle. As Hernández Díaz observed, recalls *78b*, a figure derived from Schongauer. Also related to *144n*.

235. SAINT ANDREW. Marchena, Parish church, Sacristy. 181 × 109 cm. 1635–7.

History and Lit: See *227*.

Blue tunic and ochre mantle. Frontal view. An imposing, patriarchal type.

236. THE IMMACULATE CONCEPTION. Lisbon, Private collection. 128 × 98 cm. About 1645–50.   Figure 157

History: Probably F. A. White et al. sale, Sotheby's, London, May 9, 1934, No. 126, 127 × 97 cm., to E. Spielman, £6.
Dating: Most closely related to *200*, of 1645–50, where the Virgin also looks heavenward. The modelling, brushwork, and vaporous treatment of *236* also suggest a fairly late date. In the much earlier prototype, *66*, the Virgin addresses the spectator.
Known to the author from a photograph only, making further study desirable, and reserving a final opinion until the original has been seen.

237. THE VISION OF SAINT FRANCIS. Northwick Park, Blockley, Moreton-in-Marsh, Gloucestershire, Captain E. G. Spencer-Churchill. 198 × 155 cm. Signed: Franco de Zurbaran/1661.   Figure 158

History: Unknown.
Lit: Unknown.
If the Vision of St. Francis in the Porciuncula is represented, see *40*, it seems most unusual to show Christ as a young child. The Virgin

FIG. 158   Cat. No. 237

and the little Jesus correspond to other late representations of this group by Zurbarán. A precedent for the column at the right is found in *200*.

238. SAINT FRANCIS. Mexico City, Count Felipe Subervielle. 204 × 112 cm. About 1631–2.

History: Marquis of Leganés collection, Madrid, seventeenth century; Marquis of Salamanca sale, Paris, June 3–6, 1867, No. 51, frs. 1480, bought in; sold again, 1875, No. 44, frs. 2200, to the grandfather of the owner.
Dating: The drapery folds, hands and skull are modelled similar to *61*, of 1632, which may be slightly later. *44* is evidently a smaller, far less accomplished replica.
Hitherto unpublished and not mentioned in the literature, this important picture came to light as a result of the publication of the first edition. Called 'A Gray Penitent' in the Salamanca catalogue, the identification as Saint Francis is assured by the tiny red wound in the right chest. Extraordinary sculpturesque form and great power of design distinguish this new iconographic invention.

2. So far not a single picture painted at Llerena before 1625 has been rediscovered. Judging from a good photograph, the *Christ at the Column with a Dominican*, said to be signed in 1620 (A. L. Mayer, *Monatshefte für Kunstwissenschaft*, 1920, p. 88) appears not to be by Zurbarán.

50. Rome, Private Collection.
Recent detailed photographs, sent me by courtesy of Dr. Alessandro Morandotti, indicate that the picture is by Zurbarán, except for the horizontal part of the loincloth which may have been repainted.

51. History: Gift of the Canon Ibarburu of Seville Cathedral, a native of Motrico, to his family chapel there, which now belongs to the Counts of Motrico.
In the two versions in Peru, the head leans towards the right shoulder.

55. Tentatively identified as Fray Alonso de Sotomayor y Caro, of Carmona, later archbishop of Oristano in Sardinia (1657–1663), then archbishop of Barcelona, and General of the Mercedarian Order (died 1683), by the Marquis of Saltillo, *Arte Español*, X, 1930–31, p. 191, who compares Zurbarán's portrait to one done of this cleric in 1657 by J. Valdés Leal.

64. History: From the collection of the Marquis of Prado Alegre, grandfather of the owner.

68–70. Dated about 1629–35 by J. Hernández Díaz, *Arch. esp. de arte*, 1953, No. 101, p. 33. In dating this series about 1633, the author has kept in mind the specific location and purpose for which these paintings were executed, as well as the somewhat archaic style of their graphic sources.

86. Although this scene is rare in art, most illustrated versions of the *Acts of the Apostles* contained it, including those by Bernard Salomon, Lyon, 1553, at Jean Tournes; and by Geoffrey Ballain, Antwerp, 1573, at Christopher Plantin.

86–90. J. Hernández Díaz, *Arch. esp. de arte*, 1953, No. 101, p. 33, agrees with a date in the 1630's, first suggested by the author.

129. A replica, or more likely an earlier study, is at the E. and A.

Silberman Galleries, New York, 117 × 59.7 cm., on canvas. The left hand, the right hand except the fingers, the chalice and the small Child in it, the white Carthusian garments except for some folds at the very bottom, the cape up to the elbow, and the swan of Stowe appear to be by Zurbarán, the rest, i.e. most of the cape, the fingers of the right hand, the head and some of the folds at the bottom are obviously repainted. An earlier date would seem indicated especially by the modelling of the left hand. Exhibited at Milwaukee 1951 as by the circle of Zurbarán.

131–132. See *Revel*. VIII, 3: 'And another angel came and stood at the altar, having a golden censer.'

144. J. Hernández Díaz, *Arch. esp. de arte*, 1953, No. 101, p. 35, proposes a date of about 1640.

159. Juan Gómez' version of this subject, painted in 1593 for the Escorial and still there, is so similar in the arrangement as to suggest a common graphic source (see the reproduction in J. Zarco Cuevas, *Pintores españoles en San Lorenzo el Real de el Escorial*, Madrid, 1931).

178. Charles Sterling, *La nature morte de l'antiquité à nos jours*, Paris, 1952, p. 132, sees in this picture a 'scattered composition of little monumentality, and a fragile graphic quality, which do not appear to agree with Zurbarán'. However, the painting seems to me to possess the simplicity, the monumentality and the construction in large tectonic planes one associates with Zurbarán. Until a more convincing attribution within the school of Seville is suggested, *178* should be retained as a work by Zurbarán, particularly since the modelling of flowers and fruits corresponds so closely to the artist's personal style.

185. History: Acquired in 1905 from José Fernández Pintado, Écija (possibly identical with No. 86, Votive painting, 175 × 220 cm., owned by José Fernández Pintado, Écija, in the Zurbarán exhibition of 1905 at Madrid).

219. Probably more accurately to be dated between 1635 and 1640, thus providing an additional reason against identifying the standing figure with the artist. Such identification is surely erroneous, no matter when the picture was painted.

BIBLIOGRAPHY

BIBLIOGRAPHY

A. *Sources prior to 1808:*

[1]Ceán Bermúdez, J. A., *Diccionario histórico de los más ilustres profesores de las bellas artes en España*, Madrid, 1800, VI, pp. 44–52. Quoted as Ceán.

Correspondencia de D. Antonio Ponz con el Conde de Aguila, published by Carriazo, *Archivo español de arte y arqueología*, 1929, V, no. 14, pp. 159–180.

Matute, J., *Adiciones y correcciones de D. Justino Matute al tomo IX del Viaje de España de D. Antonio Ponz*, published by Gestoso, *Archivo Hispalense*, Seville, 1886–8, III.

[2]Palomino, A., *Museo pictórico y escala óptica*, Madrid, 1724, III, pp. 355–6 (used in the edition by M. Aguilar, Madrid, 1947, 108, pp. 937–8). Quoted as Pal. III.

[3]Ponz, A., *Viaje de España*, Madrid, 1777, IX (used in the edition by M. Aguilar, Madrid, 1947).

B. *Sources between 1808 and 1850:*

Amador de los Ríos, J., *Sevilla pintoresca, o descripción de sus más célebres monumentos artísticos*, Seville, 1844.

Gómez Imaz, M., *Inventario de los cuadros sustraídos por el Gobierno intruso en Sevilla el año 1810*, Seville, 1917, second edition.

González de León, F., *Noticia artística, histórica y curiosa de todos los edificios . . . de Sevilla*, Seville, 1844.

C. *Documents:*

[4]Cascales Muñoz, J., *España moderna*, 1905, CIIC, p. 21.

Cascales Muñoz, J., *Francisco de Zurbarán*, Madrid, 1911; second edition, 1931. Quoted as Cascales.

[5]Caturla, María Luisa, Zurbarán en el salón de Reinos, *Archivo español de arte*, 1945, no. 71, pp. 292–300.

[6]Caturla, María Luisa, Zurbarán en Llerena, *Archivo español de arte*, 1947, no. 80, pp. 265–284. Quoted as Caturla.

Caturla, María Luisa, Noticias sobre la familia de Zurbarán, *Archivo español de arte*, 1948, no. 82, pp. 125–7.

Caturla, María Luisa, Conjunto de Zurbarán en Zafra, *ABC*, Madrid, April 20, 1948.

[7]Caturla, María Luisa, Zurbarán exporta a Buenos Aires, *Anales del Instituto de Arte Americano e Investigaciones Estéticas*, no. 4, 1951, pp. 27–30.

[7a]Caturla, María Luisa, A Retable by Zurbarán, *Burlington Magazine*, 1952, XCIV, pp. 45–49.

[8]Caturla, María Luisa, Lecture, *ABC*, Madrid, April, 1950.

[9]Cruzada Villamil, G., *Revista de Europa*, 1874, II, pp. 106–107.

[10]Gestoso Pérez, J., *Ensayo de un diccionario de los artífices que florecieron en Sevilla*, Seville, 1900, II, 126.

[11]Hernández Díaz, J., *Universidad de Sevilla, Laboratorio de arte, Documentos para la historia de arte en Andalucía*, Seville, 1927–30, I–II. Quoted as Documentos I and II.

[12]López Martínez, C., *Retablos y esculturas de traza sevillana*, Seville, 1928. Quoted as López Martínez I.

[13]López Martínez, C., *Arquitectos, escultores y pintores vecinos de Sevilla*, Seville, 1928. Quoted as López Martínez II.

[14]López Martínez, C., *Desde Jerónimo Hernández hasta Martínez Montañés*, Seville, 1929. Quoted as López Martínez III.

[15]López Martínez, C., *Desde Martínez Montañés hasta Pedro Roldán*, Seville, 1932. Quoted as López Martínez IV.

[16]López Martínez, C., Correspondence.

[17]Manzano Garias, A., *Aportación a la biografía de Zurbarán*, Badajoz, 1947.

[18]Montoto de Sedas, S., *Zurbarán, nuevos documentos para illustrar su biografía*, Seville, 1922. (Also published in *Arte español*, 1920–21, V, pp. 400–4.) Quoted as Montoto.

Rodríguez de Rivas, M., Autógrafos de artistas españoles, *Revista española de arte*, 1932, IX, p. 232.

[19]Sánchez Cantón, F. J., *Fuentes literarias para la historia del arte español*, Madrid, I–V, 1923–41.

D. *Monographs:*

Calzada, A. M., and Santa Marina, L., *Estampas de Zurbarán*, Barcelona, 1929.

[20]Cascales Muñoz, J., *Francisco de Zurbarán*, Madrid, 1911; second edition, 1931; English translation by Evans, New York, 1918. Of 77 paintings reproduced as by Zurbarán, 49 are listed in this catalogue.

[21]Caturla, María Luisa, *Bodas y obras juveniles de Zurbarán, Anejos del Boletín de la Universidad de Granada*, Granada, 1948.

Gaya Nuño, J. A., *Zurbarán*, Barcelona, 1948.

[22]Guinard, P., Réflexions sur Zurbarán, *Cahiers de Belgique*, 1931, IV, pp. 255–66.

[23]Guinard, P., Los conjuntos dispersos o desaparecidos de Zurbarán: Anotaciones a Ceán Bermúdez, *Archivo español de arte*, 1946, no. 76, pp. 249–73; 1947, no. 79, pp. 161–201; 1949, no. 85, pp. 1–38. Quoted as G. I; G. II; G. III.

[24]Kehrer, H., *Francisco de Zurbarán*, Munich, 1918. Quoted as K.

Lafond, P., *Ribera et Zurbarán*, Paris, 1909.

Maugham, W. S., Zurbarán, *The Cornhill Magazine*, 1950, pp. 396–420.

[25]Mier, E. de, Francisco de Zurbarán, *El arte en España*, 1863, II, pp. 181–6.

Pantorba, B. de, *Francisco de Zurbarán*, Barcelona, 1946.

Pompey, F., *Francisco de Zurbarán*, Barcelona, 1948. Of 91 paintings reproduced as by Zurbarán, 54 are listed in this catalogue.

Plá Cargol, J., *Ribera y Zurbarán*, Gerona, 1939.

Rodríguez Codolá, M., *Zurbarán*, Barcelona, 1943 (also published in *Arquitectura*, Barcelona, 1905).

[26]Sánchez Cantón, F. J., *La sensibilidad de Zurbarán, Anejos del Boletín de la Universidad de Granada*, Granada, 1944.

[27]Soria, M. S., Francisco de Zurbarán. A study of his style, *Gazette des Beaux-Arts*, January and March 1944, XXV, pp. 33–48, 153–74. Quoted as S. I.

Soria, M.S., *Francisco de Zurbarán: His Life and Works*, Ph. D. thesis, Harvard University, 1949, manuscript at Harvard University Library.

Tormo, E., Un resumen de Zurbarán, *Enciclopedia Italiana*, 1937, XXXV, p. 1059; reprinted in *Boletín de la sociedad española de excursiones*, 1941, XLIX, pp. 1 et seq.

Vollmer, H., Zurbarán, *Thieme-Becker, Allgemeines Künstlerlexikon*, 1947, XXXVI, pp. 600–3. Of 168 paintings mentioned as by Zurbarán, 113 are listed in this catalogue.

E. *Articles:*

Albocácer, Fray A. de, San Francisco y Zurbarán, *Coleccionismo*, 1918, pp. 76–82.

Amorós, J., Bodegones de Zurbarán, *Boletín de la sociedad española de excursiones*, 1927, XXXV, pp. 138–142.

[28]Angulo Iñíguez, D., *La Academia de Bellas Artes de México y sus pinturas españolas*, Seville, 1935.

[29]Angulo Iñíguez, D., Francisco de Zurbarán. Mártires mercedarios, San Carlos Borromeo, *Archivo español de arte*, 1941, no. 46, pp. 365–76.

Angulo Iñíguez, D., Cinco nuevos cuadros de Zurbarán, *Archivo español de arte*, 1944, no. 61, pp. 1–9.

Angulo Iñíguez, D., El apostolado de Zurbarán, *Archivo español de arte*, 1945, no. 70, pp. 233–5.

Angulo Iñíguez, D., Tres nuevos mártires mercedarios del taller de Zurbarán, *Archivo español de arte*, 1947, no. 78, p. 146.

[30]Angulo Iñíguez, D., El apostolado zurbaranesco de Sto. Domingo de Guatemala, *Archivo español de arte*, 1949, no. 86, pp. 169–70.

Angulo Iñíguez, D., Una variante del Agnus Dei del Museo de San Diego Estados Unidos, *Archivo español de arte*, 1950, no. 89, pp. 77–8.

Caturla, María Luisa, New Facts on Zurbarán, *Burlington Magazine*, 1945, LXXXVII, pp. 303 *et seq.*

Ford, R., Sale of Louis Philippe and Standish Spanish Pictures, *Atheneum*, London, May 14, 21, 28, June 4, 11, 18, 1853.

Fry, R., Still Life Painting by Zurbarán, *Burlington Magazine*, 1933, LXII, p. 253.

Garas, C., Un nouveau tableau de Zurbarán au Musée Hongrois des Beaux-Arts, *Bulletin du Musée Hongrois des Beaux-Arts*, September 1949, pp. 24–7.

[31]Gautier, T., *Oeuvres*, Paris, 1890, II, pp. 105, 152.

Ghilarov, S. A., Juan de Zurbarán, *Burlington Magazine*, 1938, LXXVIII, p. 190.

Gómez Castillo, A., *Discursos leídos ante la Real Academia de Bellas Artes de Santa Isabel de Hungría de Sevilla*, Madrid, 1950.

[32]Guinard, P., Zurbarán et la 'découverte' de la peinture espagnole, en France sous Louis Philippe, *Hommage à Ernest Martinenche*, Paris, 1939, pp. 23–33.

[33]Justi, K., Das Leben des heiligen Bonaventura gemalt von Herrera dem Älteren und Zurbarán, *Jahrbuch der Königlich Preussischen Kunstsammlungen*, 1883, IV, pp. 152–62.

Justi, K., Zurbarán und kein Ende, *Zeitschrift für bildende Kunst*, 1911, XLVII, p. 25.

Kehrer, H., Neues über Francisco de Zurbarán, *Zeitschrift für bildende Kunst*, 1920–21, LV, pp. 248–52.

[34]Kleinschmidt, Father B., Das Leben des Hl. Buenaventura in einem Gemäldezyklus von Fr. Herrera und Fr. Zurbarán, *Archivium Historicum Franciscanum*, 1926, XIX, pp. 3–16.

Lafuente Ferrari, E., La peinture de bodegones en Espagne, *Gazette des Beaux-Arts*, 1935, pp. 168–83.

Longhi, R., *Vita artistica*, 1927, II, p. 8.

Lozoya, Marquis of, *Mercurio Peruano*, 1942, XXIV, pp. 177 *et seq.*

[35]Lozoya, Marquis of, Zurbarán en el Perú, *Archivo español de arte*, 1943, no. 55, pp. 1–6.

Malitskaya, K. M., Zurbarán in the Moscow Museum of Fine Arts, *Burlington Magazine*, 1930, p. 16.

[36]Mayer, A. L., Zurbarán in America, *Arts and Decoration*, 1916, VI, pp. 219–22.

[37]Mayer, A. L., The Education of the Virgin, by Zurbarán, *Burlington Magazine*, 1924, XLIV, p. 212.

Mayer, A. L., A Still Life by Zurbarán, *Burlington Magazine*, 1926, IL, p. 55.

[38]Mayer, A. L., Still Lifes by Zurbarán and Van der Hamen, *Burlington Magazine*, 1927, LI, p. 320.

[39]Mayer, A. L., Some Unknown Works by Zurbarán, *Apollo*, 1928, VII, pp. 180–1.

Mayer, A. L., Unbekannte Werke Zurbaráns, *Zeitschrift für bildende Kunst*, 1927–28, LXI, pp. 289–92.

Mayer, A. L., Anotaciones a cuadros de Velázquez, Zurbarán, Murillo y Goya en el Prado y en la Academia de San Fernando, *Boletín de la sociedad española de excursiones*, 1936, XLIV, pp. 41–6.

[40]Museu Nacional de Arte Antiga, O 'Apostolado' de Zurbarán, Lisboa 1945.

Orozco Díaz, E., Un Zurbarán desconocido, *Cuadernos de arte de la facultad de letras*, Granada, 1937 (1939), II, pp. 399–402.

[41]Orozco Díaz, E., Para la interpretación de un tema de la pintura de Zurbarán, *Arte español*, 1942, XIV, p. 3. (Reprinted in Orozco Díaz, E., *Temas del Barroco*, Granada, 1947, pp. 31–35.)

Pemán, C., Zurbarán y el arte zurbaranesco en colecciones gaditanas, *Archivo español de arte*, 1946, no. 74, pp. 160–8. Quoted as Pemán I.

[42]Pemán, C., La serie de los hijos de Jacob y otras pinturas zurbanarescas, *Archivo español de arte*, 1948, no. 83, pp. 153–72. Quoted as Pemán II.

Pemán, C., Nuevas pinturas de Zurbarán en Inglaterra, *Archivo español de arte*, 1949, no. 87, pp. 207–13. Quoted as Pemán III.

Pemán, C., El linaje vasco de Zurbarán, *Archivo español de arte*, 1949, no. 88, pp. 353–5.

Pemán, C., La reconstrucción del retablo de la Cartuja de Jerez de la Frontera, *Archivo español de arte*, 1950, no. 91, pp. 203–27. Quoted as Pemán IV.

[42a]Perera, A. Algunos cuadros poco conocidos—Castro Urdiales, Santa María, El Cristo de la Agonía, *Boletín de la sociedad española de excursiones*, 1949, LIII, pp. 214–5.

Robinson, F. W., Notes on a Painting by Zurbarán, *Bulletin of the Museum of Cincinnati*, 1936, p. 17.

Romero de Torres, E., Los Zurbaranes del Museo de Cádiz, *Boletín de la Comisión Provincial de Monumentos de Cádiz*, 1908–09, I, pp. 97–108.

Saltillo, Marquis of, *Investigación y Progreso*, 1928, II, pp. 33–4.

San José de Serra, Marquis of, and Hernández Díaz, J., *Discursos leídos ante la Academia de Bellas Artes de Santa Isabel de Hungría de Sevilla*, Seville, 1934.

San José de Serra, Marquis of, Los cuadros del monasterio de las Cuevas, *Archivo Hispalense*, 1950, nos. 43–4.

Sánchez Cantón, F. J., El retrato de un hijo ilegítimo de Felipe IV, pintado por Zurbarán, *Archivo español de arte y arqueología*, 1928, IV, p. 160.

Sánchez Cantón, F. J., Cuatro jícaras más y un molinillo, *Correo erudito*, 1940, p. 102.

Santos, R. dos, El apostolado de Zurbarán en Lisboa, *Archivo español de arte*, 1945, no. 70, pp. 189–92.

[42b]Schenone, H., Pinturas zurbaranescas . . . en Sucre, Bolivia, *Anales del Instituto de Arte Americano e Investigaciones Estéticas*, no. 4, 1951, pp. 61–5.

Sebastián y Bandarán, Father J., La nueva sala de Zurbarán en el Museo de Sevilla, *Boletín de la Academia de Bellas Artes de Santa Isabel de Hungría*, 1935, II, pp. 64–5.

Seckel, H. P. G., Francisco de Zurbarán as a Painter of Still Life, *Gazette des Beaux-Arts*, 1946, XXX, pp. 279–300.

[43]Sentenach y Cabañas, N., Francisco de Zurbarán Pintor del Rey, *Boletín de la sociedad española de excursiones*, 1909, XVII, pp. 194–8.

Soria, M. S., Zurbarán, Right and Wrong, *Art in America*, 1944, XXXII, pp. 126–40. Quoted as S. II.

Soria, M. S., A Zurbarán for San Diego, *Art Quarterly*, Winter 1947, X, pp. 66–9. Quoted as S. III.

[44]Soria, M. S., Some Flemish Sources of Baroque Painting in Spain, *Art Bulletin*, 1948, XXX, pp. 253–7. Quoted as S. IV.

Soria, M. S., Sobre una Anunciación de Zurbarán, *Boletín de la sociedad española de excursiones*, 1948, LII, pp. 149–51.

[45]Soria, M. S., German Prints as Sources for Zurbarán, *Art Bulletin*, 1949, XXXI, pp. 74–5. Quoted as S. V.

[46]Soria, M. S., Zurbarán's Altar of Saint Peter, *Art Bulletin*, 1951, XXXIII, pp. 165–73. Quoted as S. VI.

[47]Soria, M. S., Two early paintings by Zurbarán, *Art Quarterly*, Autumn 1951, XIV, pp. 254, 256–60. Quoted as S. VII.

[48]Tormo, E., *El monasterio de Guadalupe y los cuadros de Zurbarán*, Madrid, 1905.

[49]Tormo, E., Five articles on Zurbarán, *Época*, March 31, April 14, May 12, May 27, June 6, 1905.

Tormo, E., Un Zurbarán, el Cristo de Motrico, *Cultura española*, 1906, IV, p. 1140.

Tormo, E., El despojo de los Zurbaranes de Cádiz, el viaje de Taylor y la efímera galería española del Louvre, *Cultura española*, 1909, VII, pp. 25–39.

[50]Tormo, E., Velázquez, el salón de los Reinos del Buen Retiro y el poeta del palacio y del pintor, *Boletín de la sociedad española de excursiones*, 1911 and 1912. (Reprinted in Tormo, *Pintura, escultura y arquitectura en España*, Madrid, 1949, pp. 144, 187–94).

[51]Zervos, Ch., Revisions: Francisco Zurbarán, *Cahiers d'Art*, 1927, II, pp. 85–92.

F. *General Works and Catalogues:*

[52]Angulo Iñíguez, D., La Encarnación de Mohedano, *Archivo español de arte*, 1944, no. 62, pp. 65–9.

[53]Carducho, V., *Diálogos de la pintura*, Madrid, 1633.

Gestoso Pérez, J., *Catálogo de las pinturas y esculturas del Museo Provincial de Sevilla*, Madrid, 1912.

Gudiol, J., *Spanish Painting*, Toledo, Ohio, 1941, pp. 107–9.

Guinard, P., and Baticle, J., *Histoire de la Peinture Espagnole*, Paris, 1950.

Harris, E., *Spanish Painting*, London, 1938, pp. 19–20, 39, pl. 62–66.

[54]Jameson, A., *Legends of Monastic Orders*, London, 1891.

Kehrer, H., *Spanische Kunst*, Munich, 1926, pp. 181–222.

Lafuente Ferrari, E., *El realismo en la pintura del siglo XVII*, Historia de arte Labor, Barcelona, 1934, second edition, 1945.

[55]Lafuente Ferrari, E., *Breve historia de la pintura española*, Madrid 1946, third edition.

[56]Leepa, A., *The Challenge of Modern Art*, New York, 1949, chapter 7.

Loga, V. von, *Die Malerei in Spanien*, Berlin, 1923, pp. 267–84.

Longhi, R., and Mayer, A. L., *The Old Spanish Masters from the Contini-Bonacossi Collection*, Rome, 1930.

[57]Louis Philippe Collection, *Notice des tableaux de la Galerie Espagnole exposés dans les salles du . . . Louvre*, Paris, 1838.

Louis Philippe Collection, Sale Catalogue, at Christie's, London, May 5–21, 1853.

MacLaren, N., *National Gallery Catalogues, The Spanish School*, London, 1952.

Malitskaya, K. M., *The Spanish Painting of XVI–XVII Centuries*, Moscow, 1947.

Mayer, A. L., *Die Sevillaner Malerschule*, Leipzig, 1911, pp. 147–61.

Mayer, A. L., *La pintura española*, Barcelona, 1926, pp. 147–52.

Mayer, A. L., *Historia de la pintura española*, Barcelona, second edition, 1942, pp. 328–47.

[58]Pacheco, F., *El arte de la pintura*, Seville, 1649.

Pemán y Pemartín, C., *Museo Provincial de Bellas Artes de Cádiz, Catálogo de las pinturas*, Cadiz, 1952.

Poland, R., and Andrews, J. G., *The Fine Arts Gallery, A Catalogue of European Paintings*, San Diego, California, 1947.

[59]Post, Ch. R., *A History of Spanish Painting*, Cambridge, Mass., 1935, vol. V.

[60]Raczynski, Count A., *Les arts en Portugal*, Paris, 1846, pp. 489–90 and 501.

Salamanca, Marquis of, Collection, Sale Catalogue, Hotel Drouot, Paris, June 3–6, 1867, and January 25–26, 1875.

Sánchez Cantón, F. J., *Catálogo del Museo del Prado*, Madrid, 1949.

Sentenach y Cabañas, N., *The Painters of the School of Seville*, London, 19—.

Soult Collection, Sale Catalogue, Paris, May 19–22, 1852.

Standish Collection, *Catalogue des tableaux, dessins et gravures de la Collection Standish*, Paris, 1842.

Standish Collection, Sale Catalogue, at Christie's, London, May 27–28, 1853.

Trapier, E. du G., *Catalogue of Paintings (sixteenth, seventeenth, and eighteenth centuries)*, Hispanic Society of America, New York, 1929.

Viñaza, Count, *Adiciones al Diccionario . . . de Ceán Bermúdez*, Madrid, 1894, IV, pp. 71–2.

[61]Viniegra, S., *Catálogo oficial ilustrado de la exposición de obras de Francisco de Zurbarán*, Madrid, 1905.

[62]Vossler, K., *Die Poesie der Einsamkeit in Spanien*, Munich, 1941.

Wehle, H. B., *The Metropolitan Museum of Art. A Catalogue of Italian, Spanish and Byzantine Paintings*, New York, 1940.

[63]White, J., Developments in Renaissance Perspective, *Journal of the Warburg and Courtauld Institutes*, 1949, XII, pp. 58–79; 1951, XIV, pp. 42–69.

INDICES

LOCATION OF PAINTINGS

AMERICA

Argentina

Buenos Aires, Javier Serra, 72
Dr. Alejandro E. Shaw, 61

Brasil

São Paulo, Museu de Arte, 17a

Canada

Montreal, Van Horne Collection, 179

Colombia

Bogotá, San Francisco Church, 172

Guatemala

Guatemala City, Santo Domingo Church, 145

Mexico

Mexico City, School of Plastic Arts, 164–5, 174, 176,
Count Felipe Subervielle, 238
Puebla, José Luis Bello y Zetina, 217

Peru

Lima, San Camilo de Lelis (Buenamuerte) Monastery, 171
San Francisco Church, 144

United States

Boston, I. S. Gardner Museum, 214
Museum of Fine Arts, 42–3, 184
Chicago, Art Institute, 148, 178, 225
Cincinnati, Art Museum, 32
Dallas, Texas, Col. Harry E. Stewart, 33
Hartford, Wadsworth Atheneum, 28
New York, Paul O. Berliz, 218
Oscar B. Cintas, 182
Hispanic Society of America, 178
Kleinberger & Co., 187
Knoedler & Co., 19
Samuel H. Kress Foundation, 198
Metropolitan Museum of Art, 3, 67, 133
Frederick A. Mont, 53
Philadelphia, Museum of Art, 210
Saint Louis, City Art Museum, 44
San Diego, Fine Arts Gallery, 75, 188, 206
Washington, National Gallery of Art, 2

TITLES OF PAINTINGS

The Persons of the Trinity

God the Father, 121
The Adoration of the Shepherds, 138
The Adoration of the Magi, 139
The Circumcision, 140
The Christ Child Blessing, 13
The Christ Child Contemplating the Crown of Thorns, 20
Christ Blessing, 113
The Double Trinity, 190
Christ as Saviour of the World, 146
Et ponit vestimenta Sua, 220
Christ after the Flagellation, 221
Christ Carrying the Cross, 204
The Veil of Saint Veronica, 63, 64, 64a, 147
The Crucifixion, 21, 23, 38, 50, 51
Christ Giving up the Ghost, 8
The Dead Christ on the Cross, 22, 37, 62, 114, 225, 227
The Dead Christ on the Cross with a Donor, 170
Saint Luke before the Crucified, 219
Christ at Emmaus, 176
The Pentecost, 123

Life of the Virgin

The Immaculate Conception, 1, 88, 200, 222, 226, 228, 236
The Immaculate Conception with Two Children, 59
The Immaculate Conception Cerralbo, 66
The Immaculate Conception with Saints Joachim and Anne, 143
The Birth of the Virgin, 10
The Young Virgin Praying, 67, 211, 212
The Young Virgin Asleep, 18
The Virgin and her Parents, 11
The Annunciation, 137, 210
Magnificat anima mea Dominum, 52
The Virgin in Clouds, 112
The Virgin with a Dish of Fruit, 182
The Virgin and Child Seated in Clouds, 199
The Virgin Nursing the Christ Child, 207
The Virgin with Sleeping Christ Child, 208
The Virgin and Christ Child with Saint John, 206, 218, 223
The Holy Family, 209
The Holy Family with Saints Anne, Joachim and John, 12
Virgin of Mercy with Two Mercedarians, 122
The Virgin as Protectress of the Carthusians, 68
Virgin of the Rosary with Carthusians, 134

Angels and Apostles

Saint Gabriel, 48
Saint Michael, 3, 192
Angel with Censer, 131, 132
The Twelve Apostles, 78, 144, 145

Scenes with Saints and Friars

Life of Saint Bonaventure, 24–27
Carthusian Scenes, 68–70
Marriage of Saint Catherine of Siena, 9
Dominican Miracles, 4–5
Vision of Saint Francis in La Porciuncula, 40, 237
The Virgin Bestowing the Chasuble upon St. Ildephonse, 189
Life of Saint Jerome, 159–161
Saint Jerome with Saints Paula and Eustochium, 198
Miracles of Jeronymite Friars, 151–158
Christ Crowning Saint Joseph, 120
Life of Saint Peter, 86–87, 89–90
Life of Saint Peter Nolasco, 30–33
Vision of the Blessed Alonso Rodríguez, 39
Apotheosis of Saint Thomas Aquinas, 41

Single Male Saints

Blessed Nicholas Albergati, 128
Saint Ambrose, 15
Saint Andrew, 47, 196, 235
Saint Anthelmus, 125
Saint Anthony Abbot, 118, 173, 186
Saint Anthony of Padua, 7, 17a, 202
Saint Augustine, 65, 164, 171b, 177
Saint Barnabas, 197
Saint Bartholomew, 233
Saint Benedict, 187
Saint Bernard of Clairvaux, 171a
Saint Blaise, 45
Saint Bruno, 106, 126, 141, 142, 171c (also 70)
Saint Carmelo, 83, 84
Saint Cyril of Constantinople, 43
Saint Diego of Alcalá, 54, 92, 201
Saint Dominic, 107 , 171i (also 4–5)
Saint Ferdinand, 53
Founders of Monastic Orders, 171
Saint Francis, 44, 91, 108, 171h, 238, (also 40, 237)
Saint Francis Kneeling, 61, 166, 167, 168, 169, 172, 216
Saint Francis Standing, 183, 184, 185
Saint Francis in Meditation, 215
Saint Gregory, 14
Blessed John Houghton, 127
Saint Hugh of Grenoble, 124 (also 69)
Saint Hugh of Lincoln, 129
Saint James Major, 230
Saint James of the Marches, 213
Saint Jerome, 16, 171g, 188, 193, (also 159–61, 198)
Jeronymite Saints, 162
Saint John the Baptist, 49, 105, 135, 191, 229
Saint John the Evangelist, 234
Saint John of God, 165
Saint Lawrence, 117, 136
Saint Louis Bertram, 150
Mercedarian Martyrs, 163

SOURCES OF PHOTOGRAPHS

The photographs used for the illustrations are from the following sources: courtesy of the owners: figs. XII, XIII, 1–3, 6, 13–4, 19, 23, 30, 36–7, 39, 45–6, 48, 72, 75–6, 79, 83, 112, 116–7, 120–1, 125, 129–30, 132–3, 146, 151, 158, pls. 2, 4, 8, 15, 17, 23, 24, 30–1, 33–4, 39, 47, 51–2, 62, 77, 87–9, 90, 93–4, 97 ; Alinari, Florence : pls. 10–1 ; Anderson, Rome : figs. I, III, 8, 22, 103, pls. 7, 22, 27, 41–2, 46, 63, 78 ; Annan, Glasgow : figs. XI, 98, pl. 36 ; Archives Photographiques, Paris : figs. XIV, 33, 94–5, pls. 69–70 ; Archivo Mas, Barcelona : figs. II, IV–IX, 12, 20, 31, 34, 47, 50, 56–7, 59, 73, 82, 84–90, 93, 96–7, 104–9, 111, 141, 144–5, 148–9, pls. 5, 12, 16, 18–9, 25, 28, 35, 37–8, 40, 43–5, 50, 60–1, 65–7, 74–6, 79–86, 93, 99 ; Bruckmann, Munich : pls. 9, 14 ; Bulloz, Paris : pls. 71–2 ; Federico Cantú, Mexico City : fig. 123 ; Sra. María Luisa Caturla, Madrid (photographs by V. Moreno) : figs. 134–40 ; A. C. Cooper, London : fig. 5 ; José Domínguez, Madrid : figs. 65–70, pls. 55–9 ; A. Fankhauser, Basle : pls. 20–21 ; Frick Art Reference Library, New York : fig. 102 ; J. Gérard, Paris : figs. 16–7, 35, 43–4, 63–4, 71, 81, 91, 126–7 ; Giraudon, Paris : figs. 24, 26, pl. 68 ; Paul Guinard, Madrid :fig. 11 ; Hanfstaengl & Co., Munich : fig. 92, pls. 92, 100 ; J. Hernández Diaz and Laboratorio de Arte, Universidad de Sevilla : fig. 156; Hugo Kehrer, Munich : fig. 110 ; Pál Kelemen, Norfolk, Conn. : pl. 95 ; Knoedler & Co., New York : figs. 25, 124, pl. 73 ; Laboratorio de Arte, Universidad de Sevilla, Seville : figs. 55, 58, 142, pls. 53–4 ; J. Lacoste, Madrid : fig. 147 ; Lilienfeld Galleries, New York : pl. 96 ; Photo Marburg, Marburg : fig. 115 ; Franz Mayer, Mexico City : figs. 113–4 ; Dr. A. Morandotti, Rome : fig. 27 ; Vicente Moreno, Madrid : figs. 18, 21, 42, 49, 61–2, 128, 150, 152, pls. 1, 3, 13, 32, 49, 64, 98 ; Ruiz Vernacci, Madrid : figs. 15, 40–1, 51, 131, 143 ; Rafael Salas, Seville : pl. 6 ; J. Sebastián y Bandarán, Seville : fig. 155 ; Serrano, Seville : figs. 4, 9–10, 38, 53–4 ; M. S. Soria, East Lansing, Mich. : figs. X, 28–9, 32, 60, 77–8, 99–101, 118–9, pls. 26, 29, 48, 91.

LIST OF COLOUR PLATES

We wish to express our gratitude to the following private collectors and gallery authorities for permission to reproduce, in full colour, paintings in their possession and for the facilities and co-operation accorded to us: Mr. Paul O. Berliz, New York; Count Contini-Bonacossi, Florence; Dr. Alejandro E. Shaw, Buenos Aires; the curators of the Samuel H. Kress Foundation, New York, of the Art Institute of Chicago, and of the museums in Cincinnati, Grenoble and Montpellier.

Credit for taking the colour photographs is due to:

H. Hinz (the paintings in Grenoble and Montpellier)

Alinari (Florence)

Richard J. Brittain (Chicago)

F. van Houten Raymond (Cincinnati).

LIST OF ILLUSTRATIONS IN THE INTRODUCTION